S0-AIP-058

365.66
P95

111481

DATE DUE			
Nov 30 '81			
Nov 24 '82			
Dec 1C '82			

WITHDRAWN

Psychiatric Aspects

of Imprisonment

This volume is published in association with the
Institute for the Study and Treatment of Delinquency

To the memory of Dr. Peter Scott

Psychiatric Aspects
of Imprisonment

John Gunn, Graham Robertson
Susanne Dell, Cynthia Way

With the Assistance of Evelyn Maxwell

Institute of Psychiatry
London

CARL A. RUDISILL LIBRARY
LENOIR RHYNE COLLEGE

1978

ACADEMIC PRESS

LONDON · NEW YORK · SAN FRANCISCO

A Subsidiary of Harcourt Brace Jovanovich, Publishers

ACADEMIC PRESS INC. (LONDON) LTD.
24/28 Oval Road,
London NW1

United States Edition published by
ACADEMIC PRESS INC.
111 Fifth Avenue
New York, New York 10003

365.66
P95
111481
oct.1979

Copyright © 1978 by
ACADEMIC PRESS INC. (LONDON) LTD

All Rights Reserved

No part of this book may be reproduced in any form by photostat, microfilm, or any
other means, without written permission from the publishers

Library of Congress Catalog Card Number: 77-71819
ISBN: 0-12-306550-X

Printed in Great Britain by The Lavenham Press Ltd., Lavenham, Suffolk

Preface

In recent years there has been a remarkable growth of interest in forensic psychiatry. This interest has been stimulated by a series of issues. A small number of well publicised violent assaults by ex-mental hospital patients; the treatment by psychiatrists of political dissidents in the Soviet Union; major legal and political clashes in the United States about the psychiatric treatment of violent offenders; the rights of psychiatric patients to receive treatment and the power and skill of the psychiatrist to diagnose dangerousness; a general international re-examination of the role of the psychiatrist in the law courts, are just a few of these issues. Many countries are introducing new mental health legislation and the pioneer English Act is also under Government scrutiny.

One debate of major international importance that has occurred during this period of uncertainty concerns itself with the place of psychiatry within a penal system. England is a good place to conduct research into this issue as it has a Prison Medical Service which is separate from the National Health Service, and which provides a variety of psychiatric services to prisoners. Furthermore, since July 1962, The English Prison Medical Service has undertaken one of the worlds most important experiments in prison psychiatry. Grendon prison is almost unique and receives a steady stream of visitors from all over the world.

In 1970 Professor Gibbens, Professor of Forensic Psychiatry at the Institute of Psychiatry in London was asked by the Home Office Research Unit to conduct a series of studies into psychiatric aspects of imprisonment. He decided to examine five areas: 1. the remand into custody for a psychiatric report; 2. the problems presented by very disruptive long term prisoners; 3. the prevalence of psychiatric disorder in the prison population; 4. the operation of a standard psychiatric service in prison, as exemplified by the oldest such service at Wormwood Scrubs prison, and 5. the operation of the special psychiatric prison at Grendon Underwood. The first study is being published as a Maudsley Monograph by Professor Gibbens and Dr. Soothill, the second a study of prisoners in maximum security prisons carried out by Mr. Patrick Pope was published in the *Prison Service Journal* (HMSO) in May 1976; this book deals with the other three projects. Part of the work presented here was successfully submitted by Dr. Graham Robertson to the University of London, as a PhD. thesis.

We hope our studies will help penologists throughout the world to think about the number and type of psychiatric cases locked away within prisons, whether it is really appropriate to deal with mentally abnormal offenders in this way, and what role psychiatric services should play within prisons. We particularly hope that the study of Grendon will help prison authorities in any country to evaluate the place and purpose of voluntary therapeutic communities within a penal system.

Acknowledgements

As a rule it is difficult if not impossible for ivory tower academics, such as ourselves, satisfactorily to carry out research in closed institutions. Such institutions do not usually take kindly to a group of outsiders observing their day to day activities whilst they the practitioners have no control over the final report. It is therefore with particular gratitude that we would like to pay tribute to the Prison Medical Service as a whole and to the staff of Wormwood Scrubs and Grendon in particular for their tolerance and cooperation. The staff at Grendon had a great deal to put up with from us because for weeks on end one or two of us were always hanging about wanting to interview prisoners, give out questionnaires, and generally make a nuisance of ourselves. To Dr. W. Gray, medical superintendent of Grendon at the time must go a very special mention because he personally saw to it that we had all the access to prisoners and records that we required. The prison officer staff at all the prisons we visited or wrote to absorbed most of the inconvenience, and they did so cheerfully in the belief that they were facilitating some important research. We blush to think what they will now make of our efforts; we hope they are not too disappointed.

Of course the project would never have been conceived, let alone facilitated, if three key people had not developed good personal relationships and each shown that degree of far-sightedness which is essential for research to flourish: Mr. I. J. Croft, Director of the Home

Office Research Unit, Dr. I. Pickering, then Director of the Prison Medical Service, and Professor T. C. N. Gibbens.

Professor Gibbens has that happy knack of steering his research projects with just the right level of control, plenty at the beginning to set the programme off down the right track and less and less as time proceeds so that at the end others can apparently take all the credit. We are determined therefore to make it clear that whilst this book was written by members of his research staff, and all the mistakes in it are ours, the inspiration for it was his.

Dr. Paul Bowden, lecturer in the Department of Forensic Psychiatry, took a special interest in our study of the prisoners' drinking behaviour and carried out some extra studies using part of our sample. We are most grateful to him for his assistance with this part of our work.

The valiant few who are still with us at Chapter 11 would like to know that the eleven Maudsley psychiatrists who assisted us with the validation interviews were Dr. Robin Anderson, Dr. Dennis Bainbridge, Dr. Michael Bowman, Dr. Angus Campbell, Dr. Anthony Clare, Dr. (now Professor) John Copeland, Dr. Paul Debenham, Dr. Brian Harwin, Dr. Michael Kelleher, Dr. Rori Nicol and Dr. Derek Steinberg. Some of these have since established themselves as national and international authorities. We cannot claim that this study has had any bearing on their success! We would, however, like to thank them for their help. The census study was in fact auxillary to a much larger census carried out by the Home Office Research Unit and conducted by Dr. Charlotte Banks and Mr. Stephen Brodie. We are grateful to them for access to their sample, access to their data, and administrative assistance.

Statistical advice has been sought and gratefully received from Dr. Ray Hodgson, Miss Margaret Vaughan, Mr. Owen White, and Mr. Peter Nicholls. Extensive use has been made of five programmes developed by Miss Barbara Kinsley, who was formerly a member of the Biometrics Unit in the Institute of Psychiatry. All frequency distribution tables, 't' test comparisons, correlations, chi squared comparisons, and pattern analysis of data have been provided by these programmes. All analyses of variance comparisons have utilised a programme by Finn (1968).

The Hofmann-la-Roche company provided free computer facilities for analysing MMPI answer sheets. This service has greatly enhanced the use which has been made of this particular test and we are especially grateful to Drs. J. F. F. Rooney, P. Blaser, and P. Jager for their help. Almost 300 MMPI protocols were analysed.

Dr. Patrick Slater and Dr. Jane Chetwynd gave advice about the repertory grid technique we used and provided the computer program and service for the grid analyses under the special MRC service set up by Dr. Slater.

Various members of the Home Office Research Unit, in particular Mr. Chris Nuttall and his assistants, have been extremely helpful in providing access to information concerning general prison population data.

Typing is an undervalued and underpaid skill. Which author or research worker could do without it? We owe a very great deal to Sybil Halliwell, Maureen Bartholomew and Celia Gunn.

January 1978   J.C.G.

Contents

Preface   v

Acknowledgements   vi

Chapter 1   The History of the Prison Psychiatry Services

The beginnings of prison medicine   1

The beginnings of prison psychiatry...   4

The Gladstone committee and the end of the nineteenth century   8

Quasi-criminal groups   10

The beginnings of psychotherapy   14

The non-sane non-insane   17

The East-Hubert report   19

Post second world war developments   22

The impact of the 1959 Mental Health Act   26

Grendon prison and after   31

Chapter 2   Orientation and Methods

Personality disorder and psychopathic personality   36

Outline of research   39

Methodology   44

Chapter 3   The Grendon Population

Demographic and social data   53

Criminal histories   56

Psychiatric characteristics   58

Personality characteristics   61

Attitude assessments   65

Current offences, sentences and referral to Grendon   ...   68

Men transferred from Grendon   71

Summary   74

Chapter 4   The Grendon Regime

A day in the life of   81
The officers   88
Doctors and other staff   91
Comparisons between wings and between occasions   ...   93
Links with the outside   98
Summary   100

Chapter 5   Changes During Treatment in Grendon

MMPI   103
Psychiatric assessment   109
General health questionnaire   111
Attitude changes as measured by the semantic differential   113
Discussion of semantic differential results   116
Changes in attitudes to crime and psychiatry   120
Summary   121

Chapter 6   Wormwood Scrubs and Its Treatment Population

Wormwood Scrubs prison   124
Arrangements for psychiatric treatment   126
Research design   128
Source of referral, age, and sentence length   128
Psychiatric characteristics   130
Criminal histories   133
Social and demographic data   136
Personality characteristics   137
Attitudes to authority and to self   138
Attitudes to treatment and to crime   139
Summary and discussion   140

Chapter 7   Treatment in Wormwood Scrubs and Changes During Treatment

The treatment   144
Changes during treatment   146
General health questionnaire and psychiatric reassessment   147
Motivation and attitudes   150
Summary and discussion   153

Chapter 8   Wormwood Scrubs and Grendon Compared

Two treatment samples 156
Summary 164

Chapter 9   After Release (1): The Controlled Re-conviction Study

Control study 169
Discussion 176

Chapter 10   After Release (2): Group Differences and Some Case Histories

Postal enquiry 180
Re-conviction data 188
Some case histories 194
Summary 205

Chapter 11   How Many Psychiatric Cases are there in the Prison Population?

The questionnaires 211
Sample bias 214
Questionnaire results 217
Validation by interview 218
Comparisons with other studies 224
The demand for psychiatric help 226
The prevalence of psychiatric disorder 227
Previous psychiatric history 229
Some illustrative cases 229
Summary and conclusions 231

Chapter 12   Psychiatric Data from the Census Questionnaire

1. Sentence length and psychiatric characteristics 233
2. Illegal drug taking 236
3. Drinking behaviour 241
4. Gambling 247
5. Factor analysis 247
Summary 249

Chapter 13   Final Remarks

Research techniques   251
Psychiatry and crime   255
Psychiatric treatment in prison   257
The Butler report   259

Appendix 1. Social and Criminal History Review   261
Appendix 2. Heim's AH4 Intelligence Test   263
Appendix 3. Criminal Profile   265
Appendix 4. Personality Assessment Using the Minnesota Multiphasic Personality Inventory...   267
Appendix 5. Attitude to Psychiatry Questionnaire (AP) ...   274
Appendix 6. Interviewer's Assessment of Desire for Treatment   280
Appendix 7. The Attitude to Crime Scale (AC)   281
Appendix 8. Measurement of Attitudes by a Semantic Differential   286
Appendix 9. Re-interview Schedule...   290
Appendix 10. Moos Social Climate Scale for Correctional Institutions   291
Appendix 11. Post Release Follow-Up Enquiry Form   ...   296
Appendix 12. Social Performance Scales   300
Appendix 13. Census Medical History Questionnaire   ...   302
Appendix 14. The Self Rating Symptom Scale (35 Item Scale)   303
References   307
Government Reports and Legislation   313
Index   314

CHAPTER 1

The History of Prison
Psychiatric Services

This book is concerned with an examination of a few aspects of
psychiatry as it is currently practised within the prisons of England.
But before presenting the data from our research, it seemed important
to put current psychiatric practice into its historical perspective.
Without that perspective it is difficult to understand the somewhat
ambiguous system which operates today, and particularly difficult to
understand the chasm between what it is commonly supposed prison
psychiatrists should do ("cure people of crime") and what in fact they
do. In few fields, perhaps, is the gap between expectation and
performance larger than in this one: a psychiatrist has recently
complained (Rollin, 1968) that doctors nowadays are expected by the
courts to effect changes in offender patients who "require the services
not of a psychiatrist, but of an alchemist". The following pages trace
the development of the prison psychiatric service, and show how a
service that began in a strictly limited and utilitarian way, by
introducing the principles of medical care into prisons, has come to be
regarded as a key element in the elusive process of turning prisoners
away from crime.

The Beginnings of Prison Medicine

The first legislative result of John Howard's investigation into the state
of English prisons, was the passing in 1774 of "An Act for Preserving
the Health of Prisoners in Gaol and Preventing the Gaol Distemper".

Gaol fever (a form of typhus) was one of the few aspects of prison conditions that affected people other than prisoners*, and it was presumably for this reason that it was the first of the prison evils to arouse public concern. The Act required local justices to order prisons to be periodically cleansed, the prisoners to be washed, and separate sick rooms to be provided. The justices were also "to appoint an experienced surgeon or apothecary, at a stated salary, to attend each gaol". This surgeon was required to report to each quarter sessions on the health of the prisoners under his care. The Act made no other reference to his duties.

At that time, although prisons were in legal theory those of the monarch, they were in fact the responsibility of justices and other local authorities. As John Howard showed (1771), these bodies took no interest or part in prison administration; they farmed the job out to gaolers, whose only concern in it was financial. The keeping of a prison was a profit-making private enterprise, and the only way the gaoler could make money was by avoiding expense (hence, for example, irons and chains were used for safe custody, as a cheaper alternative to secure prison buildings) and by maximising the opportunities for extortion. The resultant cruelties and the appalling conditions under which prisoners were held began to become a matter of public concern as a result of Howard's work, and this was reflected in legislation passed between 1774 and 1791. But the difficulty about the legislation of this period was that there was no way of enforcing it (Webb and Webb, 1922). Parliament might pass a law but it was nobody's business to communicate the fact to the justices, and certainly no part of the Government's duty to know or to find out what the local authorities were doing, or to encourage them to do better. Thus the Acts had little effect.

Up until the end of the eighteenth century imprisonment was not in itself a penalty for crime; prisons were mainly places where persons either awaited trial, or where they awaited the punishment. For major offences the normal punishments were death or transportation; for minor offences there were fines and corporal punishments. It was not until the American War of Independence put an end to transportation to America that the country was faced with the need to reconsider its penal policy, and the government itself entered what modern

---

*"Now and again a malignant outburst of gaol fever would stretch, like the arm of an avenger, from the prison house to the court of justice, and sweep away, in a few days, judge and advocates, jurymen and witnesses alike." (Webb and Webb, 1922)

American criminologists call the confinement business. With the loss of the colonies the government was compelled to supplement the local prisons by establishments under its own management. Its first expedient was to confine the prisoners temporarily in hulks at Woolwich — an expedient which was continued for more than 80 years. Secondly, legislation was introduced in 1779 empowering the government to set up State Penitentiaries for convicts who would otherwise have been transported; but when transportation to Australia became possible soon afterwards, the need for such establishments became less pressing, and Millbank, the first to be erected, only came into use in 1821.

The Rules and Regulations of the General Penitentiary Millbank (1822), show what the government of the day considered to be the appropriate standards of prison administration. As far as the medical arrangements were concerned, the Rules spelled out the duties of two officials, the Principal Medical Superintendent and the Surgeon. The former was to be in charge of the "medical department", he was to inspect the prison monthly, and to visit the patients in the infirmary twice a week. The Surgeon was required to be resident and was to have no practice outside the prison. He had to examine all the prisoners on reception, and to attend to any who were unwell. The rules make no mention of any aspect of mental health, or of insanity. Questions of reformation were the Chaplain's province.

The failure of the local authorities to comply with the standards of prison administration laid down in Acts of Parliament, led in 1835 to the establishment of government inspectors of prisons. From that date onwards, local prison authorities became subject to increasingly detailed government inspection and control. The final step in the centralisation of the prison system was taken in 1877, when the administration of local prisons was taken over by the government. By this time the government already had considerable experience of running its own establishments, for when transportation to New South Wales came to a stop in 1840, it was realised that the hulks and Millbank would provide insufficient accommodation. A prison building programme was embarked upon, and many new convict (i.e. state) prisons were opened between 1840 and 1850.

When the government took over the local prisons it charged a body of commissioners with their superintendence. Edmund du Cane, already Chairman of the Directors of Convict Prisons, was appointed to be Chairman of the Commissioners for Local Prisons as well. His aim was to administer the two systems with the same purpose — that they should become an effective deterrent to crime. The idea of using prisons as a means of reforming their inmates, an idea which was widely held when the first state prisons were put up, had no appeal for him. He set about implementing the highly punitive recommendations of the 1863 House of Lords Committee on prison discipline — hard fare, hard labour, hard bed. The diet was intentionally made poor and unpalatable; hammocks were removed from the cells and planks substituted; the crank and treadmill were introduced. In local prisons (where the maximum sentence was two years) solitary confinement was strictly maintained throughout the whole sentence, and in convict prisons it was the rule for the first nine months. Silence at all times was enforced by the use of punishment. With formidable administrative efficiency, Du Cane ensured that these policies were uniformly implemented in both the local and convict prisons. In his own words, the object was to ensure that "punishment . . . should be carried out so as to make imprisonment a terror to evil doers" (Du Cane, 1874). In the words of a later Commissioner of Prisons, he achieved a system which substituted "for death itself . . . a living death" (Fox, 1952).

The Beginnings of Prison Psychiatry

The earliest references to the duties of the prison surgeon did not include any mention of mental health matters. But doctors who visited the local gaols of the eighteenth and early nineteenth centuries cannot have avoided contact with the insane prisoner, since this was where insane offenders who were spared trial or punishment on account of their mental state were most likely to be sent. John Howard had drawn attention to the horrible conditions under which such prisoners were held, adding "no care is taken of them, although it is probable that by medicines and proper regimen some of them might be restored to their senses and to usefulness in life" (Howard, 1977). The County Asylum Act of 1808 was a first step towards remedying this situation; it empowered local justices to set up asylums for the care of the insane, including the insane offender. Legislation empowered the Home Secretary to transfer offenders from prisons to asylums, provided that insanity had been certified by two justices and two doctors.

These measures must have tended to direct the attention of prison surgeons to the question of insanity among inmates, and from the 1840s at least, the rules required the doctors to note prisoners' liability to be affected by mental, as well as physical disorder. Moreover, the doctor was required to inform the Governor whenever he had reason to believe that either the mind or body of the prisoner was likely to be injuriously affected by prison discipline or treatment (East and Hubert, 1939). This last requirement has been incorporated in all subsequent versions of the prison rules up to the present day.

Another role for the prison surgeon in the field of mental health began to evolve at this time — that of expert witness in trials where the sanity of the prisoner was in doubt, for it had long been held that insanity should exempt an offender from ordinary punishment. Although evidence as to the lunacy of the accused might still be given by the prison governor or one of his gaolers, the prison doctor began, by the middle of the nineteenth century, to assume "the authority which was later to become a decisive factor in so many trials of the insane" (Walker, 1968).

Thus historically the prison doctor's concern with mental health was for the purpose of diagnosis rather than treatment. Diagnosis was important for three purposes: for the unsentenced, if their sanity was in question, it might determine guilt, or liability to capital punishment; for the convicted, it might secure their removal to an asylum, or failing that, it might secure an alleviation of the harshness with which prisoners were normally treated. For if the M.O. found that imprisonment was adversely affecting the health of the prisoner, the governor was bound by the rules to take appropriate action. In this respect, the surgeon's role was analogous to his function relating to corporal punishment: he was required to be present when this was administered, and the Governor had to obey his directives if he considered that the prisoner's physical health was at risk. In both the physical and mental sphere, the surgeon was thus charged with the task refereeing the punitive excesses of those who administered the penal system. From the start, therefore, his relationship with the prisoner was very different from the usual doctor-patient relationship. Mary Gordon, a Medical Inspector of Prisons writing in 1922, described it thus: "The prisoner does not consult the doctor, the State pays the doctor and consults him about the prisoner" (Gordon, 1922).

In the highly punitive prisons of the nineteenth century, the doctors' task of overseeing the health of the prisoners was an important one, as the annual prison reports show. As far as physical health was concerned, a recurring theme in the reports was whether the deliberately poor diet was having an adverse effect on the health of the inmates. Medical officers who found this to be so in individual cases were empowered to order extra food. Similarly, as far as mental health was concerned, the recurring question was the effect that prolonged solitary confinement and silence might have on the prisoners' sanity. With the authorities taking a self-justifying stand, it was all the more valuable that they printed not only their own views, but the actual reports of the various medical officers in the prisons. Dr. William Baly, who was M.O. at Millbank in the 1850s, had no doubt of "the increasing risk of insanity that attends the protraction of imprisonment", and he found that prisoners of "any considerable degree of imbecility or great dullness of intellect will certainly be rendered actually insane or idiotic by a few months separate confinement" (Baly, 1852). He endeavoured to prevent this by allowing association to prisoners who were known to be mentally infirm, and this to some extent became the custom. One of the hulks was set aside as an "invalid depot", and "weak-minded" convicts, as well as the physically ill, were sometimes sent there when it seemed advisable to avoid solitary confinement. The conditions there were, however, deplorable (Walker and McCabe, 1973).

When Dartmoor came into use in 1852, it was designated as an "invalid depot", for both the physically and mentally infirm. By 1855, Dr. John Campbell, its M.O., had 100 "weak-minded" convicts in his care, and was advocating that they should be segregated from the other prisoners and placed under "Officers having some experience in the management and peculiarities of the insane" (Campbell, 1856). Not that the insane were intended to remain in prison; they were supposed to be transferred to asylums, but there were difficulties about security, and lack of vacancies (Walker and McCabe, 1973). The need for a State Asylum for insane offenders became evident, and Broadmoor was opened as a Criminal Lunatic Asylum in 1863, receiving its first patients from asylums and from convict prisons.

The nineteenth-century lunacy laws applied to persons described in the various acts as "lunatics", "idiots", "insane" or "of unsound mind". These terms were used somewhat indiscriminately to cover the major forms of mental disorder which seriously affect the intellect or reason (Royal Commission, 1958). Thus only prisoners with the grossest forms of mental abnormality (whether of illness or defect) were liable to be transferred to asylums. But although the establishment of local asylums, and then of Broadmoor, should have ensured that such persons were removed from prison, this did not happen so smoothly. Broadmoor found that transferred convicts were more troublesome and escape-minded than its other patients, and in 1874 the transfer of insane male convicts to Broadmoor was therefore stopped and it was decided that they should henceforth be cared for within the prison system, in a wing at Woking prison.

John Campbell was the doctor put in charge of Woking's criminal lunatic wing, and he recorded some of his experiences and views in a book called "Thirty Years Experience of a Medical Officer in the English Convict Service" (Campbell, 1884). He regretted the need to conform to prison regulations and thought it wrong to deny insane prisoners indulgences such as tobacco, which they were allowed in ordinary asylums, and at Broadmoor. The majority of his patients he did not think were dangerous, but like all prison administrators of the day, he was always extremely worried lest the bad should be escaping punishment by deceiving the authorities into treating them as mad: "The utmost caution is required to discriminate between the really weak-minded and those cunning miscreants who feign mental peculiarities as a cloak for their misdeeds. These latter men belong to the worst description of criminals and are proper subjects for the most deterring punishments."

Woking ceased to be used as a criminal lunatic asylum after eleven years, and transfers to Broadmoor were resumed in the eighteen-eighties. But the prisons still had to cope with the many insane prisoners who did not warrant transfer to Broadmoor and who, for various reasons such as the shortness of sentence, or the unwillingness of the magistrates to burden the rates by signing certificates of insanity, could not be placed in local asylums. Before transfers to Broadmoor were suspended in 1874, the M.O. in Parkhurst had written that the mental invalids in his care presented "every feature of insanity and imbecility which is to be found in any ordinary asylum" (Directors of Convict Prisons, 1875).

A Home Office Circular of 1889 (Walker and McCabe, 1973) sought to discourage magistrates from sentencing insane persons to imprisonment: it advised them to obtain medical evidence in doubtful cases, and if the offender was indeed insane, to dismiss the charges and deal with him under the Lunacy Acts by committing him to an asylum. The intention was to try and reduce the supply of insane persons into the prison system. One of its effects was to put a new emphasis on the diagnostic functions of the prison medical officer, by explicitly encouraging the lower courts to remand for the purpose of psychiatric reports.

A group of offenders which the prison authorities could not hope to transfer or divert from their establishments, was the large number of mentally abnormal prisoners who were not covered by the lunacy acts.

Since these acts applied only to the severest disorders of intellect and reason, mentally defective persons other than idiots fell outside their scope. The prison authorities came to use the phrase "feeble minded" to cover a wide range of mental abnormality falling short of insanity, but the most numerous prisoners in this class were the mentally defective. Since no systematic provision was made for the care of mental defectives in the nineteenth century, it was not surprising that many got into trouble with the law and found themselves sent to prison, often repeatedly. The medical officers who dealt with them in prison emphasised the importance of segregating them and treating them separately, so as to protect them both from the rigours of ordinary penal discipline, and from incurring repeated dietary and other punishments for unwittingly breaking prison rules such as the rule of silence. The M.O. at Parkhurst deplored the imprisonment of feeble-minded men, on the grounds that in prison there was a total "exclusion of the working of the omnipotent law of human kindness and sympathy so important in the treatment of the mentally affected . . . The presence of such men in an ordinarily constituted convict prison for the discipline of which they are wholly unsuited is much to be regretted. From this class the greater number of men under punishment are supplied, nor is their mental condition likely to be improved until they are dealt with exceptionally and by those exclusively who are familiar with their mental peculiarities" (Directors of Convict Prisons, 1875 and 1879). Various prisons were used at different times for the mentally infirm, but the transfer system was haphazard and segregation at the invalid prisons was never complete. By the end of the century Parkhurst was designated as the establishment for prisoners who were in the opinion of the M.O. "unfit for ordinary penal discipline because of some mental disability other than insanity". The regime there made some allowance for the prisoners' mental condition, and certain of the rules were relaxed, e.g. prisoners were allowed to talk whilst on exercise.

The Gladstone Committee and the End of the Nineteenth Century

By the end of the century, the involvement of prison doctors in the field of mental health was sufficient to lead the Gladstone Committee in 1895 to suggest that "it might with advantage be made a condition of medical appointments in prison that the candidate should produce evidence of having given special attention to the subject of lunacy"

(Home Office, 1895). Prison doctors had the charge of large numbers of mentally defective and unstable prisoners, some of whom were cared for in separate establishments. They had played an important part in identifying and transferring the insane to asylums, and were questioning the wisdom of imprisoning the defective. They had become expert witnesses in trials where the sanity of the accused was in question, and had considerable experience of diagnosing offenders remanded on suspicion of mental disorder. Finally, they had devoted some thought to the question of how far prison conditions might themselves be productive of mental disease.

In the framework of the prison regime of that time it was not possible for the doctors, any more than the rest of the prison staff, to play a more positive or rehabilitative role towards the prisoner. The ethos and intention of the regime was not that the prisoner should be rehabilitated, but that he should be punished. How little value was set on the effect that imprisonment might have on the individual is illustrated by the following statement made by the Directors of Convict Prisons in 1873: "The fact of certain prisoners being repeatedly reconvicted is no proof that the system of a prison is defective; the truth being that if, by punishing those who have an incurable tendency to crime, we can deter fresh recruits from joining the ranks of the criminal class, the whole object of punishment is effected, and obviously if we could possibly arrive at the result that all convictions were re-convictions and none of them first sentences, we should be in a fair way to putting an end to crime altogether."

In a system intentionally organised for the purpose of inflicting deterrent punishment and suffering on its inmates, prison doctors could scarcely find a therapeutic role beyond their basic task of looking after the prisoners' physical health and trying to protect at least some of the mentally disordered from the harshest aspects of the regime. The impossibility of carrying out rehabilitative treatment in the prisons of this time is well illustrated in some of the evidence given to a departmental committee set up in 1893 consider the problem of inebriety. The Committee accepted that certain inebriate offenders should be committed to special treatment institutions; and the question was then raised as to whether these could be set up within prisons. The response of the prison authorities was decisive: they considered that it would be impossible to have treatment sections within the prison system. To treat some prisoners differently from others would not only cause trouble and discontent, "it would destroy the discipline of the prisons" (Parliamentary Papers, 1893). In this they were no doubt right;

to introduce individualised treatment into the regime of that time would have involved its destruction, for one of the things on which Du Cane prided himself was that all prisoners were treated exactly alike and that "the previous career and character of the prisoner makes no difference in the punishment to which he is subjected" (Elkin, 1957).

But the first assault on the Du Cane regime was not far off. In response to public disquiet the Home Office appointed a departmental committee in 1894 to review the state of the prisons. The findings of the Gladstone Committee are well known. Disregarding the evidence of Sir Godfrey Lushington, the Permanent Secretary at the Home Office, who said that he thought it would be impossible to introduce an effective reformatory element into the prison regime, the Committee recommended that attempts should be made to devise a system that aimed to turn the prisoners out of prison better men and women physically and morally than when they came in. Prison historians have paid tribute to the idealism of the committee, but it is worth noting that Sir Godfrey himself was not opposed to the idea of reformation; what he said was that he did not believe that it could be successful inside prisons, the chief characteristics of which were "the crushing of self respect . . . the continued association with none but criminals . . . and the denial of liberty" (Home Office, 1895).

Some of the harshest features of prison life were mitigated in the first years of the new century, after Sir Evelyn Ruggles Brise replaced Edmund du Cane. The diet was improved, talking as a privilege was tentatively introduced, and the treadmill ceased to be used. The idea that prisoners might respond to rehabilitative rather than punitive treatment was put into effect in the new borstal system, where the offenders were thought to be young enough to be amenable to good influences (Commissioners for Prisons and Directors of Convict Prisons, 1902).

Quasi-Criminal Groups

On the psychiatric side, the main development in the new century was the determination of the prison authorities to rid themselves as far as possible of the mentally abnormal offender. Their reasoning was a development of the argument that had led to the mentally infirm at Parkhurst being exempted from ordinary penal discipline. The argument, as stated by the Prison Commissioners, was simple. Since the mentally infirm were "more fitly the subjects of medical care and attention than of penal discipline", they had to be removed if prisons were to "fulfil the purpose for which they exist, viz. the punishment of crime committed by fully responsible persons" (Commissioners of Prisons and Directors of Convict Prisons, 1910).

The largest group of mentally infirm prisoners thought to need medical care rather than punishment were the mentally deficient. From 1902 onwards, the annual prison reports continually draw attention to the lack of suitable provision and control for feeble-minded offenders who were unable to cope with the outside world on their own. "The frequent recommittal of this class of prisoner seems to call for some different method of treatment other than sending to prison over and over again . . . Not infrequently it is merely owing to (their) very mental deficiency that the persons are offenders against the law" (Commissioners of Prisons and Directors of Convict Prisons, 1905). Prison doctors gave evidence to the 1904-8 Royal Commission on the Care and Control of the Feeble-Minded (Royal Commission, 1908) They emphasised the need for defectives to be subject to some kind of non-penal compulsory control, if they were to be properly cared for and prevented from coming into repeated conflict with the law. The Commission accepted this need and made recommendations for meeting it by the establishment of mental deficiency institutions.

The prison authorities warmly supported these recommendations and extended an equally heartfelt welcome to the Report of the Royal Commission on the Poor Laws, which was published in 1909 and which advised that special institutional facilities should be set up for persons coming within its remit. At the same time the 1908 Departmental Committee on Inebriety made similar recommendations in respect of the need for special institutions for the drunkenness offender. The Medical Inspector, Dr. Smalley, gave his reactions to these three reports as follows: "The function of the prison will be revolutionised by the adoption of the various proposals . . . It is a change to be welcomed with enthusiasm by all who have had practical experience of prison administration and who have learned that the greatest difficulty in the way of the rational treatment of the criminal is due to the fact that he has to be dealt with by the same methods, and in the same class of institution as the various quasi-criminal groups with whose characteristics he really has very little in common. The clearing out from our prisons of the drunkard, the tramp and the imbecile" would at long last enable "prisons to be used exclusively for the treatment of the criminal" (Commissioners of Prisons and Directors of Convict Prisons, 1910).

The first steps toward the removal of these "quasi-criminal groups" from prison were taken in relation to drunkenness offenders. The Gladstone Committee had stated in 1895 that "the physical craving for drink is a disease which requires medical treatment not provided by the present prison system" (Home Office, 1895) and had recommended that the advice of two earlier departmental committees on inebriety should be implemented. These committees (Parliamentary Papers, 1872 and 1893) having heard evidence from doctors, magistrates, and prison officials, had recommended that the courts should be given powers to commit drunkenness offenders to special inebriate institutions.

The Inebriates Act passed in 1898 enabled courts to commit inebriate offenders as defined to special reformatories. Detention orders could be made for a maximum period of three years. Two classes of offender were covered; those who were convicted in the higher courts of offences caused by, or contributed to, by drink; and habitual inebriates who had more than three drunkenness convictions in one year. Because on the recommendations of the 1872 Committee the reformatories were to be "as free from restriction and as little prison like as possible", they were unable to manage or control some of the most intractable and violent offenders. Two "State Reformatories" were therefore set up in 1901, one for women at Aylesbury and one for men at Warwick, to cater for the cases which the other institutions could not manage. The annual reports by the Inspector of Inebriate Reformatories show how the state reformatories came to grips with their task, and how the medical expert came to be regarded as the appropriate person to manage this type of reformatory institution. The first Inspector described the inmates, although not certifiably insane, as "ill-balanced borderline cases, prone to excitement and violence on the slightest provocation, and when excited little removed (if at all) from a condition of dangerous lunacy . . ." (Branthwaite, 1903). "All this", Branthwaite decided, "points to the conclusion that State Reformatories should be conducted on prison lines only so far as is necessary to ensure safe custody and control, and on strict *asylum* principles in all matters referring to the treatment of inmates. The medical aspect . . . should control the application of restraint and punishment. The line of demarcation between madness and badness is sometimes most indefinite, and it is impossible for a lay mind to properly appreciate the extent of mental defect (i.e. disorder) or even the existence of it at all in cases where there is no delusional evidence of insanity . . . Bearing in mind this aspect of the question special care has been taken . . . to place the immediate control of affairs in the hands of a Medical Governor and a Medical Officer." Seventy years later the same argument was used by Dr. Peter Scott when he was considering what role, if any, the doctor should play in the treatment of the chronic offender. The doctor's peculiar contribution, he argued, is his ability to distinguish the pathological from the non-pathological, and so to see the need for medical intervention when ordinary responses to stress develop into pathological states (Mark and Scott, 1972).

The reformatory system for inebriates ran into a number of administrative and financial difficulties and fell into disuse during the First World War. By 1921 the system had been abandoned (Royal Commission, 1932). The drunkenness offender has remained a main-stay of the prison population ever since (Home Office, 1971), despite the widely accepted view that he would be better dealt with elsewhere — a view now enacted by the Criminal Justice Acts of 1967 and 1972. The former provides for the eventual abolition of imprisonment for the offence of "drunk and disorderly", and the latter for medical treatment centres to which the police can take drunken offenders. At the time of writing, little progress has been made towards the implementation of these measures, and the inebriate offender still goes to prison. Having first refused to treat him, and then failed to transfer him, it was not until the nineteen-sixties that the prison authorities tentatively embarked on the treatment of alcoholics (Commissioners of Prisons, 1961).

In the event, only one of Smalley's "quasi-criminal" groups was effectively removed from the prison system: the mental defective. The Mental Deficiency Act, long awaited since the 1908 report of the Royal Commission, was passed in 1913 and began to take effect after the war. Four grades of deficiency were defined, the last two being conditions which had not been within the scope of the Lunacy Acts: idiots, imbeciles, feeble-minded persons, and moral imbeciles. In each case it was necessary for the defect to have existed from an early age; (this was changed in 1927 to a requirement that it should have existed before the age of eighteen). Whilst idiots, imbeciles and the feeble-minded formed three grades of rising intelligence, moral imbeciles — who were renamed "moral defectives" in 1927 — were different in kind, not degree. As re-defined in the 1927 Mental Deficiency Act, moral defectives were persons "in whose case there exists mental defectiveness coupled with strongly vicious or criminal propensities and who require care, supervision and control for the protection of others". Mental defectiveness in this context did not necessarily mean intellectual defect, but was defined as "a condition of arrested or incomplete development of mind".

The 1913 Act required local authorities to set up institutions for the mentally deficient and empowered the courts to commit to these institutions any offenders coming within the four grades of deficiency. In addition, Section 9 of the Act allowed sentenced prisoners falling within the definitions to be transferred to asylums.

It was not until some ten years after the end of the First World War that the Act was working effectively as far as offenders were concerned. There were many initial difficulties, but in due course, by providing compulsory institutional care for defectives who had previously been at risk of imprisonment, the Act relieved the prisons of the seriously subnormal offender. By 1929 (Commissioners of Prisons, 1930) the Medical Commissioner estimated that its provisions had reduced the daily average prison population by about 200. This certainly represented a successful "clearing out" from prison of at least one of the quasi-criminal elements. But in respect of one sub-group, the prison authorities were less fortunate. "Moral imbeciles" had been brought within the compass of the 1913 Act in response to evidence given to the Royal Commission by prison (and other) doctors. The former must have rejoiced that these particularly difficult offenders were now to be channelled into the new asylums. But this first attempt to deal with one group of psychopaths was ahead of its time and was rarely used (Gibbens, 1966). Doctors came to believe that in order to come within the terms of the Mental Deficiency Acts, the moral defective had also to display defective intelligence (Royal Commission, 1958). The Act was therefore mainly used for those cases where moral defectiveness was coupled with subnormal intelligence.

The Beginnings of Psychotherapy

Many obstacles lay in the way of the Prison Commissioners' dream of a prison system purged of its mad and quasi-criminal elements, and devoted only to dealing with "fully responsible persons" (Report of Commissioners of Prisons and Directors of Convict Prisons, 1910). Some of the obstacles were practical, such as the difficulty of getting alternatives established and used. But as psychological medicine developed there emerged also fundamental and conceptual difficulties about separating the bad from the mad. The prison doctors of the nineteenth century had found this task a difficult one but they had not doubted that it could be done by a sufficiently skilled and experienced medical officer. But once psychiatry entered the era of Meyer and Freud the possibility of clearly separating the quasi-criminal from the criminal and the mad from the bad became more and more elusive. It was because of this difficulty that psychotherapy got its foot inside the prison gates; for as it became accepted that psychological factors could be at the root of some "bad" behaviour, so it became evident that there were no suitable institutions to which non-certifiable prisoners of this type could be transferred. The way was thus open for the prison authorities themselves to start looking at the possibilities of the psychological treatment of offenders, and this became more possible as a result of changes in the Prison Commission which took place in the early nineteen-twenties. Ruggles Brise retired and Alexander Paterson became a Commissioner. Paterson tried to decrease the punitive elements in prison administration, e.g. the broad arrow and convict crop were dropped, and to implement the ideals of the Gladstone Committee. In this climate, ideas about the psychological treatment of criminals fell on fertile ground.

The new ideas about the psychological and psycho-analytical treatment of offenders, which in the U.S. were already being applied to juvenile delinquents, began to penetrate into the English penal system in the nineteen-twenties. In their report for 1919-20 the Commissioners of Prisons (1921), wrote as follows: "During the year there have been indications that Justices and others interested in the administration of the criminal law, have been much exercised . . . as to whether the means hitherto taken for dealing with persons committing offences are the best and most humane which ought to be adopted. The opinion has been growing in intensity for some years that mental and physical disabilities may largely contribute to the commission of crime, and that it is the duty of the community to investigate thoroughly such causes . . . to determine whether such causes are beyond the ability of the individual to control, whether they do not limit wholly, or in part, the responsibility for the commission of the offence, to what extent they should be taken into account in determining the question of punishment, and whether for some form of *treatment* rather than *punishment* by imprisonment can be devised which shall be more scientific, efficacious and humane." The Prison Commissioners attributed the development of these views to two factors: one was the Mental Deficiency Act, which had shown that people previously punished for their behaviour were, in fact, in need of medical care; the other was the release from military hospitals of ex-servicemen suffering from mental and physical disabilities caused by the war.

As a result of the initiative of the Birmingham justices, part of Birmingham prison hospital was set aside for the "reception of persons on remand whose mental condition appears such as to warrant careful investigation". A full time M.O., Dr. M. Hamblin-Smith, was appointed to carry out this work. Until this time medical remand work had been directed purely to ascertaining whether the accused was insane or mentally defective. Hamblin-Smith's approach was more positive: he believed that in suitable cases delinquent conduct would yield to treatment of the underlying disorder. But the problem was the total lack of facilities for such treatment. "In making reports to courts, if we can say that a case is (insane or) certifiably mentally defective, the procedure is easy. But beyond this we are practically bankrupt" (Hamblin-Smith, 1923). The solution, he thought, was to provide special treatment institutions. "But we need not remain helpless until such institutions have been set up. We could have prisons, or parts thereof, set apart for the purpose, in which such cases could be treated as in a mental hospital. The great point is that such persons should be regarded as patients who are to be treated" (Hamblin-Smith, 1925).

Hamblin-Smith had an optimistic and open-minded approach to the possibilities of treating offenders. He deplored the compartmentalised way in which the different agencies — education, hospital, prisons, probation — each dealt with their own corner of the crime problem, and urged "the fullest co-ordination between these different authorities, even if they cannot be unified" (Hamblin-Smith, 1925). He stressed the need to train probation officers in the psychiatric aspects of crime (Hamblin-Smith, 1926), and the importance of recruiting doctors into the forensic field: in 1922, a medical post-graduate course, the first of its kind, was held at Birmingham University on "The Medical Aspects of Crime and Punishment", and lectures and demonstrations were held in the prison (Commissioners of Prisons, 1924).

As far as the treatment of offenders by psychological (which at the time meant psycho-analytic) means was concerned, Hamblin-Smith (1922) believed this would be successful with offenders whose behaviour was caused by the conflicts of a "repressed complex", who were anxious to change, and who were not subject to unfavourable environmental influences (Hamblin-Smith, 1926); he recognised that these were only a small group in the total of offenders and prisoners. The question was whether in the absence of other facilities, treatment could effectively be carried out in a prison environment, and in 1924 the question was put to the test: Birmingham prison became a centre to which sentenced prisoners of "unstable and difficult character" were sent. Hamblin-Smith (1934) reported that "the examination and management of these prisoners . . . has been of extreme interest . . .", but his experience at Birmingham seems eventually to have led him to conclude that prisons could not be used for the effective psychological treatment of offenders (Hamblin-Smith, 1922). The main difficulty was the prison system's punitive ethos. The deliberately imposed deprivation and hardship were anti-therapeutic, and the prison regime bore no relation to the prisoners' needs: "If a penal system exists for the purpose of inducing men to live in a more social way on release, then they must have chances of doing so while under sentence" (Hamblin-Smith, 1934). Although he paid tribute to the officers at Birmingham, he doubted whether prison staff were really the right people to carry out treatment. He would have liked a different method of staff selection, one that ensured that officers would be of higher educational status "young and enthusiastic . . . free from any inclination to blame or adopt any other attitude of superiority" (Hamblin-Smith, 1934). Given the existing system, he objected to sentencers imprisoning offenders with a view to their receiving treatment: "There are the strongest objections to combining the ideas of punishment and medical treatment: the subject is certain to look upon the treatment as part of the punishment" (Hamblin-Smith, 1934). An unwilling patient could not, he believed, be helped by psycho-analytic means; treatment was only possible when the offender himself wanted to change. This, of course, constituted a fundamental difficulty about the use of psychological treatment in prisons, which are places to which offenders are sent against their will: ". . . often people talk as though some special form of institution was able to reform by itself, and quite apart from the co-operation of the subject . . . Reformation is the result of a mental process within the man . . . There is something wanting in any scheme which assumes that all reform is contained in what is done to the prisoner, and which overlooks that creative impulse for regeneration which must come from the man himself" (Hamblin-Smith, 1922).

The Non-Sane Non-Insane

Hamblin-Smith's attempt to run part of Birmingham prison as a treatment centre was ahead of its time. The more commonly expressed view, and one that was certainly more convenient to the prison authorities, was that offenders who needed treatment should not be sent to prison, but should be dealt with in separate institutions. After the Mental Deficiency Act began to take effect and the mentally defective offender ceased to be imprisoned, it became clear to the medical officers that there remained many prisoners who were mentally abnormal, though they were neither certifiably deficient nor insane. Norwood East came to categorise them as the "non-sane non-insane". The Medical Commissioner wrote as follows in his annual report for 1921-22: "Medical opinion is agreed that, besides those who are certifiable as insane or mentally deficient there exists a third category of prisoners of abnormal mentality for whom no legal provision is at present made. Such prisoners cannot be dealt with under ordinary prison rules. Punishment only aggravates the trouble . . . They are therefore treated as far as possible as patients and are under the care of the medical officers . . . But the fact remains that prisons are not suitable places for such people. They require the care of a specially trained staff and should be located, as a rule, in hospital wards. In the wards of a prison hospital there is often no room for them, and isolation in a cell, even with frequent visits, tends to aggravate the condition . . . We think that such cases should not be sent to prisons or borstals at all. Such places are for those capable of being influenced by discipline and training. The abnormals, of whom we write, cannot be reached by such means. They require careful individual attention of a different kind — curative treatment . . . If they continue to arrive (in prisons) we should be furnished with the means to provide a separate establishment with a special staff."

Norwood East regarded the "non-sane non-insane" as comprising three elements: subnormals (ranging from near normal to near mental deficiency), psychopathic personalities and neurotics (both ranging from near normal to near insanity) (East, 1949). Once the prisons were relieved of the certifiable mental defective, the problems of these remaining abnormal prisoners attracted increasing attention from the medical staff. But the general reaction of the prison medical service to the new ideas about the psychological treatment of crime seems to have been one of cautious reserve. Norwood East, who became Medical Commissioner in 1929, frequently issued warnings against the exaggerated claims made for this form of treatment: "Statements are sometimes made . . . that psychotherapy can be relied upon to cure many recidivists and most first offenders . . . No statistics are available to show how many lawbreakers in this country have been checked in their criminal careers by this means, and no medical psychotherapist as far as I know has, as yet, any extensive experience in this method of dealing with crime" (East, 1932).

The claims of psychological medicine as a cure for crime were examined by the 1931-32 Departmental Committee on Persistent Offenders (Home Office, 1932), of which Norwood East was a member. The Committee found that "there is a widespread impression that many crimes are symptoms or effects of some mental disorder and that the offender's criminal habits can be cured by appropriate psychological treatment" (para. 109). It therefore took evidence from "a number of experts who have specialised in methods of psychological examination and in psychotherapy". These included prison medical officers. The Committee found that "no witness was able to give us any precise information concerning the curative value of psychological treatment in any large number of law breakers, and the results . . . have been inconclusive in the few convicted offenders who have been so treated during the currency of their sentences" (para. 113).

The Committee also pointed out that successful treatment could only be proved after a substantial period of follow-up. It concluded that "the application of (the psychological) method of treatment in criminal cases is in its infancy and is likely to remain so for many years to come", but recommended that "in order to test thoroughly the value of this method, a systematic follow up of the cases dealt with . . . should be conducted over a prolonged period; and the results, the failures as well as the successes, should be published . . ." (para. 116). Since there were very few outpatient clinics, the Committee recommended that part of this trial should take place in selected prisons or borstals.

The East-Hubert Report

In response to this recommendation, Dr. W. H. de Hubert from St. Thomas's Hospital was in 1933 appointed to carry out psychological treatment of selected prisoners at Wormwood Scrubs. The purpose of his four-year investigation was "to determine how far psychiatric and psychotherapeutic experience in the management and treatment of psychotic and psycho-neurotic illnesses and various forms of behaviour disorder could be applied with profit to offenders serving prison sentences" (East and Hubert, 1939). Dr. Hubert used two modes of treatment described in the Hubert and East Report respectively as the

"simple" and "complex" method. The former consisted of discussions
with the patient, designed to give him a better intellectual grasp of his
problems. The latter involved the development of a transference
situation, and the use of the "analytical therapeutic method". Medical
officers all over the country were invited to suggest suitable cases for
treatment: the broad criteria were that the prisoner should be under 40
willing to have treatment, serving at least six months and convicted of
offences considered to be due to some "remedial" condition (para. 34);
unstable adolescents were also potential candidates. No prisoner with
certifiable mental disorder was eligible. Four hundred and six referred
cases were seen by Dr. Hubert, of which 214 were approved for
treatment.

The report gives full case histories for many of the referrals
(including those found unsuitable for treatment) and shows their
response to psychotherapy whilst in prison. Unfortunately there was no
follow-up data. "As, at the most, any treated cases in our series can
only have been out of prison four years at the present time, while the
majority have been at liberty for much shorter periods, and some, in
fact, are still serving their sentences, it is not possible to show the result
of our investigations statistically" (para. 158). No information on
subsequent mental health or criminal career are therefore given, and
in this respect the report wholly failed to fulfil the requirements of the
Persistent Offenders Committee. Nevertheless on the basis of
"observation, investigation and careful consideration of all the data",
Hubert and East (1939) felt justified in reaching certain conclusions.
One of these was that "psychotherapy as an adjunct to an ordinary
prison sentence appears to be effective in preventing, or in reducing the
chance of, future antisocial behaviour" (para. 158). But the number of
disorders thought likely to respond to psychotherapy was "comparatively small" (para. 160) and "it is more than probable that skilled
direction, management, specialised training and other general
psychiatric methods of treatment are applicable to a very much larger
number of cases and to a wider range of conditions than is
psychotherapy alone" (para. 163).

The main recommendation of the report (para. 172) was that "the
most satisfactory method of dealing with abnormal and unusual types
of criminal would be by the creation of a penal institution of a special
kind". This was intended to serve three functions. First, as a clinic and
hospital, where cases could be investigated and if necessary treated,
and where criminological research could also be centred. Secondly, as
an institution in which selected prisoners could live under special

conditions of training and treatment: these would be offenders who had not responded to the methods used in ordinary prisons and the aim would be "by the application of psychiatric experience, to achieve alterations where future behaviour is concerned". Thirdly, as a colony for offenders who had proved themselves quite unable to adapt to ordinary social life, but for whom reformative measures seemed useless. It was recommended that the medical staff at the proposed institution should be psychiatrically trained and that the super-intendent should be a prison psychiatrist (para. 173).

By recommending that the proposed new establishment should be part of the prison system, Hubert and East rejected the traditional view and ideal of the prison authorities, that the abnormal offender should be shunted right out of the prisons. On the contrary, they believed that the prison medical service had a competence and expertise in the field that made them *more* suitable than other authorities, to undertake the treatment of the mentally abnormal offender. Their distrust both of non-medical psychologists and of doctors without adequate forensic experience seems to have been the reason for this: "In this field enthusiasm not uncommonly outruns discretion and it would be a great misfortune if the psychiatric approach to crime became discredited by irresponsible exponents unaware, perhaps, of the complexity of the problem involved" (para. 167).

The East-Hubert report, although its recommendations were not implemented for about 25 years, marks a turning point in the history of British prison psychiatry. In the first place, it shows the prison medical authority anxious to take on, rather than to shed, the task of treating the mentally abnormal prisoner. Secondly, it defines the objective for that treatment—not a medical objective but a behavioural one: "The main object of psychotherapy in criminal work is to prevent crime being committed and repeated by the individual" (para. 58). By explicitly defining the main purpose of prison psychiatry as the prevention of recidivism, the authors ensured that the prison authorities would, in their search for ways of making prisons reformative, henceforward pay increasing attention to the views of psychiatrists. Thus the prison psychiatrist came to a new role, not unlike the role of the chaplain in earlier times; he came to be regarded as an expert in the business of turning criminals away from crime*.

The third turning point was that the Home Office and the Prison Commissioners accepted the report and its treatment concepts. Instead of pursuing the traditional policy of seeking to transfer from the prison system those abnormal offenders who were unsuited to ordinary penal discipline, the authorities were henceforward committed to trying to adapt the prison system so as to make it suit the mentally abnormal inmate. This point was illustrated by the way in which Dr. Methven, who succeeded Norwood East, welcomed the recommendations of the report: "The value of such an institution as is proposed . . . lies in the fact that it will not follow the usual run of prisons — within its boundaries treatment to meet the needs of each individual can be applied" (Commissioners of Prisons, 1939).

Post Second World War Developments

The outbreak of the war brought developments to a stop; Wormwood Scrubs was closed, and psychiatric work ceased. It was not resumed until 1943 when Dr. Mackwood was appointed as a part-time psychotherapist at the re-opened Wormwood Scrubs. Although only a very small proportion of the cases referred to him were found to be suitable for treatment (18 out of 70 in 1943), hopes of success were high, as the Senior Medical Officer's annual report showed: "Since 1934 a large amount of information has been collected on the type of case which is likely to be cured by psychotherapy in prison, and on the possibility, failing a cure, of bringing about a practical modification of his abnormal psychological processes. This is being applied, as far as circumstances permit, in the prevention and cure of criminal tendencies associated with such defects" (Commissioners of Prisons, 1945). The 1945 Prison Medical Officers' Conference had as its main topic "Psychotherapy in Prisons": the object was to review the selection

---

*It is interesting that when confidence in religion as a reformative method was at its height, it was thought suitable and appropriate for a clergyman to be both Chaplain and Governor. No more dreadful warning to the modern Medical Superintendent and Governor could exist than the picture painted by Hamblin-Smith of what happened at Millbank in the early nineteenth century when the Governor was the Rev. Daniel Nihil: "He attempted to organise a complete system of religious work . . . He insisted that his . . . officers should set what he termed a proper example. The result was the production of a system of gross hypocrisy. The officers were well aware that their promotion . . . depended on the opinion of Mr. Nihil as to their spiritual zeal . . . They sought to obtain credit . . . by professions of piety, the use of scriptural language and the ostentatious carrying of bibles." The prisoners did the same and spent much time in discussing matters of religion with the Governor. The system is said ultimately to have resulted in complete chaos (Hamblin-Smith, 1934).

of cases referred to Wormwood Scrubs for treatment. Among those regarded as unsuitable were the certifiable, the subnormal, those with cerebral changes, those with "constitutional psychopathy" and those whose criminal careers showed "marked chronicity".

During the war, group methods of psychotherapy were developed and used in certain hospitals that treated psychiatric disturbances among servicemen (Northfield Experiment). It was not long before the value of the ideas underlying these methods was recognised by psychiatrists working in prisons. In 1947 the Principal Medical Officer at Wormwood Scrubs wrote as follows: "Many of the mental illnesses from which man suffers and which are amenable to psychotherapy arise from the setting of man in relation to the society in which he lives. His relationship with others has caused his illness or demonstrated its existence and therefore it would appear rational that he should be treated in a supervised relationship with his fellows . . . The value of group psychotherapy is being increasingly recognised as a useful method of psychiatric treatment and it has a definite place in prison practice" (Commissioners of Prisons, 1948). In 1946 Dr. Mackwood started a trial of group treatment for men already receiving individual psychotherapy. He found it was advantageous in various ways, including its suitability for a wider selection of prisoners. But he considered the constraints of prison conditions and of fixed sentences to be handicaps in the treatment, as was the lack of aftercare: "On getting back into civil life after feeling an accepted member of a socialised group in prison, with a morale that he values, the ex-prisoner finds that . . . acceptance is too often denied him. Then his morale begins to flag" (Commissioners of Prisons, 1950).

Increasing experience of group and therapeutic community methods eventually led to the decision that the psychiatric prison which Hubert and East had recommended should be run on these lines. The advent into prisons of the idea of the therapeutic community — the idea that the inmate community itself can be made into a powerful instrument of rehabilitation — was an important step. It constituted a serious assault on Sir Godfrey Lushington's argument (Home Office, 1895) that imprisonment could never be reformative, because it involved "the continual association with none but criminals", and gave new ammunition to those who believed that prisons could be made into instruments of treatment and reform.

The establishment of a National Health Service in 1946 left the prison medical service unaffected and independent, and in the decade after the war the Commissioners went ahead with a considerable expansion of their psychiatric services. It took a rather different form from that which Hubert and East had advised, for they had been emphatic about the importance of centralising psychiatric facilities. Post-war economic conditions ruled out any immediate prospect of a special psychiatric institution being built, but such developments as took place in the psychiatric field were not in the direction of centralisation: the services were spread more widely, as well as expanded. Wakefield became a centre for psychiatric treatment in 1946 and was intended to serve the prisons of the north as Wormwood Scrubs served the south.

The expansion of the psychiatric services in the post-war decade is illustrated by two extracts from the annual reports. In 1946 the Medical Commissioner had written that "There is a considerable amount of medical and surgical work to be done in the prisons and though the psychiatric work is equally important it does not represent by any means the major part" (Commissioners of Prisons, 1947). By 1950 the assessment was different: "While prison medical practice affords considerable opportunity for experience in physical medicine, it is recognised that the greater part of the work lies in the psychiatric field" (Commissioners of Prisons, 1951). Most of the psychiatric work centred on diagnosis rather than treatment. In 1957, for example, when there were 16,000 sentenced men in prison, the number receiving psychotherapy was about 200, while over 5,000 men were remanded in custody for psychiatric reports in that year (Commissioners of Prisons, 1958).

Part of the impetus for the expansion on the diagnostic side can be attributed to the Criminal Justice Act of 1948. This required the courts to consider the prison authorities' "suitability" reports on mental and physical health, before imposing sentences of corrective training, preventive detention, or borstal training. The Act also introduced two new "psychiatric" sentences: probation with a condition of mental treatment, and, for magistrates' courts, hospital reception orders for offenders coming within the scope of the Lunacy Acts. These changes meant an increased demand for pre-sentence psychiatric examinations and reports. In addition, the internal requirements of the prison system, with its growing emphasis on classification, involved the medical staff in further diagnostic work. To assist with this and also with treatment, ancillary psychiatric services were developed. More emphasis was given to the psychiatric training of hospital officers; psychiatric social workers were appointed at the prisons with psychiatric facilities; and in 1950 the prison psychologists became established.

Two other developments in the post-war decade were of interest. One was the introduction into prisons of visiting psychotherapists from local hospitals. The original idea was that short term prisoners in need of treatment would then continue to visit the same therapist after release. Earlier attempts to attain the same objective by sending the prisoners out to local clinics for treatment had been discontinued as unsuccessful "largely owing to the sharp contrast between the clinic and the prison, repeated at each visit". This contrast, the prison authorities believed, "tends to obscure the function of a prison to reclaim its inmates by emphasising the punitive aspect in the mind of the prisoner" (Commissioners of Prisons, 1949).

Another development was the wider variety of psychiatric or psychological methods of treatment that came into use — ECT, narcoanalysis, ether abreaction, aversion therapy (the case of a fetishist treated at Wormwood Scrubs was described in the 1957 report) and psychodrama. Attempts were also made at some establishments to run selected wings as therapeutic communities. These treatments were often described in the Annual Reports as having beneficial results, but little information on the exact nature of the benefits was given.

There was in fact no agreed view as to what psychiatric treatment in prison was intended to achieve. Hubert and East had been specific that one of its objects was to prevent the prisoner from offending again. By 1947, however, the Medical Commissioner was expressing a more limited view: "It is sometimes assumed that cure by psychological treatment is, or should be, a sure preventive of further criminal activity. Criminal acts may arise from abnormal psychological factors of which the subject is unaware or only partially aware. The function of psychotherapy is to bring these factors into consciousness in such a way that any repetition of the act can only take place if the subject has the will and intention to do it. To expect more from psychological treatment is to give it credit for greater power than it possesses." In 1949 Dr. Gould, one of the psychiatrists at Wormwood Scrubs, explicitly drew attention to two very different possible roles for prison psychiatry: "In the prison service general physical care is provided for prisoners, and as ancillary to the general care provided by the medical staff of the prison service there are available consultants and specialists in surgery, ophthalmology etc . . . Psychological treatment could conceivably be organised in a similar way, namely to treat the incidental psychiatric illness of the prison population with no special regard to underlying factors in their future behaviour, or to put it from a different point of view, the psychiatrist or psychotherapist would be primarily concerned with psychological illness in prisoners, but not primarily concerned with the psychiatric aspects of antisocial behaviour. With this approach . . . prisoners would then be selected for treatment who responded rapidly and easily to orthodox methods of approach as used in general civil practice, and the problem of the reform of the prisoner would be left where it has always lain traditionally, with the discipline staff of the prison. The current social outlook, however, and current psychiatric thought are apt to regard psychiatry as capable of making a direct contribution to the treatment of anti-social behaviour . . . The enlightened public conscience perhaps must decide whether the role of psychiatry in prison should be the treatment of those who respond readily to orthodox forms of therapy (and thus regard psychiatry as an ancillary service) or whether psychiatry be applied as a fundamental method of approach to those whose antisocial behaviour is psychologically motivated . . ." (Commissioners of Prisons, 1950). Dr. Gould himself believed that our techniques for achieving this second objective had yet to be developed.

The fundamental questions raised by Dr. Gould were not, at any rate publicly, further examined by the prison medical authorities. But by 1956, the Director of Medical Services (Dr. Snell) was assuming that both of the two functions discussed by Dr. Gould were the task of prison medical officers: "If we are to fit men and women to lead good and useful lives every effort must be made not only to care for their well being and ordinary health while they are in our care, but to seek out, and if possible to remedy, physical disabilities and maladjustments of personality which may hinder vocational fitness or social relationships and make it more difficult for them to regain a place in law abiding society" (Commissioners of Prisons, 1957). This view was endorsed in the government White Paper of 1959, *Penal Practice in a Changing Society* (Home Office, 1959).

The Impact of the 1959 Mental Health Act

Meanwhile, half a century after the appointment of the Radnor Commission (Royal Commission, 1908), the Percy Royal Commission on the law relating to mental illness and mental deficiency was set up (Royal Commission, 1958). The evidence concerning mentally abnormal offenders that was presented to the Commission centred largely round the moral defective or psychopath. Although there had been a suggestion in the 1946 Annual Report that the prison medical service would have welcomed a wider definition of moral defectiveness, so as to achieve the transfer of certain psychopathic prisoners into long-term asylums, the Home Office in its evidence to the Royal Commission did not suggest any such course. Not only did it resist the opportunity of proposing that these difficult inmates should be decanted from the prisons into the health services, but it also firmly accepted responsibility for the treatment of mentally abnormal prisoners in general. A number of bodies, however, pressed for changes. The British Medical Association and the Royal Medico-Psychological Association asked for the definition of the moral defective to be widened so as clearly to include persons of normal intelligence and those in whom the condition developed after the age of 18. As for the question of where these persons were to be treated: "Care and treatment under compulsory conditions can be and are in a number of cases provided by means of a prison sentence . . . Treatment under prison conditions is not however always appropriate and its duration is always limited by the length of the sentence." The BMA and RMPA therefore suggested that a variety of new institutions should be set up for the psychopath (whether or not his behaviour was criminal), and that these should include at least one institution on "colony" lines, one on the therapeutic community model and others of a purely medical character for the treatment of alcoholics and drug addicts.

Although these and other witnesses pressed for the expansion of non-prison facilities, it is interesting that not only the Home Office but virtually all the doctors who gave evidence to the Percy Commission accepted prisons as places where offenders in need of treatment could suitably be sent. For example, Dr. Maxwell Jones told the Commission that he believed that ". . . special units either in relation to psychiatric hospitals or prisons, or both, and run on the lines of a therapeutic community offer the best chance of resocialising anti-social character disorders". The Royal Commission accepted that for some psychopathic offenders "it may be desirable to combine the deterrent aspects of imprisonment . . . with psychiatric treatment" and that "at present this combination of treatment and detention can be provided for some patients in prison" (para. 344). But they were conscious of the difficulty that treatment in prison could only be provided for the fixed term of the sentence, and that some psychopathic offenders needed longer or indeterminate periods of treatment. Their recommendation was that a psychopathic offender should be liable to compulsory hospitalisation "only if the court is satisfied that normal penal measures alone are insufficient or inappropriate" (para. 356).

The Mental Health Act of 1959 which followed the report of the Royal Commission made major changes in the law relating to the mentally abnormal offender. First, courts were empowered to make hospital orders when imprisonable offences were committed by persons suffering from mental disorder, and the new definition of mental disorder covered a far wider range of conditions than had previously been subject to compulsory care under the Mental Deficiency and Lunacy Acts. Sentenced prisoners suffering from disorder could be transferred to hospital by the Home Secretary's direction. Secondly, no offender could be made subject to a hospital order unless a hospital was willing to accept him: in the previous legislation, hospitals had no right to refuse a certified patient committed by the criminal courts. Thirdly, the term "moral defective" was abandoned and the considerably wider definition of "psychopathic disorder" was substituted — "a persistent disorder or disability of mind (whether or not including subnormality of intelligence) which results in abnormally agressive or seriously irresponsible conduct on the part of the patient, and requires or is susceptible to medical treatment".

One might have thought that this definition together with the other provisions of the Act would have sufficed to transfer a considerable proportion of the population at risk of imprisonment into mental hospitals; but a number of factors have prevented this. One has been the development of psychotropic drug treatments which have enabled hospitals to help and discharge certain types of patients much more rapidly than before. Secondly, there was the spread of the open door policy which went with the more permissive and humane regimes introduced in mental hospitals after the war. This, together with the requirement that a hospital order could only be made when a specific hospital was willing to accept the offender, meant that hospital doctors became unwilling to accept difficult patients such as chronic schizophrenics or aggressive "psychopaths" whom they felt they could not help, nor even hold. It also meant that for offenders, psychopathic or otherwise, who were committed to ordinary hospitals, there was little compulsion to stay: as Dr. Rollin (1968) puts it "they are fed . . . from the prison system into the mental hospital system only again to be discharged, or allowed to discharge themselves, or to abscond". Walker and McCabe have now examined this revolving door system in some detail. They show that although some thousand hospital orders are made annually, a combination of factors, including the prevalence of absconding, prevents many of the recipients from staying long in hospital. The result is that many offender patients made subject to hospital orders are soon free again to come into conflict with the law and run the risk of imprisonment — a risk which is considerable, since Walker and McCabe (1973) show that 60% of the men and 42% of the women in their sample of hospital order cases had two or more previous convictions.

Thus the Mental Health Act has provided only limited relief for the prisons, as far as the mentally abnormal offender is concerned. In 1972 the prison authorities reported that because of the difficulty of obtaining mental hospital beds for offenders who had been remanded for psychiatric examination, "a senior medical officer at one establishment . . . conducted a short trial of the treatment of chronic psychotics in prison by recommending to courts, in cases which had several times been the subject of orders under Section 60 of the Act, that a short period of imprisonment might be just as beneficial as a few months in a mental hospital. None of the magistrates demurred . . ." (Home Office, 1973). Thus fifty years after the Birmingham magistrates had first questioned the wisdom and justice of imprisoning mentally abnormal offenders, the reluctance of hospitals to accept them for treatment, even when psychotic, seems to be channelling them back into prison (see also Bowden, 1975a). A contributing difficulty has been the absence within the National Health Service of secure hospital units: despite the recommendations for such units made by the 1961 Working Party on Special Hospitals (Ministry of Health, 1961), the potentially aggressive offender who is mentally abnormal and is thought to need security is still catered for only by the Special Hospitals and the prisons. The Butler Committee, which was appointed in 1972 to examine the law and facilities relating to the mentally abnormal offender, produced in 1974 a strongly worded interim report (Home Office, DHSS, 1974) which re-emphasised the recommendations of the 1961 Working Party and urged the building of security units within the National Health Service. The Government has accepted the need for this, and has undertaken to make some funds available for the purpose (Hansard, 1974). But in the meantime shortage of space in the Special Hospitals, together with the reluctance of ordinary hospitals to accept offender patients, has made it difficult for the prison authorities to find vacancies not only for remanded offenders, but for sentenced prisoners whose mental illness requires hospitalisation.

In the same year as the Mental Health Act became law, the Government published a general review and analysis of its penal policy, *Penal Practice in a Changing Society* (Home Office, 1959).

After stating that work on a psychiatric prison hospital would soon be started at Grendon, the paper went on ". . . when this is ready the major psychotherapy now carried out at the three clinics (Wormwood Scrubs, Wakefield and Holloway) will be concentrated in one place . . . But the value of psychiatry is not limited to the treatment of those abnormal states of mind which require the kind of psychotherapy that will be given in the new establishment. A psychiatrically experienced doctor can do much to help disturbed prisoners not only to adjust themselves to prison life but also to change their general attitudes so that they make a better adjustment in society after release." The paper recommended that such services should be available in most of the larger prisons. This represented an attitude to the psychiatrist's role that was very different from the one that Hubert and East had taken. He was no longer simply to be the doctor who could treat selected "cases" by psychiatric methods; he was also a specialist in helping prisoners "to change their general attitudes". In this new role he was to be found a place in every major prison. While East and Hubert had wanted to see the psychiatric services centralised and used mainly in an establishment that was run on psychiatric lines, the idea now was to spread the services throughout the prison system without necessarily remodelling it; indeed, one of the psychiatrist's functions was to help prisoners "to adjust themselves to prison life".

The White Paper recognised two difficulties about the proposed policy. One was the shortage of prison psychiatrists, and the other was the fact that they spent most of their time examining remand prisoners for the courts. The solution proposed was that separate establishments should be set up for remand prisoners: "When the proposed remand and observation centres are established the medical officers in the ordinary prisons may hope to be free to devote much more of their time to the mental care of those prisoners whom they can help." In the event, this never happened. With one exception (Risley), the only remand centres to be set up were for young persons, and in the large local prisons the psychiatrists still spend much of their time on work for the courts. This aspect of prison psychiatry expanded at an unprecedented rate after the Mental Health Act came into force, an expansion which the authors of the White Paper had not foreseen; between 1959 and 1969 the number of prisoners remanded for psychiatric reports increased from 5,700 to 13,400.

East and Hubert (1939) could hardly have anticipated that psychiatric remands would reach these proportions, but they had in their report drawn attention to the "danger that for the sake of securing an expert medical examination . . . the courts may commit to custody persons who could properly be examined on bail". They had therefore suggested that in areas where outpatient clinics were not available, the prison medical officers should be enabled to carry out examinations on an outpatient basis. It was not until 1971 that a few such facilities were established. The 1964 Working Party on the Organisation of the Prison Medical Service (Home Office, 1964) had stressed the need to prevent the prison psychiatric service from becoming too self-contained. As one way of avoiding this, they had recommended that there should be joint appointments of psychiatrists to serve part-time in prison, and part-time in the forensic field outside: this, like the use of visiting psychotherapists, is fostering links between psychiatric practice inside and outside prisons. The logical long-term development may well be the integration of the prison medical service with the national health service.

Grendon Prison and After

The psychiatric prison recommended by East and Hubert was eventually built at Grendon Underwood in Buckinghamshire and opened in July 1962. Its objectives were defined by the prison authorities as follows: "Grendon's three primary tasks will be to investigate and treat mental disorders generally recognised as responsive to treatment, to investigate offenders whose offences in themselves suggest mental morbidity, and to explore the problem of dealing with the psychopath. The prisoners . . . selected will be those whose mental disorder is not of such nature and degree to qualify for . . . transfer to a hospital under Section 72 of the Mental Health Act but who require psychiatric treatment and management" (Commissioners of Prisons, 1963).

The form which the psychiatric prison took and which is described in Chapter 4, is rather different from what East and Hubert envisaged; nor, contrary to their plans, did the new institution centralise within itself the whole of the prison psychiatric service. Grendon only takes some 200 men and it was inevitable that treatment would continue to be given at other prisons. Nevertheless, the proportion of the prison population receiving treatment remains small. Much of the prison psychiatrist's time is spent on work other than treatment: the demand for reports is heavy, not only from the courts, but from within the prison service, and from the parole board. Detailed figures of the number of inmates receiving psychiatric treatment are no longer published in the annual reports, but the ratio of staff to prisoners gives an indication of what is possible: in 1971 when the total prison population averaged almost 39,000, there were 97 full-time medical officers in post, 45 of whom had a diploma in psychological medicine, and the number of part-time visiting psychotherapists was 50 (Home Office, 1972).

These figures are relevant to a problem which has dogged the prison psychiatric service since the twenties: the disparity between what the service can achieve, and what it is believed it can achieve. From the very beginning the prison medical authorities were at pains to emphasise that only a very small proportion of prisoners was likely to be "cured" of crime by psychological or psychiatric treatment. Norwood East repeated this again and again, as have done most of his successors. But in spite of the cautions issued by the practitioners of prison psychiatry, the courts have invested it with tremendous potency. Of course even before the advent of psychological treatment, courts have always been ready to send problem cases to prison; Hobhouse and Brockway (1922) surveying their fellow prisoners during the First World War came to the conclusion that "the official assurance 'he will be well looked after in prison' is too readily accepted". Since then psychiatry has acquired an immense prestige and mystique, in which doctors working in the forensic field have shared. It seems that sentencers may have an exaggerated view both of the size of the prison psychiatric service, and of what it can hope to achieve. This together with the fact that the prisons, unlike the hospitals, are secure and cannot refuse to accept a mentally abnormal offender, is inevitably affecting sentencing policy. Hamblin-Smith would almost certainly have been disconcerted to find the Court of Appeal announcing in 1969 that within limits "it may be perfectly proper to increase the sentence to enable a cure (for alcoholism) to be undertaken whilst in prison" (Thomas, 1970). He would probably have taken exception both to the principle and to the language: the principle of making punitive detention a pre-requisite of treatment, and the language which suggested that the cure for alcoholism could be taken or administered rather like a bottle of iron tablets for anaemia. Today such cures are no more readily available than in Hamblin-Smith's time, but sentencers are reluctant to accept this fact. Offenders who are sent to prison may be assured that the intention is purely therapeutic — "We are not doing it to punish you" (Thomas, 1970) — or that it is therapeutic as well as punitive. In 1968 the Court of Appeal refused to reduce a five-year sentence on a twenty-one year old drug addict. Although the offender had not been co-operative in treatment in prison, the Court noted that "he is under Dr . . . (a visiting psychotherapist) who perhaps is one of the greatest experts on drugs . . . and albeit we are told he is only visited by Dr . . . once a month, it is a satisfaction to the court to know that even that is happening". The Court upheld the sentence, "not merely as a punishment to this man, but as producing the conditions where a cure is most hopeful" (Glasse, 1968).

CHAPTER 2

Orientation and Methods

It is clear from the previous chapter that to some extent psychiatry has become entwined with penology: a belief has developed that anti-social behaviour is a form of sickness, a mental aberration, which comes within the psychiatrist's province to treat. The belief has a number of origins, not all of them Freudian. At the simplest level it may be argued that since it is only sensible and sane, acting in one's own best interests, to conform to the law, those that break the law seriously or repeatedly must be in some way mentally abnormal. This argument is strengthened by the knowledge that (a) some forms of mental illness lead to illegal behaviour (e.g. a man suffering from a severe depression may believe that life is so bad and hopeless that he must kill himself and all his family) and (b) whenever prison populations are examined a considerable number of mentally disturbed people are found. However, the argument neglects some important factors. It is not always sane and sensible to obey the law; there are circumstances where breaking the law is likely to prove a more rewarding course for a particular individual. Merton (1938) has argued that for those who cannot legitimately achieve the goals of society, such as affluence, illegal or criminal methods are among the few available alternatives. Other sociologists (Mannheim, 1965) have demonstrated how far crime is socially determined, and how environmental and situational factors, as well as personal ones, may be criminogenic. Psychiatrists have therefore to be scrupulous in refusing to diagnose mental disturbance on the basis of anti-social or illegal behaviour alone; Sir Aubrey Lewis (1953) has warned us against this trap. Illegal behaviour may give a clue to mental disturbance, but the diagnosis of psychiatric disorder must be made on other grounds independent of the illegality.

Also to be resisted is the assumption that because prisons contain a large number of people suffering from psychiatric disturbance, it necessarily follows that criminality is a form of mental disorder. The prison population represents only a small and highly selected minority of all convicted offenders and studies of people in prison are unlikely to throw light on the general relationship between crime and mental abnormality. Sentencing policy determines who is sent to prison, and is itself determined by a great variety of factors and influences, among them the availability of alternative provision for people who break the law. We saw in the previous chapter how the setting up of mental deficiency institutions led to the exodus from prisons of the seriously mentally subnormal offender; and how, more recently, trends in the Health Service have prevented certain mentally ill offenders from being accepted by hospitals, and have channelled them back once more into the penal system. Penrose (1939) pointed out that countries with large mental hospital populations have low prison populations and vice versa, and it is certainly interesting to see that, as the mental hospital population has been declining in England and Wales since the 1950s, so the prison population has been rising.

Comparisons between levels of morbidity in the general population and in the prison population are difficult to make. One needs to know what level of mental abnormality has been caused by the aftermath of the crime and by the imprisonment. For example, it is very difficult to establish, unless several helpful informants are available, whether a depressed murderer is depressed because he has been imprisoned for life, depressed because of the conditions in which he is imprisoned, depressed by the enormity of his crime, or whether he committed murder because he was depressed in the first place.

In view of all these factors, it cannot be assumed that because prisons contain a large number of disturbed people there is a fundamental relationship between crime and mental disorder. This, of course, does not make it inappropriate to have psychiatrists offering treatment in prisons, any more than it is inappropriate for a general physician to offer treatment in a prison: both are essential for humane care. But although, as we have seen, doctors entered the prison system for this reason, psychiatrists gradually came to be regarded as specialists with the task of curing crime by medical methods. Inevitably, therefore, the question of what prison psychiatrists actually do, and what they could be expected to do, has loomed large in our minds throughout our research.

Personality Disorder and Psychopathic Personality

The idea that crime is, or is linked with, mental abnormality has been given status through the development of the concept of moral defectiveness, or, as it later became, psychopathy. The concept, in the words of Walker and McCabe (1973) is of a disorder "which in the first place falls short of more definite forms of mental disorder, and secondly is associated with anti-social conduct". We have seen in the previous chapter how psychopathy was defined in the 1959 Mental Health Act, and Wootton (1959) has drawn attention to the implications of that definition: "The psychopath makes nonsense of every attempt to distinguish the sick from the healthy delinquent by the presence or absence of a psychiatric syndrome, or by symptoms of mental disorder which are independent of his objectionable behaviour . . . He is, in fact, the model of the circular process by which mental abnormality is inferred from anti-social behaviour while anti-social behaviour is explained by mental abnormality."

However circular the process, it has ensured that certain offenders, *because* of their behaviour, are regarded as the proper object of psychiatric treatment. Most contemporary systems of psychiatric diagnostic classification include a group of disorders called "personality disorders", with sub-groups for anti-social personality disorders. The current International Classification of Diseases, for example, has a code 301 which the British Glossary (General Register Office, 1968) says refers to a group of more or less well defined anomalies or deviations of personality which are not the result of psychosis or any other illness. The equivalent diagnostic manual of the American Psychiatric Association (1968) refers to a "group of disorders . . . characterised by deeply ingrained maladaptive patterns of behaviour that are perceptibly different in quality from psychotic and neurotic symptoms. Generally there are life-long patterns, often recognisable by the time of adolescence or earlier". Each of the classifications has a sub-category for "antisocial personality disorder".

The British Glossary states: "This term should be confined to those individuals who offend against society, who show a lack of sympathetic feeling, and whose behaviour is not readily modifiable by experience, including punishment. They may tend to abnormally aggressive and seriously irresponsible conduct. This category includes those individuals who are classified in the Mental Health Act 1959 (England and Wales) as suffering from 'psychopathic disorder'." The APA definition is similar: "This term is reserved for individuals who are basically unsocialised and whose behaviour pattern brings them repeatedly into conflict with society. They are incapable of significant loyalty to individuals, groups or social values. They are grossly selfish, callous, irresponsible, impulsive, and unable to feel guilt or to learn from experience and punishment. Frustration tolerance is low. They tend to blame others or offer plausible rationalisations for their behaviour. A mere history of repeated legal or social offences is not sufficient to justify this diagnosis. Group delinquent reaction of childhood (or adolescence) and social maladjustment without psychiatric disorder should be ruled out before making this diagnosis."

Clearly these are vague and diffuse definitions, and it is not surprising that in practice they are used as dustbin categories for a heterogeneous collection of problems, and that reliability between psychiatrists is very difficult to obtain (Walton and Presley, 1973). Few would doubt that chronic disturbances of psychological function do occur — analysts talk of weak ego or super ego structure — nor would many doubt the disastrous consequences of being unable to socialise effectively, i.e. to give and take love, to fit into groups with an appropriate degree of self assertiveness and submissiveness, and to take others' needs into account as well as one's own. These are the kinds of problem which the personality disorder definitions are aiming at, but they suffer from a number of serious deficiencies. The British definition, for example, makes no attempt to exclude individuals caught up in a repeated social conflict which for them may be perfectly healthy. The American definition is more careful about this point, but both definitions include, without reference to data, a whole range of traits which are necessary for the diagnosis, presumably on the assumption that such traits can be readily measured and that they correlate together. The American definition says that selfishness, callousness, impulsiveness, inability to feel guilt, low frustration tolerance, all appear in antisocial personality disorder. Using data from the present research two of us (Gunn and Robertson, 1976) examined such a hypothesis about the Grendon population, a group commonly described as being composed entirely of psychopaths. We found it very difficult to get reliability between the two interviewers on important traits such as sexual adjustment and impulsiveness, and think this indicates that there are areas of difficulty in measuring personality traits which cannot lightly be dismissed. Moreover for those traits where we did obtain reliability there was little inter-correlation between one and another. The results deterred us from attempting, by means of a factor analysis, to extract a general component of personality disorder.

For all these reasons we have largely eschewed the terms personality disorder, and psychopathy, in this book. Our decision may be regarded as an academic eccentricity, or valid only for research projects, but this is not our view. We believe that the concept of psychopathic disorder is used as a dumping zone for a host of problems which do not necessarily interrelate, and that it has overtones of despair in clinical work because it is regarded as a fixed pattern with little potential for change. People who are given the diagnosis are not a homogenous group in aetiological or therapeutic terms, and the label tells the clinician nothing about the patient's symptoms or about the kind of treatment or care that is appropriate. We have noted with interest that an important American text-book (Redlich and Freedman 1966) some years ago even gave up having a separate section on personality disorders. In their chapter on neurotic behaviour they state: "Asocial and antisocial behaviour varies from relatively mild cases, with unreliable and unresponsible personal relationships to very severe destructive cases. It must be remembered that value orientation influences diagnostic and therapeutic endeavours with the sociopathic group. A behaviouristic diagnosis — a list of facts — that does not include the psychosocial context in which they occurred is of little use . . . Crime is a legal, not a psychiatric term . . . The function of value judgments is particularly evident when an 'antisocial' member of one culture or social class is evaluated by a member of a culture with different mores . . . The range of impulsive disorders from the neurotic to the sociopathic is wide . . . Many persons well situated in stable social roles and professional groups show in their character problems a large 'component' of sociopathic disregard for bonds and feelings . . . clear demarcation from what is ordinarily called neurotic and psychotic behaviour is often not possible." Redlich and Freedman then go on to discuss sociopathic behaviour as a subsection of neurotic behaviour. We believe their approach more nearly takes into account the difficulties we identified than do the traditional systems.

Outline of Research

The object of the study was to examine the nature, extent and effectiveness of the psycho-therapeutic facilities available within British prisons, and to form some estimate of the demand for such facilities. Since resources allocated to the project were strictly limited — it was a five-year programme and at no time were more than three full-time workers engaged on it — it was clearly impossible to look at all aspects of prison psychiatry and three were chosen. Our largest study really chose itself: nobody could begin to comment on prison psychiatry in England without mentioning Grendon. Grendon is only just in its second decade of life but already it is controversial, famous, much visited and very much at the heart of any philosophical debate about the role of prison psychiatry. We examined the nature of the intake at Grendon, the type of prisoner who leaves Grendon prematurely, the regime applied, and the changes that occur within the individuals who stay the course. We also tried to see what happens to the men after they leave, and to increase the value of this last aspect we examined a control group of prisoners closely matched to the Grendon men.

Our second study focussed on the kind of psychiatric treatment given in a more typical prison, and the establishment chosen for this purpose was Wormwood Scrubs. It is one of the country's largest prisons, and the one in which Dr. de Hubert began his work 40 years ago. The pattern of psychiatric treatment developed there has been followed in most other prisons, so that while Grendon is unique in its conception and orientation, Wormwood Scrubs represents the more typical organisation of prison psychiatric work in Britain. Grendon is a therapeutic community where the whole regime and day is geared to treatment objectives; whereas Wormwood Scrubs is an ordinary prison, where psychotherapy is carried out by visiting psychiatrists who see their patients individually for sessions at weekly or longer intervals. Our research looked at the men selected for psychotherapy at Wormwood Scrubs, at the nature of the treatment given, and at its effect; and it compared the Grendon and Wormwood Scrubs treatments in terms of their effect on the patients whilst they are in prison.

The treatments which were the subject of this part of the study were all "talking" treatments, i.e. treatments which depend upon their effect on the interaction of patients and therapists, this being the type of treatment which a man is most likely to get within an English prison: other more controversial methods (such as surgery and aversion therapy) are little used in Great Britain. Drugs are of course used in prisons, usually to alleviate problems such as anxiety, depression and insomnia, but our research was not seeking to look at this area of psychological medicine, which is carried out in the main by prison doctors who are not necessarily psychiatrists. Our concern was with the work of psychiatrists who by means of psychotherapy seek to help their prisoner-patients with psychiatric or behavioural problems. It should be emphasised that such treatment is given only to patients who agree to have it; all the patients we studied at Wormwood Scrubs and Grendon were voluntary, and could cease having treatment whenever they wished.

The research involved, in the first place, examining what actually happened to patients in the selected prisons, and seeing what their treatment and daily prison routine consisted of. Secondly, we looked at the kind of men who were selected for treatment. Thirdly, we sought to measure the influence of psychiatric treatment on the men whilst they were in prison, by looking for psychological and attitude changes between the beginning and ending of treatment. Finally, came the most elusive part of the research — our attempts to see whether the treatment proved helpful in terms of post-release experience. It was our original hope that we would be able to keep in touch by letter with the men from the two prisons after they were released, but in the event (see Chapter 10) we were able to maintain contact with only 40% of our sample in this way. The only post-release information that we could collect for all the men was their re-conviction data. This is all too frequently assumed to be the criterion for successful treatment, but for reasons discussed more fully in Chapter 9 we do not think it is appropriate to evaluate psychiatric treatment in prison simply by means of the patients' post-release conviction records. Re-conviction depends upon a myriad of personal, environmental and situational factors, many of which the prison psychiatrist cannot be expected to influence.

Our main emphasis has therefore been to examine the effects of the treatment processes upon prisoner-patients whilst they were in prison, and for this purpose to measure changes that occurred in attitudes, psychological functioning, and symptomatology. The broad design of the study was to interview and test the men in Grendon and Wormwood Scrubs at the beginning of their treatment: this initial assessment was designed to provide information about the men's social and criminal background, about attitudes to authority figures such as the police and prison staff, about their motivation for treatment, attitudes to crime and about their psychiatric state. Personality characteristics, self-esteem and intelligence were also measured. Reassessment was then carried out at regular intervals during treatment.

The techniques used to describe the population and to measure changes are described in general terms in the body of the book, but in the interests of readability, we have put into the Appendices the more detailed material relating to the tests, their construction, form, reliability and validity. A brief outline of the questionnaires and interviews used will be found at the end of this chapter. Some of these were specifically devised for the study, others were imported ready-made, and one — the MMPI — although it fell into the latter category, was used in a rather unusual way.

The need to measure change over time was a prime consideration in the selection and construction of our assessment methods. From this point of view, the use of the concept of personality disorder, even had it not been subject to the problems discussed earlier in this chapter, would have been of little value in a research project seeking to assess treatment over periods of twelve months or so. Psychopathic or personality disorder is a diagnosis made on the basis of persistent problems throughout the life history, and changes in the condition would be measurable only if reassessments were spaced years apart. Psychiatric treatment — whether in prison or elsewhere — normally operates on a shorter time scale, and we have therefore tried to evaluate it by selecting measuring techniques capable of recording change within such time scales, techniques designed, for example, to measure the presence and severity of specific neurotic symptoms, and of manifest abnormalities.

Having looked at the nature of psychiatric treatment in two prisons and having seen what sort of men receive it, and to what effect, we come to the last area of our research. This was an attempt to estimate the size of the psychiatric problem confronting the prison service. Our approach to this question was really predetermined by circumstances. In 1972, the Home Office Research Unit undertook a census of 10% of all the sentenced prisoners in custody on one particular February night in the south-east of England, and we were asked to collaborate with this project in an attempt to estimate the number of prisoners in the south-east who could be regarded as psychiatric cases. On the face of it, this sounded like a straightforward exercise, but its inherent complexity became apparent as we looked for answers to the two crucial questions: "Who is a psychiatric case?" and "Who is a psychiatric case in prison?" The difficulty with defining the size of the psychiatric problem in a given community is that the answer obtained depends very largely on the standpoint and belief system of the observer. Unfortunately, psychiatry has not reached the stage where doctors agree largely about the presence or absence of pathology: they agree about severe pathology and absolute normality, but a large grey area of disagreement lies between these. Even if good agreement about pathology were obtainable, however, it will probably never be the case that all psychiatric pathology will or should receive treatment. Going to a doctor, asking for and accepting treatment are decisions which the individual has to make for himself, and he will make them on the basis of other factors besides pathology. For example, people with drinking problems, who may display serious pathology, vary widely in the extent to which they are prepared to regard their problems as psychiatric: some seek or accept psychiatric treatment, some do not. In clinical practice, and particularly in prison practice, the degree of motivation on the part of the patient is a crucial factor in determining the demand for psychiatric treatment. In seeking to assess the size of the prison psychiatric problem, it therefore seemed to us important not only to consider the levels of pathology in the population, but also to form an estimate of the motivation of that population to have treatment.

With the resources available to us, it was not feasible to interview a sufficiently large sample of the census population to arrive at an estimate of the proportion which could be regarded as psychiatric cases. We therefore decided to proceed by questionnaire, and a series of these was sent to all the 811 men who fell into the Home Office census sample. The questionnaires covered three areas which we regarded as crucial in determining psychiatric case status: current mental state (presence and severity of neurotic symptoms, etc.); desire for treatment, and previous psychiatric history. Shortly after the questionnaires were received back — there was a 78% response rate — a random sub-sample of the census population were given a standardised psychiatric interview. Among the psychiatric data recorded for this sub-sample was the psychiatrist's answer to the question: "Is this man suitable for specialist psychiatric care in the N.H.S.?" (i.e. is he — taking all things, including motivation, into account — to be regarded as a psychiatric case?). The questionnaires of the interviewed men were then scrutinised for the items which discriminated most between cases and non-cases and questionnaire criteria were developed for the purpose of identifying the men diagnosed as cases from their questionnaire responses. These criteria were then applied to the questionnaires of the whole census population, in order to produce an estimate of the population that could be regarded as cases.

The method by which our case identification procedure was devised is somewhat statistical, and may be of more interest to the specialist interested in developing such procedures, than to the general reader. But the results—showing that about a third of the sentenced prison population in the south-eastern region could be regarded as psychiatric cases—are of more general interest, and raise a number of important questions, including the extent to which imprisonment itself generates mental disorder.

The object of the census study was to devise a case identification procedure, but the exercise incidentally provided us with a considerable mass of information about a substantial sample of the prison population. Some aspects of this are reported in Chapter 11 and some of the material is also referred to in the first part of the book, since it gave us a valuable guide about norms in the prison population in areas such as symptomatology, attitudes to treatment, and to crime, which were of interest to us in the Grendon-Wormwood Scrubs part of the study.

The outline of the book is as follows. It begins with a description of the men who went to Grendon and a description of those who dropped out of the treatment (Chapter 3); this is followed by a description of the regime at Grendon (Chapter 4). Chapter 5 looks at the effect the treatment had on the men whilst in prison, and the way in which they changed in personality functioning, attitudes and mental health. The next two chapters go over the same ground for the Wormwood Scrubs sample, describing the men who got treatment, the kind of regime and treatment to which they were subjected, and the effect that the treatment had. Chapter 8 then compares the Grendon and Wormwood Scrubs results.

The next chapter (Chapter 9), deals with the post-release situation. It describes our attempt to assemble a matched control group for the Grendon men. The object of this exercise was to compare the post-release experiences of the Grendon men with their controls. It will be seen that in the event this part of the study was not very successful, although what we learned from it seems to us to be a matter of major importance, namely, that there is little practical hope of using matching procedures to establish satisfactory control groups for this type of research work.

The plan of our post-release study was not only to collect re-conviction data, but to try to keep in touch with our samples by letter, to find out how they were getting on. The results of this postal enquiry are outlined in Chapter 10, as are the re-conviction data. Chapter 10 also contains an account of the post-release experiences of six men. We hope that these give an indication of the complexity of the considerations involved in evaluating prison treatment, and the problems about using absence of re-conviction as the criterion of success.

The last part of the book is about our attempt to estimate the size of the psychiatric problem confronting the prison department, i.e. to assess the number of psychiatric cases in the prison population of the south-eastern region. Chapter 11 describes how from their responses to a census questionnaire, we devised a method of identifying the men who were cases. The implications of our finding — that one-third of the sentenced prison population in the region can be regarded as psychiatric cases — are also discussed in this chapter. Information about subjects of psychiatric interest (e.g. drug and alcohol problems) which emerged from the census questionnaires, are presented in Chapter 12. Finally, in Chapter 13, we discuss in more general terms, the findings of our whole research undertaking, and their implications.

Methodology

Statistical Analyses

Extensive use has been made of a number of programmes developed by Miss Barbara Kinsley, formerly a member of the Biometrics Unit at the Institute of Psychiatry. All frequency distribution tables, "t" test comparisons, correlations and chi squared comparisons have been provided by these programmes.

For those parts of the study which deal with change, for example by comparing the attitudes of men on entry to Grendon and after various intervals of time, a multivariate analysis of variance programme has been used (Finn, 1968). Amongst other things, this is designed to deal with the statistical problems caused by using a repeated measures design and takes account of factors such as the reliability of the tests or scales being used.

Outline of Interviews, Questionnaires, etc. Given to the Interviewed Samples

1. Social and Criminal History Interview

Each man was asked about his social background and criminal history. Details of the content and reliability of the interview are given in Appendix 1.

2. *Criminal Profile Rating*

This was an attempt to record the amount of offending behaviour in which a man had engaged, irrespective of whether he had been convicted of it. Seven areas of behaviour were covered: theft, fraud, sex, violence, motoring, drink and drugs. For each of them, a five-point rating scale was devised, and a man's position on each scale was determined both by the number of convictions incurred in that particular area, and by the offences he admitted in interview.

On all the scales, the lowest possible score was 0, and the highest, representing heavy involvement in the activity concerned, was 4.

One other rating scale was developed to assess the degree of each man's previous financial dependence on crime. This scale was originally constructed as part of our attempts to measure motivation for treatment (see items 4 and 5 below) for it seemed likely that the extent to which a person had previously depended on crime for a living would be related to his motivation for giving it up. A scale was therefore constructed to measure the extent of past financial dependence on crime. The highest score (4) was allocated to professional criminals who had engaged in large-scale well-planned crime, the lowest (0) to men whose offences had never involved financial gain.

Details of the scales are given in Appendix 3, and a modified version has been published elsewhere (Gunn and Robertson, 1976b).

3. *MMPI (Minnesota Multiphasic Personality Inventory)*

This personality test consists of 560 questions to be answered by the respondent, and from it something like 220 scales have been developed since the MMPI was devised some thirty years ago. We were extremely fortunate in that the Hofman La Roche Company provided us with their free computer facilities for analysing the MMPI questionnaires completed by our samples. Each man's results were given on a print-out which included his scores on 73 scales. We examined all these scales with a view to utilising those which measured personality dimensions or pathological traits in a way which was reliable, valid, and suitable for the purposes of the research and for measuring change over time. The details of this work are given in Appendix 4. Seven scales were finally selected for use in the project—not, it should be noted, as diagnostic instruments, but as measures of symptomatology and personality. The scales are: depression, hypochondriasis, manifest anxiety, ego strength, social introversion, extraversion and manifest hostility.

4. *Attitudes to Psychiatry and Treatment*

The importance of motivation in psychotherapy is accepted by all workers in the field. Prison doctors lay particular emphasis on it; since the time of Dr. Hamblin-Smith they have emphasised that psychotherapy in prison can only help those who are anxious to have it, and in the view of its founding Governor, Grendon is of benefit in the main only to men who can become motivated to have treatment, and to change their way of life.

It therefore seemed necessary, in evaluating treatment and in comparing populations receiving it, to take into account the extent to which the men were interested in entering into treatment and in finding alternatives to a criminal style of life. We also wanted to see whether in the course of treatment these attitudes changed, and whether such changes were related (as Grendon's Governor believed them to be) to successful treatment.

Two measures of attitudes towards treatment were devised:

(i) *Attitude to Psychiatry Questionnaire (AP)*. This contained seven statements about psychiatric treatment — e.g. "psychiatry is useful for people with problems", and the men were asked to indicate the extent of their agreement or disagreement. A high score reflected a positive attitude towards psychiatry; the maximum possible score was 28. Details of the scale are given in Appendix 5. The scale is sometimes referred to as the "AP".

(ii) *Desire for treatment: Interviewer's rating*. The research interviewers rated the strength of each man's desire for treatment on a five-point rating scale, taking into account, for those who wanted to have treatment, the extent to which it was wanted for extraneous reasons — e.g. the hope of pleasing the authorities, or of obtaining peripheral benefits of one kind or another. High scores reflected a strong desire for treatment, the highest (4) being given to those with strong motivation and little interest in peripheral benefits, and the lowest (0) to those evidencing no desire for treatment at all.

Details of the interview and the scale are given in Appendix 6.

5. *Attitudes to Crime (AC)*

As part of our attempts to measure motivation, a questionnaire was devised to elicit the men's attitude to crime and the strength of their wish (if any) to abandon it. The questionnaire consisted of five statements, concerning matters such as the degree of guilt felt about past offences, the strength of the wish to make money from crime, and the extent to which respondents felt themselves to be one of the criminal fraternity. The men were asked to say how far they disagreed or agreed with each statement, and their replies were scored: the maximum possible score, representing the strongest possible motivation to give up crime, was 20. Details of the instrument are given in Appendix 7.

6. *Attitudes to Authority Figures and to Self*

Attitudes to certain authority figures were measured. The figures chosen fell into three groups: first, the law enforcement officers — magistrates, and police; secondly, the prison authorities — prison doctors and governors; and thirdly, two "soft" authority figures — social workers and psychiatrists. We had also hoped to measure attitudes to figures of personal importance such as parents and siblings, but for reasons explained in Appendix 8, our attempts had to be abandoned. However, we retained one figure of a personal nature in our questionnaire — "myself". Self image is fundamental in psychotherapy, and we hoped to establish whether it was affected by treatment in prison, particularly as there is evidence (Heskin *et al.*, 1974) that imprisonment itself has an adverse effect on self esteem.

The method chosen to examine attitudes to these figures was the semantic differential. Respondents were given forms on which they were asked to rate each of the figures in ten respects; namely, how far they regarded them as helpful, sincere, hardworking, honest, considerate, narrow-minded, friendly, humane, polite and good. In the event, we found that the men were using each of the scales, with one exception, to reflect their basic evaluation of each figure as good or bad. (The exception was honesty, see Appendix 8, which, in the view of a prisoner population, is evidently somewhat divorced from the concept of goodness). The data is therefore presented in the book in the form of a single scale, which consists of the total score from all the individual scales minus honesty. This single scale represents an evaluative factor that can be regarded as good opinion, or popularity. High scores reflect high esteem (70 is the maximum possible score, 10 the minimum), and changes in score between test occasions are taken to mean changes in popularity or evaluation.

Details of the semantic differential, its construction and its reliability are given in Appendix 8.

7. Standardised Psychiatric Interview

Psychiatrists are becoming increasingly aware that it is not sufficient to say "I examined this man and found such and such an abnormality", statements of that nature must be founded, like all biological observations, on techniques of known reliability and validity. The validity of psychiatric statements is extremely difficult to test because there is no external criterion. For example, if a patient looks depressed, says he feels depressed, and expresses a range of depressive ideas he is regarded as depressed, even although there is no other external test; there is no special blood test, no typical X-ray, no prediction about his behaviour, that will be as accurate as the statements from the patient himself. For scientific purposes this makes reliability of the conversations the psychiatrist has with his patient all the more important. He must be sure that his observations and interpretations are shared by equally skilled colleagues. To put it more simply, if only one psychiatrist out of ten who interviews a patient, believes the patient to be depressed, that atypical belief may tell more about the training of the psychiatrist, the interaction between him and that particular patient, or even his own mental state than about the patient's condition.

In recent years a number of standardised psychiatric interviews have been developed in an attempt to deal with this problem. A standardised interview is one in which areas of discourse are laid down in advance, together with the sort of questions that may be useful in that area. The interviewer requires training to use such a standardised interview, and at the end of each area of discourse he has to make a rating on a scale about the phenomenon he is investigating. The main purpose of such a procedure is to make sure that each interviewer covers all the necessary points, and then to check between raters whether they agree about the points under examination, i.e. whether inter-rater reliability. has been achieved.

At the Institute of Psychiatry two important standardised psychiatric interviews have been developed in recent years. One by Wing *et al.* (1967) is primarily for use in the US/UK Diagnostic Project which is investigating national differences in psychiatric diagnoses and practices. The other by Goldberg *et al.* (1970) is a tool for examining patients in outpatient and general practice situations. We examined both and chose the second for the following reasons: it is shorter, it is specially devised to lead gently from physical to psychiatric symptoms (an important point if there is doubt about the client's fears of being examined by a psychiatrist), and it concentrated less on psychotic symptomatology. We were expecting our subjects to be fearful of, perhaps hostile towards, psychiatrists and certainly to be insulted by any implication of madness.

The interview is divided into two parts. The first is a structured section asking about ten groups of symptoms — somatic symptoms, fatigue, sleep disturbance, irritability, lack of concentration, depression, anxiety and worry, phobias, obsessions and compulsions, depersonalisation. Each symptom is then rated in a standardised way on a five-point scale; a rating of 0 means that it is absent, and a rating of 4 that it is present to a severe extent. Mean scores for individual symptoms can thus be calculated for different populations, as can a total symptom score — which is the addition of the ten individual symptom scores.

The second part of the interview requires the doctor to make ratings of the "manifest abnormalities" which he has observed in the patient. Twelve such abnormalities have to be rated: they are slowness, suspiciousness, histrionic behaviour, depression, tension, elation, incongruity, concern with bodily functions, depressive thoughts, thought disorder and delusions, hallucinations, and intellectual impairment. A five-point scale is again used, with 0 denoting absence of the abnormality, and 4 its presence to a severe degree.

Details about the interview and its reliability are given in Goldberg et al. (1970). For the purposes of the present project one of us undertook training from members of the Institute general practice team, using standardised videotape interviews, and joint interviews with skilled interviewers, both in the hospital setting and in the community, until on no scale were disagreements of more than 2 points being recorded, and the overall reliability coefficient did not fall below 0·80.

8. *General Health Questionnaire (GHQ)*

This is a questionnaire developed by Goldberg (1972) as a screening device for use in community health surveys. It consists of sixty items asking "Have you recently . . ." e.g. "felt that you are ill?", or "felt that life isn't worth living?" and the subject has to rate himself by choosing one of four prescribed answers, "not all all", "no more than usual", "rather more than usual", "much more than usual". The construction, reliability and validity of the test are described by Goldberg patho- logical scores for each item are given only when the subject reports having experienced problems more than usual. Nearly all the items on the questionnaire concern neurotic symptoms, and a high total score on the questionnaire reflects that the respondent has recently been feeling tense, anxious and depressed.

From the point of view of our research, the questionnaire had two deficiencies. First, by asking about recent symptoms (in the instructions the past few weeks are specified) it concentrated upon acute symptoms. Many of our subjects complained of symptoms they had had for years but these they had to rate as "no more than usual", a non-pathological score. Secondly, the variance generated by the test was so great that a sample would generate a large standard deviation that was often larger than the corresponding mean: this meant that for comparing groups or the progress of one group it was an insensitive instrument and minimised real differences and changes.

It should be noted that we omitted two items in the questionnaire which referred to current civilian life ("have you been late in getting to work?" and "have you been getting out of the house?"), so our results are based on a fifty-eight item version of the test.

9. *Heim AH4 Intelligence Test*

This test was developed by Heim (1970): it seeks to provide an indication of general ability by assessing (1) verbal and numerical ability and (2) ability to manipulate spatial relationships. Details about the test, and how it was used in the research are given in Appendix 2.

10. *Social Performance*

At the initial interview, Grendon, Wormwood Scrubs and control prisoners were asked a series of semi-standardized questions about their social performance in important areas of their life such as personal relationships, work, sexual relationships and the like. Unfortunately, for reasons which have been published elsewhere (Gunn and Robertson, 1976a), this did not prove to be entirely successful. In the event, only three scales were used in the analyses reported in this book. These are defined in Appendix 12.

11. *Re-Interview Schedule*

The men receiving treatment in Grendon and Wormwood Scrubs were periodically re-interviewed, and asked to repeat questionnaires and tests, so that changes in motivation, attitudes and psychiatric condition could be measured. Re-interviews were usually held three months and nine months after the start of treatment, and finally just before release. At each re-interview the men were asked, among other things, if they felt the treatment was helping them, if they had learned anything about themselves and how often they had seen their doctors. They were also asked if they had been involved in any fights. Details of the re-interview schedule and its reliability are given in Appendix 9.

CHAPTER 3

The Grendon Population

At the time of our research, certain of the negative East-Hubert criteria were still used in the selection of prisoners for Grendon, in that psychotic men and those of subnormal intelligence were excluded, but there were no formal qualifying attributes for admission to Grendon. Its founding Governor, Dr. William Gray, regarded it as important that the men should be intelligent and that they should have expressed anxiety about themselves. Within those broad limits it was up to medical officers in the prisons to recommend men for treatment. When they did so, the procedure required them to complete a report (form 1080) about the prisoner; this went to the Regional Medical Office, where a decision was taken as to whether the man was suitable for treatment, and if so whether he should go to Grendon or to one of the other prisons at which psychiatric treatment was available. Obviously, Grendon's limited intake was a pre-determining factor here. If treatment at Grendon was considered appropriate, a report on the prisoner would be sent to its Governor, who could, if he regarded the man as unsuitable, decline to accept him; this, however, happened only infrequently.

Prisoners could be transferred to Grendon at any time during their sentence, but, as will be seen later in this chapter, most of them were sent before they had served a year and the majority did not have more than two years still to serve. The expectation was that they would remain at Grendon until their parole or release date was reached, although some men, e.g. life prisoners, might be transferred to more open conditions when their release date approached.

The research involved a study of all the adult prisoners sent to Grendon for psychiatric treatment between 1st June 1971 and 31st May 1972: there were 107 such men. They were interviewed and tested when they first came to Grendon. This initial assessment was designed to provide information about social background, criminal history, attitudes to authority figures, and motivation for treatment. In addition, intelligence and personality characteristics were measured, and each man was examined by the research psychiatrist. Reassessment was then carried out at regular intervals.

The initial assessment began within a week or two of the men's arrival: this allowed them a little time to settle down before being bombarded with the battery of interviews and tests which had been prepared. It was explained that participation in the project was entirely on a voluntary basis and that the information collected would be treated in strict confidence. All men agreed to be interviewed and all but one were willing to embark on the initial series of tests and written questionnaires.

After their criminal records and hospital case notes had been seen, the men were interviewed by the project psychologist and psychiatrist, and a social history was taken. Details about the construction, reliability and content of the social history interview are given in Appendix 1.

Demographic and Social Data

Grendon deals with a young group of men: 72% of the sample were in their twenties, and the average age was twenty-seven. The oldest man was forty-eight. Men sent to Grendon were younger than other prisoners; only 47% of the general adult prison population are in their twenties.

The men were asked about separation from their parents in early life. Almost half had been separated for at least a year from either one or both of their natural parents before they were fifteen: 51% (54) had been separated from their fathers to that degree, and 45% (48) from their mothers.

Most of the sample had left school at the earliest possible opportunity, but there were two men with degrees, twenty who had at least one "O" level and four with some "A" levels. Although the educational attainment of the group was not high, this was not for lack of intelligence. Intellectual ability and functioning were assessed by

Table 1   Age of Grendon Prisoners

Age	No.	%	Sentenced Adult Male Prison Population* %
Under 25	46	43	26
25-29	31	29	21
30-39	23	21	31
40 +	7	7	22
	107	100	100

Mean 27·3 s.d. 6·1. *From *People in Prison* (1969) p. 119. Home Office.

means of the AH4 intelligence test as developed by Heim (1970). Details of the test are given in Appendix 2. The men completed it individually after the interview, in the presence of the interviewer.

The test has been standardised against the scores of 1,183 British naval ratings. This group is not representative of the general population at the extreme ends of the intelligence dimension — very dull youths would be screened out before recruitment, and highly intelligent young men do not often become naval ratings. But so long as this limitation is borne in mind, the norms are valuable for purposes of comparison. Heim divided her normative group into five categories; A represents the top 10% of the sample, B the next 20%, C the middle 40%, D the next 20% and E the bottom 10%. Table 2 shows the distribution both of the Grendon population and the normative group in these categories.

Table 2   Distribution of Heim's Intelligence Test Scores

Category	Grendon Men No.	%	Naval Ratings %
A	19	18	10
B	11	10	20
C	32	30	40
D	21	20	20
E	23	22	10
	106*	100	100

*One man refused to be tested.

The extreme ends of the Grendon population are relatively high, as is to be expected given the nature of the normative population, but the difference between the means of the two groups was not statistically significant. (Grendon mean 71·90, s.d. 20·56; naval ratings' mean 75·23, s.d. 14·58, t = 1·609.)

Asked about employment at the time of their current offence, a quarter of the men (28) said they had been unemployed for several months. The rest were asked to describe their work in sufficient detail for it to be classified into the census social class categories. Table 3 shows that compared with the general working population, the lowest social class is over-represented among Grendon's employed prisoners, and classes one and two are under-represented; it has, however, to be remembered that the age structure of the Grendon population is very different from that of the general working population.

Table 3 Social Class of Employed Grendon Men

Social Class	No.	%	Male Working Population* %
1. Professional, etc.	—	—	4
2. Intermediate occupations	4	5	16
3. Skilled occupations	30	38	50
4. Partly skilled occupations	20	25	21
5. Unskilled	25	32	9
	79	100	100

*From 1966 *Sample Census, Economic Activity Tables, No. 29.*

Few of the men had as yet enjoyed marital relationships of a stable character. Only half (58 men) had experienced marriage, or long-term (two years or more) cohabitation and only 28 prisoners in the whole sample were planning to return to wives on release. Indeed, many men had no home at all to return to. A glimpse of their social isolation was obtained when they were asked if, after release, they expected to have any dependents looking to them for financial support. The majority (62%) answered in the negative: 29% expected to be responsible for a wife and/or children, and another 9% said that others, usually parents, were dependent on them.

Criminal Histories

The majority of the men had started to come before the courts as juveniles: Table 4 shows the age at which they first appeared in court in connection with an offence.

Table 4   Age at First Court Appearance for an Offence

Age	No.	%
8-11	16	15
12-13	16	15
14-16	41	38
17-20	18	17
21-24	11	10
25-29	4	4
30-31	1	1
	107	100

Mean 15·74, (s.d. 4·48) range 8-31.

Information about previous offences was obtained both from the interviews and from the criminal records. It is never easy to decide on the best way of presenting this information. Each different counting method has it own disadvantage, and all are subject to the vagaries of the criminal process, in that undetected or unprosecuted offences are left unrecorded.

In the present work two different approaches were used. One attempted to measure the extent of the men's involvement in defined areas of criminal activity (theft, violence, drugs etc.), whether or not prosecution had followed. Details of this method of assessment are given in Appendix 3. The other method used for recording the men's criminal history was a simple count of their convictions. By this method three convictions — whether they were incurred at one hearing, or on different occasions — are counted as such. This way of counting gives a complete picture of prisoners' official criminal histories, but it has the disadvantage of preventing comparisons from being made with the official prison statistics on previous convictions, since these treat offenders who have incurred several convictions at one court appearance as having one conviction only. Offences "taken into consideration" were excluded from our conviction count.

The most common offence for the Grendon prisoner, as for prisoners and offenders in general, was theft. Only 10 out of the 107 men had no convictions for it, and 70% of the sample had six or more. Many of these convictions were for taking and driving away — over half the men (53%) had incurred such convictions, usually repeatedly.

Although the majority of the men were heavily involved in property offences, only a small proportion could be regarded as at all professional: no more than 17% of the sample was assessed as having been financially dependent on crime to a large extent (details of the scale used for this assessment will be found in Appendix 3).

Because of the high prevalence of taking and driving away offences, there was a concomitant prevalence of related motoring offences — driving while uninsured, driving while disqualified, driving without a licence, etc. Sixty per cent of the men had motoring convictions, the great majority of which (68%) were related to taking and driving away offences. Convictions for dangerous driving were rare, accounting for only 3% of all the motoring offences.

After theft, violence was clearly the major problem for the Grendon population: 52% of the men had convictions for violence against the person, including four men with convictions for homicide. Eleven prisoners had four or more violence convictions, but the conviction count was obviously an inadequate measure of the severity of the problem, for much violence, especially in the home, goes unreported. The interviews gave a much fuller picture, and on the basis of the information obtained from them (Appendix 3 describes the assessment methods used) only 41 men (38% of the sample) were rated as non-violent or responsible only for minimal violence. A third of the men (35) had been involved in episodes of violence which had seriously endangered another person's life or health. These incidents were often unreported. For example, a prisoner expressed continuing guilt about an occasion when, after a night of disturbance from his fretful baby son, he had hurled the baby across the room in explosive anger. No serious harm was done, but clearly the incident could have resulted in the baby's death.

A summary of the conviction count is presented in Table 5. It will be seen that only 12 men had been convicted of drug offences, but this figure gave little indication of the extent to which the group had been involved in drug taking: 39 men (37%) confessed to having been involved in frequent drug-taking activities (i.e. they were rated 2, 3 or 4 on the scale shown in Appendix 3). The small number of men with convictions for drunkenness (14) was also no measure of the extent to

Table 5   Type and Number of Convictions
(Current convictions included)

Offences	Men with Convictions		No. of Convictions		
	No.	%	Range	Mean	s.d.
Theft*	97	91	0-50	10·9	8·7
Motoring	67	63	0-31	4·5	6·0
Violence	56	52	0-11	1·4	2·1
Fraud	49	43	0-38	2·6	6·3
Robbery	17	16	0- 3		
Sex	16	15	0-12		
Drink	14	13	0- 8		
Drugs	12	11	0- 6		
Arson	6	6	0- 4		
Total	107	100	1-62	20·9	12·5

*Including taking and driving away of cars, etc.

which the men had serious drinking problems: 30 prisoners, 28% of the sample, were diagnosed as alcoholic by the research psychiatrist.

The average number of convictions for the sample was twenty-one (s.d. 12·5); 37% of the men had between eleven and twenty convictions, a fifth had fewer than eleven, a fifth had between twenty-one and thirty, and a fifth had more than thirty-one. There is no doubt that the average Grendon prisoner had both a long and a dense record of crime.

As the number of their convictions might suggest, the majority of the men had been in prison, borstal, and/or detention centres, repeatedly before the present sentence: young as they were, almost 40% had already spent more than three years in such custody, and a fifth had spent more than five years inside. These figures relate to time actually served. For the great majority, the present sentence was just one more dose of a medicine which the courts had been prescribing for years.

Psychiatric Characteristics

How disturbed or mentally disordered were the men? Almost half of them (48 men) said they had been in-patients in mental hospitals. (The true figure may have been higher, since only those men were

Table 6   Time Served in Custody Before Present Sentence
(Actual time spent on sentence in prison, borstal or detention centres)

Months	No.	%
0	17	16
1-12	13	12
13-24	21	19
25-36	16	15
37-48	10	9
49-60	10	9
61-72	4	4
73 +	16	16
	107	100

Range 0-200 months. Mean 36·7. (s.d. 37·5).

counted who said they had been in-patients, and where the hospital concerned confirmed it). Forty-four men said they had attempted suicide, eight of them having made four or more attempts.

All the men were psychiatrically interviewed soon after their admission, with the standard psychiatric interview previously mentioned (p. 48). It involves rating both the patient's manifest abnormalities and the current neurotic symptoms which he reports: both are assessed on a severity scale. Table 7 sets out for each symptom enquired about, the proportion of men who reported its presence to a pathological degree. It will be seen that nearly a third of the men

Table 7   Reported Neurotic Symptoms Among 107 Grendon Men

Symptom*	Men with Significant Pathology	
	No.	%
Anxiety	33	31
Lack of concentration	33	31
Sleep disturbance	29	27
Depression	25	23
Fatigue	18	17
Irritability	18	17
Somatic symptoms	16	15
Obsessions and compulsions	7	7
Phobias	6	6
Depersonalisation	—	—

*Not mutually exclusive.

complained of pathological anxiety, and lack of concentration, and about a quarter reported a pathological degree of depression and sleep disturbance.

The same standardised psychiatric interview was also used in the census study (see Chapters 11 and 12) to assess a small sample of the ordinary prison population representing 1% of all men imprisoned in the South-Eastern region on February 2nd 1972. The sample was too small to be properly representative of prisoners in general, but it certainly suggested that the amount of pathology found among the Grendon men was greater than that present in a group of prisoners taken at random: the Grendon men had significantly higher scores than the S.-E. population both for neurotic symptoms and for manifest abnormalities. When the individual symptom scores were added together to give a total score for all neurotic symptoms, the mean for the 107 Grendon men was 10·6 (s.d. 7·2) while that of 81 South-Eastern men serving sentences of over 18 months (nearly all the Grendon men were serving over 18 months) was 5·33 (s.d. 5·4) t = 5·73 p < 0·01. Similarly, when a total score for manifest abnormalities was calculated, the mean for the Grendon sample was 5·9 (s.d. 3·8) compared with the South-Eastern prisoners' mean of 2·10 (s.d. 2·7) t = 7·97, p < 0·01.

On the basis of the clinical interview, taking both neurotic symptoms and manifest abnormalities into account, the overall severity of each man's disturbance was assessed. Fifty-nine per cent of the sample were assessed as pathologically disturbed, and another 23% as suffering from a sub-clinical degree of disturbance; the remaining 18% were not rated as disturbed. This of course does not imply that they should not have been in Grendon; current psychiatric disorder is obviously not the only factor taken into account when men are transferred.

The difficulties of psychiatric diagnosis in a population of this kind are well known. A large number of the men could have been classified as "personality disordered"; almost all those who had been in mental hospitals had at some stage had this label attached to them. For reasons discussed in Chapter 2 such a diagnosis has not been used in this study. Table 8 gives the numbers in the sample diagnosed as suffering from other disorders as defined in the International Classification of Diseases.

Although only fourteen men were given the diagnosis of "drug abuse", there were in all twenty-eight men (26% of the total) who had become sufficiently dependent upon drugs to experience withdrawal symptoms when they stopped taking them.

The general picture emerging from the psychiatric interview was of

Table 8   Summary of Psychiatric Diagnoses

Diagnosis*	No.	%
Alcoholism	30	28
Anxiety states	16	15
Drug abuse	14	13
Sexual deviance	12	11
Depression	9	8
Pathological gambling	4	4
Epilepsy	3	3
Schizophrenia	1	1
Obsessive-Compulsive state	1	1

*The diagnoses are not mutually exclusive.

a group of men displaying considerable evidence of past and present disturbance. But when the psychiatric findings were correlated with the information about criminal history, it was found that apart from the well-known relationship between alcoholism and violence offences and the obvious one between alcoholism and drinking offences, there were few correlations of even moderate strength. The lack of relationship between criminal and psychiatric variables, although it may seem surprising to some, suggests that it is wrong to see criminal behaviour in illness terms, except in specific well-defined areas (e.g. drunkenness). It follows that it is unrealistic to expect that treatment for psychiatric disorders will of itself lead to an end to offending behaviour.

Personality Characteristics

Among the battery of tests and questionnaires which the men were asked to complete on their own after they had been interviewed, was the Minnesota Multiphasic Personality Inventory (MMPI). It covers a very wide area of human functioning, with questions relating to social and family relationships, self-image, feelings of anxiety and depression, and so on. Since the research was seeking to examine what changes, if any, occurred in the course of treatment, the wide range of behaviour covered by the MMPI and its inclusion of many items relating to symptoms, made it a particularly suitable instrument to use. It does, however, have the disadvantage that American norms have to be relied upon for purposes of comparison, since normative data has never been collected from a sample of British people.

Completion of the MMPI is quite an onerous task — it takes up to two hours to cover the 566 items. Only one man declined to do the test. It was interesting that whilst the results showed the Grendon men to be a very abnormal group, they did not deviate from the norm of the "lie" scale. Although one or two men may not have taken the test entirely seriously, the response from the group as a whole has been accepted as genuine and valid.

As mentioned before the Hofmann-La-Roche drug company provided us with free computer facilities for analysing the MMPI data. These facilities were designed primarily for clinical purposes and the programme included a print-out for each individual of "clinical statements" which are designed to describe areas of possible pathology for further investigation by the clinician (Fowler, 1969). In the present study these statements are used as a way of describing the pathological characteristics of the Grendon men, by giving a picture of the most frequent types of disturbance pointed to by the computer's analysis of the test results. Table 9 shows the types of statements that were most frequently made.

The general picture shows the men as neurotic, depressed, and unable to relate properly to other people. A good indication of the personality of a newly arrived Grendon inmate is given in the following frequently used statement: "A resentful, constricted and apprehensive

Table 9   Types of Clinical Statement on MMPI Printouts
for 106 Grendon Men

Statement Type	No. of Men	%
Patient described as being anxious and tense	84	79
Patient has problems with personal relationships: difficulties in establishing personal relationships	81	76
Patient is depressed at the moment: chronically depressed	73	69
Patient's test results are strongly suggestive of a major emotional disorder	57	53
Patient shows mistrust of others: chronic tendency to misinterpret the motives of others	51	43
Patient tends to be impulsive: has difficulty in controlling his actions	43	41
Patient has difficulty in sleeping: suffers from insomnia	43	41
Patient has problems related to sexual behaviour, or is homosexually oriented	28	26

person who feels disillusioned and embittered. His distrustful, suspicious and querulous style of life alienates people and impairs the efficiency of his social interactions."

When the MMPI was originally constructed, its authors, hoping to use it as a diagnostic aid, developed nine clinical scales from the items, each one of which was intended to serve a different diagnostic function. Since then, over two hundred scales have been derived from the test to fulfil various purposes. The Roche print-outs provided scores for 73 scales in all.

All these scales were examined with a view to utilising those which measured personality dimensions or pathological traits in a way which was reliable, valid and suitable for the purposes of the research. This operation is reported in detail in Appendix 4. Seven scales were finally selected for use in the present work, not as diagnostic instruments but as measures of symptomatology and personality. The scales are: depression, hypochondriasis, manifest anxiety, ego-strength, social introversion, extraversion and manifest hostility. Details about them are given in Appendix 4.

The depression scale was selected to measure the state of mind described by the authors of the MMPI as being "characterised by poor morale, lack of hope in the future, and dissatisfaction with the patient's own status generally" (Welsh and Dahlstrom 1956). A high score reflects this depressed and unhappy mood. The hypochondriasis scale is used as a measure of health concern — high scores reflect abnormal concern about bodily health and functions. The manifest anxiety scale reflects a person's potential to react in a neurotic, maladaptive way; a high score suggests a high level of underlying instability and neuroticism. The ego strength scale, selected because of its specific applicability to the present study, was developed as an instrument for predicting the response of neurotic patients to psychotherapy. The items of this scale were selected by its author (Barron, 1953) on the basis of their relationship with improvement during psychotherapy in an out-patient clinic. The person with a high ego-strength score reports little ill-health, is in good contact with reality, emotionally "open" and feels self-confident and adequate; in other words, high ego-strength reflects good personality. A low score on the scale reflects a constricted, rigid and neurotic outlook on life.

The extraversion scale was devised as a measure of extraversion that was independent of the neurotic dimension: it reflects social extraversion. In the words of its authors, a person scoring highly on the scale would be "the stereotype of an extravert . . . someone who is socially aggressive, full of energy, and likes to be with people" (Giedt and Downing, 1961). The social introversion scale reflects unwillingness to take part in group activities and a withdrawal from social activities in general. Although it is shown among the extraversion measures in Table 10, there is a strong neurotic component to this scale. The last scale, which also has a neurotic component, is "manifest hostility": it measures the amount of social hostility a person expresses. People with high scores on this scale report "a tendency to be grouchy, competitive, argumentative, uncooperative and retaliatory in inter-personal relationships" (Wiggins, 1969).

Table 10   MMPI Scale Results: T scores of 106 Grendon Men

	Mean	s.d.	t	p
Neuroticism Scales				
Manifest anxiety	83·16	17·9	26·64	0·001
Ego strength	43·95	13·9	3·63	0·001
Hypochondriasis	60·37	15·1	5·89	0·001
Depression	74·9	16·9	13·04	0·001
Extraversion Scales				
Social introversion	61·78	12·6	7·51	0·001
Extraversion	45·97	10·9	2·78	0·01
Manifest hostility	54·03	10·9	2·78	0·01

The Grendon men's average scores on the seven selected scales at the initial occasion of testing are given in Table 10. To facilitate comparisons with the scores of the normative (American) population, the results for each scale are presented as standardised T scores, in which the normative population has a mean of 50, and a standard deviation of 10. This enables the difference between the mean scores of the Grendon men and of the normative group to be easily assessed, and the last column in the table shows the significance of the differences between Grendon and the normal population for each scale.

On the first four scales, which can be regarded as measures of neuroticism, the Grendon population produces responses which are highly different from those of the American normative population. It is unfortunate that comparisons cannot be made with a British population, but it is extremely unlikely that cultural differences could account for the enormous deviance from the norm which the Grendon group produces. They report a much greater degree of anxiety and depression than the normative sample, complain of poor health more often, show less self-confidence, and generally present a picture of a neurotic, maladaptive and emotionally constricted group.

The extraversion scales similarly present an abnormal picture; on each one the Grendon men differ significantly from the normative population. As a group they report themselves as being introverted, socially anxious and withdrawn, prone to hostile and retaliatory relationships with others. Given their low mean score on the extraversion scale, one would have expected a similarly low score to have been obtained on the Manifest Hostility Scale, for both these scales are loaded heavily on a general factor of extraversion (see Appendix 4). The fact that these two scales lie in opposite directions, one significantly below and the other significantly above the normative mean, provides an indication of the ambivalent and overwrought nature of the group's social functioning.

Altogether the results of the MMPI analyses present a picture of a neurotic group expressing a very considerable degree of abnormality. Depression, anxiety and social withdrawal characterise the Grendon inmate; he is unable either to relate properly to others or to deal effectively with his own feelings. He is likely to misinterpret the behaviour of other people towards him, and the bitterness and resentment which are common features of his make-up are often relieved by overt hostility or impulsive acting-out behaviour.

Attitude Assessments

In order to examine the effects of treatment it seemed necessary to look not only at psychiatric and psychological variables, but also to examine attitudes which might be relevant to a person's response to psychiatric treatment, or to his future criminal career. Attitudes in three main areas were examined: attitudes to psychiatry, to crime and to authority figures.

1. *Attitudes to Psychiatry and Treatment*

The original impetus to investigate the motivation of the men in the study came from Grendon's Governor, Dr. Gray. He had put to us a three-fold hypothesis: (1) that those who are well motivated for treatment when they come to Grendon do well as a group; (2) that men who are not well motivated when they arrive, and whose motivation does not improve, do not do well; and (3) that men who are not well motivated when they come to Grendon, but improve in motivation during their stay there, do best of all.

The problem about testing this hypothesis lay in the difficulty of finding some way of defining and assessing motivation, and the views of the prison doctors and psychiatrists were canvassed on this point. Their replies suggested that some of them regarded motivation as comprising two elements: a wish to enter into a treatment situation in order to produce psychological change, and a wish to turn away from criminal activity. Rating scales were therefore developed, designed to reflect a man's attitude in these two areas. These were introduced in Chapter 2 as the Attitude to Crime scale (AC), the Attitude to Psychiatry scale (AP), and the interviewer's rating of the desire for treatment (see also Appendices 5, 6 and 7).

The AP questionnaire was given to the census sample of prisoners in the South-Eastern region, as well as to the Grendon men. When the results were compared, the average score of the Grendon prisoners was found to be significantly higher: the Grendon mean for 106 men was 19·78 (s.d. 3·46), the South-Eastern prisoners' mean for 613 men was 16·36 (s.d. 5·18), $t = 7·81$, $p < 0·001$. It was of course to be expected that the Grendon men, all of whom had agreed to accept treatment in a psychiatric prison, would express as a group an above average amount of faith in psychiatry. More interesting was the finding that a substantial proportion of them (39%) had low scores, suggesting considerable scepticism about the value of treatment.

In addition to the questionnaire about attitudes to psychiatry, desire for treatment was assessed by the interviewers. We found that the men ranged from the one or two who had no interest in treatment at all, but had come to Grendon "just for the ride", to those for whom treatment was of prime importance. Like the results from the questionnaire, the interviews showed that a substantial proportion of the men had reservations about entering into treatment (Table 11). Less than half (42%) were regarded as strongly motivated, a fifth were frankly ambivalent, and 12% had little or no interest.

2. *Attitude to Crime (AC)*

This questionnaire was an attempt to measure the men's motivation to abandon crime: they were asked to complete it on their own after they

Table 11   Interviewers' Rating of Desire for Treatment
(for details see Appendix 6)

Rating	No. of men	%
(0) No desire for treatment	3	3
(1) No desire for treatment, but would accept if offered, for whatever reasons	10	9
(2) Ambivalent attitude towards personal suitability for treatment	22	21
(3) Wishes treatment partly for peripheral benefits	27	25
(4) Strong desire for treatment, expresses little or no interest in peripheral benefits	44	42
	106*	100

*Data missing for one man.

had been interviewed. Details of the construction and reliability of the questionnaire are given in Appendix 7, but it should be said here that it was not possible conclusively to demonstrate its validity.

As with the AP the questionnaire was given to the census sample of men in the prisons of the South-Eastern region, as well as to the Grendon men, and there was no significant difference in the mean scores of the two groups. (Mean of 106 Grendon men was 13·4 (s.d. 3·7); mean score of 607 South-Eastern prisoners was 13·25 (s.d. 4·3), (t = 0·35)). In so far as the questionnaire was measuring it, the desire to abandon criminal activity was no stronger among Grendon's newly arrived inmates than it was among the general prison population.

3. Attitudes to Authority Figures and to Self

As previously indicated these were measured by the semantic differential technique. Details of its construction and reliability are given in Appendix 8. The adjectives used for rating the eight figures (listed in Table 12) were selected from those suggested by a group of prisoners who took part in a pilot study. Ten pairs of adjectives were selected: helpful/unhelpful; sincere/insincere; hardworking/lazy; dishonest/honest; considerate/inconsiderate; narrow-minded/broad-minded; friendly/unfriendly; inhumane/humane; good/bad; rude/polite.

A principal components analysis showed that the men were using the different scales to reflect their basic evaluation of each figure as good or bad. The semantic differential data is therefore presented in the form of a single scale, which consists of the total score from all the individual scales except honesty. This total score represents an evaluative factor that can be regarded as good opinion, or popularity. High scores reflect high esteem.

The purpose of the semantic differential was to see whether attitude changes would occur over time. It was nevertheless of some interest to see how the men initially regarded the various figures who were named in the questionnaire. It has to be remembered that at the time they completed it, the men were fresh from having spent, on average, twelve months in conventional prisons. Table 12 reflects some of their feelings about the experience: the prison authorities, and the police and magistrates who delivered the men into the hands of those authorities, are rated negatively. A fairly clear division is drawn between these "bad" elements and the "good" ones—social workers, psychiatrists, and myself. Prison governors seem to occupy a mid-way position (Goffman, 1961).

Table 12   Mean "Popularity" Rating of Figures in the Semantic Differential. 93 Grendon Men at Initial Testing*

	Mean	s.d.
Psychiatrists	60·3	7·9
Social Workers	54·5	11·0
Myself	52·2	9·0
Prison Governors	43·2	13·9
Prison Doctors	39·8	15·1
Magistrates	38·8	13·3
Police	38·5	14·4
Prison Officers	37·4	14·6

The maximum possible score was 70, the minimum was 10.
*Seven men who had been in Grendon before were excluded, and seven others failed to complete the test.

Current Offences, Sentences and Referral to Grendon

Having described some of the attitudes and the criminal, psychiatric and personality characteristics of the Grendon sample, it remains finally to examine the factors more specifically related to the men's situation in prison. For what offences were they imprisoned, how long were their sentences, how much time did they still have to serve, and how did they come to be sent to Grendon?

Categorising the offences for which the men were serving their present sentence was not a straightforward task, since the great majority had been convicted of more than one crime. The table below shows the principal offence, i.e. that attracting the longest sentence, for which the men were imprisoned.

Table 13   Principal Offence for which 107 Grendon Men were Imprisoned

Type of Offence	No. of Men	%
Property Offences		
Theft, Burglary, Fraud	61	57
Robbery	9	8
Violence against the person		
Homicide	3	3
Other	16	14
Sex	7	7
Arson	5	5
Drugs	3	3
Driving	3	3
	107	100

The length of the aggregate sentences is shown in the next table: only 13% of the sample were serving less than two years and 60% had sentences of between two and four years.

Table 14   Length of Present Sentence

Months	No. of Men	%
12-18	10	10
19-23	4	4
24-36	49	46
37-48	15	14
60 +	26	24
Life	3	3
	107	100

Mean, excluding lifers = 42·28 (s.d. = 22·92) range 12-144, and life.

The next table shows how much of their sentences the men had served before they reached Grendon:

Table 15   Time Served on Present Sentence before Transfer to Grendon.

Months	No. of Men	%
0- 3	1	1
4- 6	27	25
7-12	51	48
13-24	22	21
25 +	6	5
	107	100

Mean 12·9. s.d. 13·9.

Three-quarters of the men reached Grendon within a year of starting their sentences; prisoners who had served more than two years were rare.

The length of sentence which still lay before the men at the time of their transfer is set out in the next table. Just over half the sample (57%) were transferred when they had less than fourteen months left to serve, while a third had between fourteen and thirty-one months before them. Nine men were more than thirty-one months away from their earliest date of release. Prisoners with life sentences are excluded from the table.

Table 16   Time Still to be Served
(From arrival in Grendon until earliest date of release)

Months	No. of Men	%
4-10	39	38
11-13	20	19
14-22	21	20
23-31	15	14
32 +	9	9
	104*	100

Mean 15·9 range 4-52.
*Three prisoners with life sentences are excluded from the table.

In order to see which agencies had been instrumental in referring them to Grendon, the men were asked how they had come to be transferred, and the files were also searched for this information. Table 17 presents the results. It was noted earlier that before a prisoner can be transferred for psychiatric treatment, the prison medical officer has to recommend this course. In some cases, however, a prison doctor may make the recommendation less because he believes treatment to be essential, than because he considers it right to endorse other pressures for it, e.g. from a court. In Table 17, referrals of this kind are not shown as being due to the prison medical officer.

Table 17   Analysis of Referral Agencies

Prison Medical Officer	36
Prison Medical Officer and Court request	31
Prison Medical Officer and outside pressure	14
Prison Medical Officer and Court request and outside pressure	11
Outside pressure	6
Court request and outside pressure	5
Court request	4
	107

The Prison Medical Department was solely responsible for recommending the transfer of one-third of the men. Recommendations from the courts were a factor in almost half (51) of all referrals, but the proportion of cases in which court requests did not result in transfer could, of course, not be gauged from the present study. For about a third of the sample, outside pressures — e.g. from a probation officer — were a factor in bringing about the transfer.

Men Transferred from Grendon

As will be seen in the next chapter, the Grendon regime makes heavy demands upon both its staff and its inmates. A proportion of each are found to be unsuitable, and a further proportion decide of their own accord to opt out of participation. Who are the prisoners who do not stay the course?

Of the 107 men in the sample, 27 (25%) were transferred away from Grendon prematurely, i.e. before their release or parole date. One of these was sent to a Special Hospital shortly before his release date; he had done well in his ten months at Grendon but was considered too dangerous to be released. Another man, after fifteen months in Grendon, had an acute psychotic breakdown and had to be hospitalised. A third man who had done well was transferred after a year to a prison considered more suitable to his needs.

Of the remaining 24 men, 10 were sent away for disciplinary reasons. Although Grendon generally avoided a disciplinary approach to behaviour problems, not all breaches of the rules were treated as "acting out", and some were inevitably dealt with more formally. The decision as to whether to transfer a man for disciplinary reasons always involved a number of factors, but probably the main consideration was whether, despite the offence, he appeared genuinely to be interested in participating in the regime and continuing with treatment. Drug smuggling, for example, was likely to be regarded as a certain sign that the offender had no genuine wish to come to grips with his drug-taking problem. The men transferred for disciplinary reasons included some who had tried to smuggle in drugs, some who had used strong arm methods to try to enforce gambling debts, one who absconded from home leave, and three who had been involved in incidents of violence.

Apart from those transferred for disciplinary reasons, six men were transferred because it was thought they had no genuine interest in taking part in treatment. They had spent between three and ten months in Grendon. Another three men were transferred (after 2-7 months) because they were regarded as "too damaged" to make use of the regime. Nearly all these nine men came from one wing, where the doctor had a much more positive attitude towards "weeding out" than did the staff on other wings.

Finally, there were five men who left at their own request: they had spent between two and six months in Grendon. One still had four years to serve and said he could not face so long a period of "aggro", although he was interested in returning to Grendon nearer his release date. Another man — a compulsive gambler — had come to Grendon expecting to receive aversion therapy, and asked to leave when he found that it was not forthcoming.

Six of the 27 transferred men had done well at Grendon and participated actively in the regime before they were transferred. Was there anything distinctive about the remaining 21 that differentiated them from the rest of the sample? Comparisons were made between these 21 men (called hereafter the "unsuitable") and the rest of the sample (the "suitable") on all the variables collected at the initial assessment. Differences were found only in three areas. One related to the extent to which the men had previously been financially dependent upon crime. There were more men among the unsuitable group who were rated as having been heavily dependent, 33% as compared with 13% among the suitable (chi² = 3·72, p < 0·10). The average score of the unsuitable men on the scale which assessed financial dependence on crime was also higher (2·10, s.d. 1·22, compared with 1·42 s.d. 1·05 among the suitable, t = 2·57, p < 0·05). The unsuitable men as a group were evidently more professionally involved in crime. The second difference related to the men's early history: the unsuitable had been separated from their natural fathers more frequently. Eighty-two per cent of them (16 men) had been separated for more than a year before they were fifteen, compared with 45% (38) of the "suitable" men (chi² = 5·69, 1 d.f., p < 0·01).

The third area of difference related to the men's mental state, and to the characteristics measured by the MMPI. On both these indices, the unsuitable men had at the initial assessment been found to be less disturbed and abnormal than the suitable. At the psychiatric interview 43% (9) of the transferred men were found to be suffering from a clinically significant degree of disturbance, compared with 63% (54) of the non-transferred (chi² = 2·83, 1 d.f., p < 0·1). The MMPI results showed that on all the scales there was a trend for unsuitable men as a group to have less deviant scores than the rest of the sample. For three of the scales, the differences reached statistical significance. The manifest anxiety scores showed the unsuitable to be less unstable and neurotic than the suitable men (the mean T score of the 21 unsuitable men was 77·14, s.d. 17·18, compared with the mean of the 86 suitable men of 84·92, s.d. 18·12, t = 2·239, p < 0·05). On the ego-strength scale, which measures what is in effect good personality, the unsuitable did not deviate at all from the American normative population, whilst the suitable were significantly weaker (the mean T score of the unsuitable was 50·52, s.d. 23·47; that of the suitable was 42·33, s.d. 15·31, t = 2·484, p < 0·05). The other scale on which the unsuitable men had more normal scores was social introversion, reflecting that as a group they were less socially withdrawn, and more willing to take part in group activities than the rest of the sample. (Unsuitable mean = 56·14, s.d. 11·84, suitable mean = 63·18, s.d. 12·57, t = 2·333, p < 0·05.) Thus both the psychiatric assessment and the MMPI show the transferred men as a group to be more stable, socially adequate, and less neurotic than those who remain in Grendon.

Apart from the three areas discussed, the initial assessment data did not point to any significant differences between men who stayed and those who did not stay the course. Their motivation for treatment, their attitudes to authority figures, and their criminal histories were similar, although none of the small number of men with arson and homicide convictions appeared among the unsuitable. All in all, the picture suggests that a social or environmental basis underlies the criminal behaviour of the "unsuitable" men, whilst the rest of the sample for the most part are less stable, with criminal careers related perhaps more to the irrational relief of tension and frustration, than to the achievement of financial gain. But whilst the differences between the suitable and unsuitable men are suggestive, they are only differences of degree, and do not provide a dividing line clear enough to enable the unsuitable to be identified in advance. Only one sub-group among the unsuitable could have been identified before transfer to Grendon; this was a small group of men with well-integrated personalities and mono-symptomatic problems, such as gambling. Because Grendon is known as a "psychiatric" prison, men of this kind may be referred there in the mistaken belief that they will receive behaviour therapy or individual psychotherapy. No such treatment is given in Grendon, and as we shall see the problems of these men are unlikely to respond to the Grendon approach: there is no reason to expect that a compulsive gambler with an otherwise stable personality should be helped by a regime which assumes that the gambling represents merely an outward symptom of an underlying disorder. Men of this sort would not have been sent to Grendon had they, or the referring medical officer, had an accurate understanding of what the Grendon regime involved.

Summary

About a fifth of our sample of 107 men were transferred away from Grendon on grounds of their unsuitability. They tended to be the more stable, less neurotic men, and those with a more professional approach to crime.

The general picture of the 1971-2 intake that emerged from our data was of a young population — average age 27 — which for the most part had been heavily, though not often professionally, involved for many years in criminal activities. The average number of convictions for the group was twenty-one. Almost every type of offending behaviour was represented, but offences of theft (incurred by 91% of the sample) of motoring (63%), and of violence (52%) were the most common. Young as they were, the men had already spent a substantial proportion of their adult lives in custody: the mean figure of actual time served before the present sentence, was over three years. The average length of the current sentence was 3½ years, and the men usually reached Grendon before they had served a year.

As their penal histories would suggest, the men generally expressed unfavourable attitudes to authority figures such as police and prison officers. Nor, when compared with the ordinary prison population, did they express any particularly strong desire to abandon criminal activities. It was clear that as far as their criminal characteristics were concerned, Grendon prisoners were not chosen for their hopeful prognosis.

The social histories showed that before they were fifteen almost half of the men had been separated from one or both parents for at least a year. Many complained of unhappy lives in childhood. Few had established stable matrimonial relationships, almost half were un-married, and separation was common among those who had married. The distribution of intelligence in the sample was similar to that of the general population, but not many of the men had realised their potential either at school or at work.

Compared with the inmates of ordinary prisons, the newly arrived Grendon men expressed an above average faith in the value of psychiatry but over a third of them had negative or ambivalent feelings about receiving treatment. The psychiatric examination and the MMPI both gave a picture of a disturbed, unstable and neurotic group, anxious, depressed and unable to relate properly to other people. At the psychiatric examination 59% of the sample were found to be suffering from a clinically significant degree of disturbance, and the MMPI forms returned by the great majority of the prisoners showed very abnormal responses.

The material presented in this chapter suggests that as regards criminal history, social background, mental state, personality, and attitudes to crime and authority, a definitely negative answer has to be given to the question: "Does Grendon receive the prison system's 'good' cases?"

CHAPTER 4

The Grendon Regime

Grendon is a maximum security prison as much subject to the prison rules as any other penal establishment. It lies in the heart of rural Buckinghamshire several miles from the nearest town. Most of its staff live on an estate built around the prison. The general direction of the regime was determined when Dr. Gray, a senior prison doctor at the time he was appointed as Grendon's first Governor, opened the prison in 1962. He told us that his experience in prison hospitals had persuaded him that much of the aggression and psychiatric disturbance that sent prisoners into these hospitals had its origins in the repressions and tensions of the ordinary prison regime. He took the decision to base Grendon on a system of communication which would prevent this traditional atmosphere from developing, and to run Grendon as a therapeutic community.

A pre-requisite for the achievement of both of these aims was to prevent the ordinary sub-culture of the prison community from gaining a hold in Grendon. As Gray (1973a) has pointed out, the values of this subculture are not only anti-social but grossly anti-therapeutic, yet they become the most powerful influence upon the prisoner whilst he is in prison. In order to create an institution that should as far as possible be free of this influence, the new prison was opened gradually. For several months staff lived and trained there together, becoming a community and developing a joint approach before the prisoners arrived. Then the first wing was opened and began to receive prisoners in very small numbers, so that the new arrivals would become absorbed into the atmosphere, instead of flooding it with the values and traditions of the conventional prison system which they brought with them. One by one, the other wings were opened, receiving only a few men at a time. In this way Grendon's therapeutic atmosphere, having been carefully constructed, was deliberately fostered and preserved. Upon it the functioning of Grendon as a therapeutic community still depends, and the Governor has always continued to exercise close control over the rate at which new inmates are admitted. An influx of too many men coming at one time could quickly weaken or destroy Grendon's approach, for as was seen in the last chapter, those sent there have had much previous experience of imprisonment and are steeped in the traditions of prison sub-culture. These traditions are irreconcileable with participation in a therapeutic community, which requires people to examine themselves and to change in the light of what they experience in the community. The values of the sub-culture demand the opposite approach: they depend on rigid stereotyping, on a gulf between prisoners and staff, and on an inflexible code of conduct.

Dr. Gray has recently given an account of Grendon's ideology and methods: "The treatment philosophy towards which Grendon aims is that of the therapeutic community, that is, a system in which all the resources of the institution — staff, patient and relations — are mobilised in the interests of treatment . . . Treatment takes place in small groups . . . and in larger community meetings of thirty or forty people living in the same wing . . . Therapy takes place by the elucidating and working through of personal relationships.

"Side by side with this involvement of patients in each others' treatment an endeavour is made . . . to get patients to participate in the organisation of their own activities and in making important decisions about each other.

"The activities into which patients at Grendon are pressurised are likely to be more rehabilitative than the customary institutionalised dependency . . . A population . . . who are grossly disturbed in their capacity for personal relationships . . . benefit from a situation which maximises the possibility of such relationships. Since disturbed individuals are notoriously prone to distorted ideas of reality it is hoped that frequent meeting with other patients may constitute an opportunity for genuine reality confrontation.

"The essence of the system is to help patients to mature by giving them a high degree of responsibility (in an) atmosphere less authoritarian than usual . . .

"Care is taken that decisions on the running of the institution shall, as far as possible, be democratically arrived at by all grades of staff and patients, rather than by a fiat of the Medical Superintendent.

"Within this system, Grendon has evolved a culture based on assumptions very different from those of the traditional prison. That it has been in operation for ten years without major incidents such as escapes or serious overt violence has been largely due to the group values which confront new arrivals and to the close staff/inmate relationships" (Gray, 1973a).

When the other doctors at Grendon were asked informally how they saw their task, they expressed their aims in terms similar to those used by Dr. Gray. The psychiatrist in charge of one wing said he was trying to give the men a chance to develop, to learn how to make relationships, and to create an environment where these things would be possible. The doctor of another wing said that his aim was to help the men to gain sufficient strength and self-organisation to enable them to cope more effectively with life outside. On the third wing, a doctor described his objective as helping the men to find and to stick to a realistic goal, and giving them the encouragement they needed for this difficult task.

The following account of the Grendon regime relates to the period of our research in 1971-3. At that time, as we saw in the last chapter, Grendon men were on average serving sentences of some 3½ years: they had usually spent the first part of the sentence in ordinary prisons, and were transferred to Grendon for the last 1-2 years. At the time of our study Grendon had about 200 inmates, half of them youths under the age of 21, with whom our research was not concerned. For the prison as a whole the staff ratio was unusually favourable: there were some 70 uniformed officers, 7 psychiatrists, 4 psychologists and 4 welfare officers. The adult part of the prison comprised three physically distinct wings, each one housing between thirty to forty men. Each wing had a permanent staff consisting of a psychiatrist, psychologist, welfare officer and ten uniformed prison officers. About half the officers, including the Principal Officer on each wing, held the Prison Nursing Certificate.

On arrival, each new inmate was allocated to a wing, and he remained a member of this throughout his stay. Although allocation to the wings was not made on a random basis, our research showed that there were no significant differences between the men on the different wings, on any of the variables measured (age, offence, personality characteristics, etc.).

Most of the inmates' activities were centred on the wing: they slept there, ate there, spent most of their leisure time there, and group and community meetings took place there. Although men from the different wings met each other in the prison's communal areas at work, games, or evening classes, most of their time was spent in the company of other members of their wing. The extent to which the three wings formed separate, even isolated, communities was striking, and each developed considerable solidarity. Differences between the wings are discussed below.

Staff relationships were of an unusual character in that they lacked the hierarchial and military features traditional to the prison service. Between the various ranks of officers, and between officers and non-uniformed staff, there was easy mixing, use of first names, and straightforward exchange of views. Decisions on the wing were reached by staff consensus, or vote, not by order. On one wing, for example, where the officers differed from the doctor as to the desirability of retaining a man at Grendon, a vote was taken; the doctor accepted the majority decision, saying that he recognised that no prisoner could be successfully treated on the wing if the majority of the staff did not want him to be there. Among the features making for close staff relationships within each wing, was the system of regular staff meetings. On two of the wings these meetings were held daily, and on the third twice or three times a week. Attended by all staff members — doctors, officers, welfare officers and psychologists — and lasting for anything from fifteen minutes to an hour, these meetings enabled the staff to exchange information, to discuss difficulties as they arose, and to give each other support. This last function was particularly important in a regime where the prisoners had an unaccustomed freedom to act out, and where the staff, particularly the officers, had to bear the full weight of this acting-out behaviour. As Dr. Gray puts it: "It must be emphasised how exposed their position is. An important responsibility of the doctors is to give the officers adequate support in this situation" (Gray, 1973a).

In addition to the regular staff meetings on the wings there were also inter-wing staff meetings. Every day began with an informal meeting of the Governor and all the doctors, and this was followed by the more formal "morning meeting" attended by the Governor, the doctors, welfare officers, psychologists and principal officers from all the wings, as well as by the Chief Officer and the security staff. At this the Governor read the occurrence book from each wing, and matters of management — either of a general kind, or relating to individual prisoners — were discussed. In addition to these daily meetings there were fortnightly meetings of the entire Grendon staff.

Grendon thus set an extremely high value on communication

between staff members. Its supportive and democratic staff relationships were the basis for its therapeutic and non-authoritarian regime:
without them, it would probably have been impossible for the staff to
cope with the anxieties and hostilities raised by the behaviour of their
patients.

The type of prisoner sent to Grendon was described in the last
chapter, but two features of the selection system that had an important
bearing on the regime should be referred to here. First, the apparent
paradox that while Grendon is described as a psychiatric prison, those
suffering from psychotic illness were excluded, as were those of
subnormal intelligence. Although officially inmates were termed
"patients" (a term which many officers deliberately eschewed) the tone
of the prison did not encourage the prisoner to regard himself as a sick
person, and indeed there was little that was obviously "psychiatric"
about the place. The orthodox methods of psychiatry were conspicuous
by their absence; individual psychotherapy was hardly practised, drugs
were rarely used, and the doctors gave no other specific "treatments".
Treatment in Grendon consisted of the patients learning from their
interaction with each other and with the largely non-medical staff. If a
prisoner developed a mental illness he was removed from his wing to
the prison hospital, and not returned to the wing until he was regarded
as fit; if his illness persisted, he was transferred away from Grendon.
Although designated as a psychiatric prison, Grendon was in fact an
institution which stressed the health and normality of its inmates, and
discouraged them from regarding themselves as "patients" whose
problems have medical answers.

A second feature of the selection system which had an important
bearing on the regime was that no prisoner was sent there against his
will, and no prisoner remained there against his will. It was constantly
emphasised by the staff that Grendon did not seek to do things *to* the
inmates—the aim was to give the men a chance to make use of the
place in the way most suitable to their needs: the onus was on them to
utilise it. The philosophy of the regime thus demanded both that the
men should be mentally fully responsible, and that they should be
volunteers.

Grendon has a "no violence" rule, and prisoners were warned on
arrival that breaches of it would automatically lead to expulsion. In
practice, however, the rule was not rigidly applied. Violence was in
fact rare—a remarkable achievement given that over half the inmates
had violence convictions to their name. In the interviews, the men
were asked whether they had been involved in any fighting; after three

months 5%, and after nine months 9% said they had been involved in a fight, but most of these incidents had been of a very minor nature. Of the 107 men admitted to Grendon between June 1971 and May 1972, only three were transferred away because of aggressive behaviour.

Fear of being transferred was no doubt an inducement for the Grendon prisoner to respect the "no violence" rule, but a more important factor seemed to be the general lack of tension in the prison. One middle-aged man in our sample had a history of violence dating back to his early childhood. In the police record he was described as "extremely dangerous", and all his past prison sentences had been characterised by aggression against the staff. Whilst at Grendon he was involved in no incidents of violence at all, a fact which he himself attributed to the absence of tension and the relaxed atmosphere between prisoners and staff.

One way of looking at an institution's regime is to follow a man through a day of it. The routine in Grendon is more or less the same for all inmates — as one officer put it, "they all get the same medicine". The way that things are done does however change with time, since the wings are free to evolve changing responses to their ever changing problems. The following account gives a general impression of the situation in 1972.

A Day in the Life of . . .

The Grendon prisoner's day was certainly less harrowing than that of Ivan Denisovich (Solzhenitsyn, 1968). At 5 a.m. when Ivan was awoken by morning reveille, the Grendon men were still asleep. Most of the men slept in single cells, but each wing also had two dormitories. The way in which these were used varied from wing to wing and from time to time. One wing reserved its two dormitories for the members of two groups, the idea being that the group members, by being together in the evenings, would develop closer relationships than would otherwise be possible. On other wings prisoners went into or out from the dormitories at their own request, according to the need they felt for company or support.

The cells and dormitories were unlocked at 7 a.m. and not locked again until 8.30 p.m. Meals were taken in the dining room on each wing. After breakfast, work began at 8 a.m. In the course of his sentence, each man would do a variety of jobs; slightly more than half the population were employed on work concerned with the running of the prison. The most popular of these servicing jobs was the gardening party, which employed about ten men; other jobs involved work in the kitchens, in the stores, library, etc., but about a quarter of the men were engaged in domestic cleaning work. Those who were not employed on servicing jobs worked either in the laundry — an industrial concern processing work for institutions besides Grendon — or in the workshops of which there were two, a weaving shop and a light assembly shop. Except for the wing cleaners, the time spent at work was their main opportunity to meet people from other wings, and to escape from both the company and from the atmosphere of their own.

The scarcity of work, and the low calibre of jobs available were handicaps to a regime seeking to develop the social competence and confidence of its members. Did the work perform any function in Grendon other than as a means of servicing the institution and providing some occupation for its inmates? In discussing this question a number of staff pointed to the discrepancy between the theory and the practice. One of the psychiatrists said that ideally the patient at work should be subject to examination in the same way as he was subject to it in all other "here and now" situations in a therapeutic community: problems with the job, with his instructor, or with his peers should be observed and brought up for discussion in group meetings. But this therapist, like a number of other staff members, found that the feed-back from work to the wing was inadequate, for wing members worked all over the prison, and the staff in charge of them might sometimes have more interest in the work being done (for example — getting the food prepared on time), than in the man doing it. It was to overcome such difficulties that one wing had exclusive use of one of the workshops.

Whilst aware of the imperfections of the work programme, the staff nevertheless tried to bring it into the treatment. Weekly work groups were held, attended by the men and officers engaged in that work, at which matters relating to the work could be discussed: these might include personal relationships, poor performance, or dissatisfaction with the type of work available. Another way in which the wing staff tried to maximise the therapeutic role of work was through the allocation process: as far as possible, men's needs were taken into account when work was assigned. On one wing, job allocation was decided by vote at wing meetings: applicants had to argue their case at the meeting, and decisions were reached by majority votes. If staff or prisoners had reason for thinking that an applicant should not have the job he applied for, the subject would be publicly debated.

A prisoner who was knotting the fringes of bedspreads in a workshop, remarked to one of the research team that it was not so different from sewing mailbags: but he added: "In Grendon therapy comes first, work is just an extra." This was certainly true in the sense that the time allocated to work was limited by the time allocated to "therapy": there were rarely more than five hours of time available for work on any given day. However, the staff were well aware that at the time of our research, the scarcity, the nature and to some degree the organisation of the work in Grendon was limiting its therapeutic potential, and to that extent work was indeed an extra.

Twice a week, after two hours work in the mornings, the men returned to their wings for group therapy meetings. There could be between five and nine prisoners in each group, and one or two members of staff. The meetings lasted an hour, and attendance was obligatory. The men were allocated to a group soon after arriving in Grendon, and stayed on it until discharge. Close group relationships therefore built up over time.

In Dr. Gray's words the rationale for the group system is that "therapy takes place by the elucidating and working through of personal relationships". The prisoners themselves generally regarded group meetings as the most valuable activity carried on at Grendon. Within the group they could talk about their past, about fears and plans for the future, and about current problems and relationships in prison and outside. In the words of one man: "The best thing is being able to get things off your mind—to talk to people and not feel embarrassed. You always find someone else has had the same experience." In the event of a sudden crisis, e.g. if a man received a farewell letter from his wife, he or his fellow group members could ask for a special meeting to be convened forthwith. The size and atmosphere of the groups ensured that each member had an understanding yet realistic set of people helping to consider his behaviour and his problems; and the knowledge that others had problems and difficulties like his own was a source of reassurance and support.

The small group system was the heart of the Grendon regime, and its main therapeutic instrument. Within the freedom and security offered by the group, the men were expected to come to terms with themselves and their environment. For most of them it was a new and at first difficult experience to communicate at all with other people on personal matters; feelings of social anxiety and isolation, and inability to relate to others were, as was seen in the last chapter, characteristic of the population. But within the security of the group, members come to appreciate that others are like themselves and that they are like other people, and communication becomes easier. As one man put it, when he looked back on the experience a year after his release: "You find you all have the same fears . . . You get to understand people . . . You become more balanced."

All the doctors and psychologists conducted groups, but the majority were taken by prison officers. They were usually given a short initial training course for this work, but in practice they acquired much of their knowledge by observing sessions conducted by experienced staff. The way that different staff members conducted their groups varied considerably, for the training was brief and non-directive, there was no supervision of group work, and moreover staff members (including doctors and psychologists) differed from each other in their views about the best approach. Thus while one doctor might be conducting a psycho-therapeutic group, another would be using methods more akin to group counselling; and whilst one officer might believe in a wholly non-directive approach, another might prefer to "confront" the men with their offences. Although there was little central guidance as to how group leaders should work, they had the opportunity to meet together regularly to discuss problems and methods: twice a week an inter-wing meeting took place for this purpose.

The small group system was central to Grendon's regime not only as a treatment method but also because it was the foundation for the atmosphere of tolerance in the prison. By giving group members a direct insight into each others' problems, the traditional stereotyping of prison culture was undermined. Sex offenders for example came to be accepted as human, however much their offences were disapproved of, and similarly the "we/they" barrier between staff and prisoners was eroded, enabling both sides to see and treat each other as individuals. The result was a relaxed, and often warm relationship between staff and prisoners. An officer, in talking about a man with a serious history of violence, demonstrated how this process affected relationships and conduct on both sides: "In a conventional prison he is an animal—I wouldn't approach him with a ten-foot pole. But here I would let him play with my children."

An officer gave us an interesting account of what it had been like on his wing when small groups had once been temporarily abandoned because of staff difficulties. He said that the standard of order and behaviour on the wing began to deteriorate. The staff found themselves pressing for tighter discipline, because without the groups they found it impossible to grapple with the problems of 30-40 men. Thus for management purposes, apart from therapeutic ones, groups were found to be an essential component in the regime and had, as he put it, to be "re-invented". The relationships they foster enabled Grendon's officers to achieve order on the basis of understanding and trust rather than discipline.

After attending the morning group sessions, the prisoners had lunch. This was followed by a leisure period which included thirty minutes optional exercise in the playing field. Work was resumed at about 2 p.m. but on three days a week it ceased at 3.30 p.m. for the men and staff to return to their respective wings for the wing meeting.

As a rule wing meetings were attended by all members of the wing, staff and prisoners. There was normally no agenda, and no chairman in the formal sense. The room was filled with anything between 30-45 people sitting in armchairs set up all the way around the walls, and whoever wanted to speak simply did so. Staff might or might not play a part, but they did not often play a dominant one. The meetings lasted an hour.

Anything could be raised and discussed at wing meetings, but there was an understanding that no-one would be discussed in his absence. The subjects that arose most frequently were (1) problems of personal relationships between individual prisoners, or between a prisoner and a staff member; (2) the behaviour or progress of an individual prisoner; (3) general questions affecting staff/prisoner relationships; and (4) matters concerning the running of the prison.

The way in which any of these or other subjects were handled varied from occasion to occasion, depending partly on the prevailing atmosphere in the wing. For example, on one occasion a man's complaint that an officer was behaving dictatorially, could set off a wave of similar complaints and lead to an airing of staff/prisoner tensions, whilst on another occasion it might lead to the complainant's own behaviour being questioned and discussed. For both staff and prisoners, being discussed at a large meeting could be an ordeal, and comments were often made about how inmates would engage in discussion of "trivial" matters (e.g. the food), in order to delay the onset of possibly more threatening subjects. Many men were habitually silent at wing meetings, and from time to time there were discussions about how to get this silent majority to contribute, since both staff and the more active inmates were uneasy about the number of men who were thought to be silently "riding" the system.

On the other hand, both staff and prisoners were aware of the danger that, for the sake of pleasing the authorities and appearing to be "therapeutic", men might be led to make spurious contributions. After a wing meeting at which the problems and progress of a prisoner had been very sympathetically discussed, one of the officers expressed his doubts to the rest of the staff as to what had taken place. Was it "therapy" he asked, or were the prisoners simply trying to make the staff feel good, by telling them what they wanted to hear?

If wing meetings sometimes gave rise to irritation or a sense of wasted opportunity, they also fulfilled positive functions. Tensions and anger could be openly expressed. People became more confident in expressing themselves and making others understand them. Difficulties in relationships could be openly examined, and the opinion of every prisoner and staff member could be sought. Staff members frequently responded to criticism by changing or modifying the way things were done. But the chief and unique value of the wing meeting was that all parties were present, so that whatever was discussed or whatever accusations were made, every person concerned could put his point of view. In this way it became difficult for distorted or unreal views about other people to survive, or for grievances to build up.

Were wing meetings in any sense the instrument of democratic government in the prison? The formal answer is certainly no; Grendon is a prison, and it is not the inmates who run prisons. This fact, together with Grendon's security classification, limited the role for prisoners in decision making. Nevertheless, there is a sense in which it could be argued that inmate power had some reality, for to a large extent Grendon relied upon its more experienced inmates to demonstrate the system to newcomers — staff as well as prisoners. The success of the regime depended upon a careful control of intake: an excess of new inmates coming on to a wing over a period meant that there would be too few men skilled and experienced in Grendon ways to absorb them, with the result that the traditional values of prison culture gained ascendency. This seemed to be occurring on one of the wings during the research period: considerable difficulties arose, which the staff attributed to recent turnover in the population. Too many of the experienced men had been discharged, and it had consequently been impossible for the wing to assimilate the new intake. However skilled the staff, they cannot alone sustain a therapeutic community, and in this sense it can be held that the prisoners in Grendon exercise genuine responsibility in the running of the institution.

After the wing meeting, tea was served at 5 p.m. and from then on the evening was the prisoner's own. During term time, he could attend educational and recreational classes, or take part in drama groups. Otherwise men could watch television, listen to records, play darts or table tennis, read or talk. Some men said that they felt so agitated by their increasing self-awareness that they found it hard to concentrate on activities in the evenings. Therapy and groups, they explained to us, did not end at 5 p.m. — it was a non-stop process, from which there was no escape; informal group discussion went on throughout the evening in corridors, cells and in the wing office.

The preceding account gives an outline of the prisoner's weekday. It omits, however, any description of the general atmosphere in which these activities took place. Anyone who goes to Grendon and who has also visited conventional prisons, is struck by the difference, particularly by the easy relationship between officers and prisoners, and by the relaxed atmosphere. As one of the discharged men said, when after a year he was asked to recall the best things about Grendon: "It's the freedom . . . the really free atmosphere . . . it's the atmosphere, rather than anything specific." Another man, still in Grendon when he spoke, put it this way: "Here you have freedom to drop any fronts, to be yourself. You don't have to live a lie. You don't have to pretend to be a big-time gangster. Here I can say I'm a petty thief. And sex cases don't have to cower in a corner."

An Anecdote

One of our sample, a recidivist and a professional criminal, was unexpectedly transferred away from Grendon. On enquiry it was learned that for a number of weeks prior to his transfer he had opted out of the treatment and had been asking to leave. This in itself was not a particularly unusual occurrence and did not arouse much interest at the time. It was not until several months had passed that the real reasons for his actions came to light. It seemed that a number of men in the prison from which he had originally come had a score to settle with him. He had "grassed" and his punishment was that he receive a beating. In the normal course of events this would have been commissioned by the men in his previous prison and carried out in his present one. Word was passed into Grendon by the usual prison grapevine but it was not possible to persuade anyone there to carry out the job. Eventually a girl-friend of the man was threatened and so he precipitated his transfer back to an ordinary prison to take the beating.

The Officers

The work of the officers was the pre-requisite for the favourable atmosphere; they were the staff with whom the prisoners had by far the most contact. It was the officers who were on the wings all day, who unlocked the men in the mornings, supervised work, and saw to the smooth running of the wing. Their wing office had its door open from morning to night, constituting a walk-in social centre which never closed. The men came and went, to talk, to listen, share jokes, air grievances, get explanations, and exchange views. What went on informally in the wing office was as important as what went on in the group meetings; in both the "we/they" barrier was undermined, and the two sides met and interacted as individuals. That some of the prisoners should maintain contact with the officers after discharge, followed naturally from the relationships that developed. Discharged men telephoned, wrote in, or asked for officers to visit them. Such visits were usually made in the officers' free time, for after-care was not one of their duties. With Grendon's catchment area covering the whole of England and Wales it would be impossible for its staff to carry out their own after-care, much as some would like to do so; the work is done by the probation service. Nevertheless, in times of crisis, the ex-prisoner may turn to a Grendon officer and the latter may respond by speeding to the rescue on his day off.

Officers are not specially selected for Grendon, and it was therefore inevitable that some would find the work less congenial or more difficult than others. For example, an officer with a self-confessed reputation as a tough and rough disciplinarian, had been transferred to Grendon after specifically requesting to go to a prison elsewhere. To outsiders like ourselves it seemed strange that staff should be sent to Grendon against their wishes, the more so as no prisoner is sent there unless he is willing to go. Yet the policy has unexpected as well as expected results. The tough disciplinarian found himself in Grendon not only geographically, but ideologically, far from where he wished to be. He was wholly out of sympathy with the system, and refused to attend wing meetings on the grounds that he had no wish to hear what inmates had to say. But over a period of time his attitude changed; asked to describe what happened he said "At 'X' (the prison he had come from) they were all cons. Here they're blokes". He started to attend wing meetings; and later on became a group officer, saying that he had begun to appreciate the value of getting people to look at themselves. Another officer, who came to Grendon after considerable experience in other prisons said "I've changed a lot since then. If the system changes the staff so much, it must change the men". (He went on to say that there should be 30 establishments like Grendon — it was the best thing that had ever happened to the prison system). In any assessment of Grendon's work, its effect on staff should not be overlooked. It comes about not through any training programme but through the officers (like the inmates) being exposed to the atmosphere and relationships of their wings. But whilst the work of re-orientating the authoritarian officer was a valuable function — albeit a by-product — it also represented a substantial burden on the existing staff. If officers hostile to the regime were retained on the wings for an undue period of time, staff morale and efficiency could be undermined. The officer in charge of one wing explained how the presence of such men could be thoroughly demoralising, especially when "therapy" seemed not to be going well. He was rejoicing in the fact that for the first time in many years, his wing had no "loud-mouthed anti-Grendon officer" on its complement.

Many officers commented how the "rule book", which they are trained to use and rely upon, plays no role in Grendon. Breaches of the rules were usually treated as problems of behaviour rather than as challenges to authority. For example, a prisoner who explodes with abuse towards an officer would in an ordinary prison find himself "on report" the next day: at Grendon, although it was open to staff to take such action, their usual way of handling such an incident was to try to bring into the open the emotions which had caused the outburst. Staff authority stemmed more from skill in personal relationships, than from status; and this, for men trained in a basically authoritarian approach to discipline, was often a difficult transition to make. Probably few officers remained untouched by their experience at Grendon, but inevitably, given the lack of selection, some found the work too difficult or uncongenial. They could either seek a transfer, or ask to be moved away from the wings, on to one of the "centre" jobs, i.e. jobs, such as manning the gate, the central services, or the administrative offices, which are necessary to the running of a prison, but which do not involve much personal contact with the inmates. As a result of this process, the officers who became disenchanted with the regime on the wings, accumulated in centre types of employment and were known as the "centre group". The centre group was perceived by the rest of the staff as radiating a certain cynical bitterness; as one young wing officer put it, their attitude was "You're wasting your time — it's all been tried and failed". When things on the wings were going well, this attitude could be regarded as challenging, or perhaps merely as teasing — a standard greeting from the centre group was, "And have you been talking therapeutically today?" — but when there were difficulties on the wing, the influence of the centre group, and indeed of the members of the wing staff who shared its views, became more threatening and undermining. It is hard for people who are straining to achieve a difficult objective to be surrounded by those who confidently assure them that they are wasting their time.

Whilst there was a clear division between the officers who were fully committed to Grendon's approach and those who were not, there was also an intermediate group who opted out, not so much because they believed the system was wrong, but because they felt they could not cope with it any longer. Their reasons centred largely round two subjects: the long hours of close and emotionally demanding contact with the men, and the feeling that they were inadequately trained for the job. The formal training for officers in Grendon consisted of a short induction course, and a later group counselling course, but basically it was by watching and participating in the regime that new officers learnt the Grendon approach. However, they learned it in a practical way, and in a fundamental sense might lack a rationale for what was done. This meant that after a point, and particularly when difficulties arose, officers could begin to feel at a loss, inferior or even guilty about their role — as, for example, when they came to feel that they were simply pandering to the prisoners. "They expect me to be more sophisticated than I am" was how one wing officer put it, when he explained his reasons for seeking a transfer to the centre. Although compared with the professional staff (doctors, psychologists, etc.) the officers were required to work longer hours and to have closer contact with the men, they lacked an advantage which the professional staff normally had, namely, training and expertise to help them to remain emotionally detached from the problems and people whom they were trying to help. Many officers stressed the mental and emotional strain of work on the wings, and how exhausting they found it. "You're told not to get emotionally involved," said one, "but how can you help it?" The supportive system of staff meetings and relationships provided a bulwark against these problems, but after a certain period some officers found the work, in conjunction with the long hours, too much for them. Prison officers are liable to find themselves on duty from 7 a.m. till 9 p.m., and at times of staff shortage, they may work for two weeks without a day off. Such hours at a job that requires constant attention to the needs and demands of others, can become a burden.

An officer who was applying for a centre job said that although the hours there would be the same, because the work would be much less intensive and exhausting he would be able to tolerate them: "You can't be therapeutic fifteen hours a day."

When the burden of the work was under discussion almost every officer referred to the additional strains imposed upon them by living together on one estate. At Grendon, the staff houses lie together in a small compact estate a few yards outside the prison gate. It is a considerable walk to the nearest village, and over ten miles from any town; public transport barely exists. Living so close to his colleagues in an isolated community composed exclusively of them, means that the officer never gets away from the prison environment. After what may have been a difficult or upsetting day at work, he can find no retreat: if he has had a row with a colleague, or handled an incident with a prisoner badly, the whole estate, including his wife, may know about it before he gets home.

Although the excessive hours proved too heavy a strain in some cases, the nature of the work, and the fact that it was demanding, was nevertheless recognised by staff as one of Grendon's greatest merits. One officer, when explaining why work in Grendon was harder than in the prison he had come from, put it thus: "At . . . prison I was a machine; here I have to decide for myself." Fatiguing and difficult as it was, and frustrating as it could be, there was no doubt that for many officers the opportunity to work closely with the men, to conduct groups, and to become personally involved in all aspects of rehabilitative work was very rewarding. The supportive staff relationships and their democratic nature, so different from what is customary in the prison service, were also appreciated, and it was the staff, as much as the inmates, who gained from the relaxed atmosphere and absence of tension which the regime fostered. One middle-aged officer, recalling his experience of abuse, aggravation and violence in other establishments concluded simply: "I know the old-fashioned way. This is a better way to run a prison."

Doctors and Other Staff

The individual prisoner had more contact with the officers than with any other members of staff. Newly arrived inmates were liable to be disconcerted when they found how little private contact they had with the doctors. Most of the doctors believed that the main therapeutic value of Grendon lay in the interaction of the individual with the community, and they therefore encouraged problems to be discussed and worked through "on the wing" rather than in the privacy of the consulting room. Indeed it was generally felt that the development of confidential one-to-one relationships would "drain away" material that should be fed into the community. The doctors on the wing thus played a rather different role from that which prisoners have come to expect from a psychiatrist; they were present at wing, group and staff meetings, and were available on the wing for much of the day, but they generally eschewed private consultations and individual psychotherapy. Even the traditional role of the doctor as drug dispenser was lacking at Grendon, for it was policy on all wings to avoid the use of psychiatric drugs except in exceptional cases. The main function of the wing doctor was in fact the leadership and management of the wing as a therapeutic community, and a major part of this responsibility consisted of giving the staff adequate support.

As well as the doctor, each wing had a psychologist and a welfare officer on its staff. The psychologists, although they carried out certain types of specialised work (such as testing, research and staff training) for the prison as a whole, were not on the wings for this purpose. On the wings they were simply one of the staff, attending meetings, taking groups and making their personalities and experience available to the common pool. Unlike the welfare officers, they did not have offices on the wings and their presence there was often limited to specific meetings.

The welfare officers constituted the prisoner's main and formal link with the post-release world. They helped with arrangements for accommodation and jobs, and they ensured that the probation officer in the area to which the prisoner was to be discharged was kept in touch with his needs. As part of the wing staff, welfare officers also took groups and attended wing and staff meetings.

One unusual feature of the staffing arrangements at Grendon was the blurring of staff roles: although officers, psychiatrists, psychologists and welfare workers had different specialised training, they did not necessarily confine themselves to their orthodox roles. For example, an officer who had a close relationship with a prisoner might perform in relation to the prisoner's family what was usually the welfare officer's function. Several staff members said that they thought that in a therapeutic community such as Grendon, there should be no formal division of roles among the staff.

Comparisons Between Wings and Between Occasions

Since the atmosphere of each wing depended partly upon the staff, and partly upon the inmates, there were obviously differences between the wings, although the basic regime was the same on each. One of our interests in the study was to look at the extent to which the three wings differed. An earlier Grendon internal research report, which suggested that different wings might have different re-conviction rates, served to remind us that penal treatment depends largely upon the interactions of staff with prisoners, and cannot be assumed to be homogeneous, even within one institution. We therefore tried to look at the differences between the wings in a systematic way, and also to see how far conditions changed over time.

Substantial problems soon became apparent. As publication was envisaged, descriptions which enabled therapists or officers to be recognised were considered undesirable and because the wings were so small, this ruled out any possibility of descriptive comparisons. In any case our resources would not have enabled us to station full time observer-research workers on the three wings throughout the study period. Most of our information was culled from the visits we made to see the men, and the contacts with prisoners and staff which developed in the course of the study. In addition, one of us was able to spend a couple of months on each wing as an observer. These contacts were not sufficient to enable us to plot anything approaching the natural history of each wing. In the end, an attempt was made to overcome some of these difficulties by asking the staff and inmates to take part in what amounted to a series of opinion polls about the prevailing conditions on each wing.

The method was to use the Moos "Social Climate" questionnaire (Moos, 1968). This was developed for the purpose of measuring the psychological and social atmospheres of mental hospitals and penal institutions. Inmates and staff in the institution are asked about the usual patterns of behaviour in their unit (ward, wing, etc.), and their replies give a picture of the institutional environment not as it appears to an outside observer, but as the respondents themselves perceive it. The questionnaire contains 140 statements which each respondent is asked to mark as true or false: e.g. "Staff order inmates around"; "Inmates get into trouble if they argue with each other"; "Inmates rarely help each other". From these items Moos derived a number of scales, designed to measure different aspects of the unit's social climate, or psychological atmosphere. In his 1971 version "C" of the instrument (Moos, 1971) he presented nine scales, each made up of ten items; but in our own work we found that most of these scales correlated significantly with each other, and that by using only three scales of the nine, there would be minimal loss of information. The details about our work on the scales, their reliability and validity, will be found in Appendix 10

The scales selected for use in the research were (1) Support, (2) Control and (3) Clarity. The Support scale was shown by our factor analysis to be largely an evaluative measure, reflecting how far respondents felt the atmosphere of their wing to be helpful or good. The scale was designed to measure the extent to which inmates were encouraged to be helpful and supportive to each other, and the extent to which the staff were supportive. Items in the scale included "Staff go out of their way to help inmates", "Inmates rarely help each other", and "Therapists have little time to encourage inmates". The Control scale measures the degree to which the social climate is authoritarian. Items from this scale included "Staff order inmates around", "Inmates get into trouble if they argue with each other", and "Inmates may criticise staff to their faces". The Clarity scale measures the extent to which inmates know what to expect of the regime and the degree to which the behaviour expected of them is made clear. Items included "Staff are always changing their minds here", "Staff tell residents when they're doing well" and "If an inmate breaks a rule, he knows what will happen to him".

We attended wing and staff meetings in order to explain what the Moos questionnaire was for, and to ask whether staff and prisoners would be prepared to take part in such an exercise. Permission to carry out the survey was given on each wing, and the test was carried out on three occasions at intervals of six months, in December 1972, and May and December 1973. The procedure on each occasion was identical. The 140-item questionnaires were issued at wing meetings, and men and staff were asked to return them in the sealed envelopes provided. In order to maximise the response, names were not put on the questionnaires, although people were told that they could sign them if they so wished. The instructions asked the respondent to mark each statement according to whether he believed it to be generally true or false on his wing. Forms issued to the staff were a different colour, so that they could be separately analysed.

On the first two occasions, questionnaires were returned by at least three-quarters of the men and staff on each wing. On the third occasion, the proportion of prisoners completing forms was 63% on

Wing 1, 72% on Wing 2 and 80% on Wing 3; staff responses were 90% on the first two of these wings, and 70% on the third.

The questionnaires were analysed to see how much each wing changed between the three occasions, and also to see how different the wings were from each other.

When the prisoners' responses were examined on the Clarity scale, they showed virtually no difference between occasions, nor did the wings differ from each other. In absolute terms it seemed that the degree of clear role definition perceived by the inmates was rather low: out of a maximum possible score of 10 on the scale, the average wing scores ranged from $3 \cdot 5$ (s.d. $1 \cdot 4$) to $4 \cdot 3$ (s.d. $1 \cdot 8$). When staff responses on each wing were compared with those of the prisoners, there was a tendency for them to have slightly higher scores, but the difference reached statistical significance only on two of the nine comparisons made: both were on the same wing.

Staff and inmate scores on the Control scale, which measures the extent to which the regime is felt to be authoritarian, are shown in Table 18. The maximum possible score on the scale, representing the maximum possible degree of authoritarian control, was 10.

Prisoners reported little change on the Control dimension within their wings over the three occasions. When the wings were compared with each other, there was a consistent trend for the inmates of Wing 1 to regard their wing as being less authoritarian than the others. In absolute terms, the degree to which the prisoners on all three wings felt that the social climate was authoritarian seemed to be low: out of the maximum possible score of 10, the wing averages ranged from $2 \cdot 3$ (s.d. $1 \cdot 7$) to $3 \cdot 5$ (s.d. $1 \cdot 8$).

When the scores of the wing staff were compared with those of the prisoners, the staff consistently reported a lower degree of control than the men: the difference was statistically significant in five of the nine comparisons which were made. The staff on each wing evidently felt the regime was operating with minimal emphasis on control.

Finally, the Support scale was examined. The results are shown in Table 19 below. Again, the maximum possible degree of supportiveness, or goodness was 10.

Inspection of the figures suggests that on Wings 1 and 2, the prisoners' evaluation changed between occasions, although not dramatically: the largest difference was on Wing 3 between the first and third testing occasion (t = $2 \cdot 50$ p < $0 \cdot 05$). When the wings were compared with each other there was on each occasion, but most markedly on the first, a tendency for Wing 3 to receive a higher rating

Table 18   Control Scale

Occasion	Wing 1			Wing 2			Wing 3			F One-way analysis of variance between Wings	P
	No.	Mean	s.d.	No.	Mean	s.d.	No.	Mean	s.d.		
Men											
1.	29	2·35	1·54	25	3·12	1·39	31	2·77	1·26	2·08	n.s.
2.	29	2·41	1·52	24	3·46	1·67	31	3·39	1·52	3·93	< 0.02
3.	19	2·37	1·57	15	3·27	1·79	29	3·45	1·62	2·60	< 0.08
Staff											
1.	13	1·08*	0·95	10	1·9+	1·37	9	1·56+	1·81	1·05	n.s.
2.	9	1·66	0·50	9	2·0+	1·5	9	1·44*	1·74	0·38	n.s.
3.	8	1·25	0·71	7	2·57	1·40	9	2·33	1·73	2·07	n.s.

+ *On these occasions the staff ratings were significantly higher than the mens, *$p < 0.01$ + $p < 0.05$.

Table 19 Support Scale

Occasion	Wing 1			Wing 2			Wing 3			F One-way analysis of variance between Wings	P
	No.	Mean	s.d.	No.	Mean	s.d.	No.	Mean	s.d.		
Men											
1.	29	5·38	2·43	25	5·84	2·36	31	7·71	1·95	9·055	<0·003
2.	29	5·90	2·91	24	4·46	2·64	31	6·23	2·31	3·35	<0·04
3.	19	5·26	2·13	15	4·87	2·72	29	6·14	2·86	1·34	n.s.
Staff											
1.	13	8·46*	1·33	10	7·70+	2·11	9	8·11	1·76	0·55	n.s.
2.	9	7·66	1·58	9	7·89*	2·09	9	8·00	2·65	0·05	n.s.
3.	8	9·0*	1·07	7	7·29	2·14	9	8·22+	1·39	2·26	n.s.

+*On these occasions staff ratings for the wing were significantly higher than the mens, *$p < 0.01$ + $p < 0.05$.

than the others. This wing was evidently regarded as a better and more helpful place by its inmates, than were the other wings. On the Support scale, as on the two others, the staff gave more favourable ratings than the men, and this was the pattern on each wing.

The findings on the three scales show that the prisoners reported some changes in the atmosphere of their wing between the test occasions, and some differences between the wings. The results can of course only be interpreted with reference to the varying proportions of men who completed the test, but this differed substantially only on the last occasion. Other factors which Moos found to be related to test results, such as inmate-staff ratio, did not vary significantly from wing to wing. Nor did the wing populations appear to differ from each other: the men allocated to the three wings did not, in the year of our research, differ significantly as regards the variables we measured (age, criminal and penal record, offence, social history, mental state, attitudes and personality). The results thus suggest that although the wings had to deal with a constantly changing population, their social climate, whilst subject to variations, did not change fundamentally over the twelve months, and was not very dissimilar from wing to wing. The similarities were highlighted by the minimal differences between the scores of the staff on the three different wings: as a whole, the staff subscribed to and operated a common Grendon approach, and the differences between the wings, both those that were observed, and those that emerged from the test results, were probably less important than the similarities.

Links with the Outside

A question frequently raised in Grendon by staff, prisoners and visitors is — how can the institution help inmates to cope better with life outside when they are kept so severely isolated from it? In discussing this question the predominant fact is that Grendon is a prison. However much the staff wish to innovate in the interests of rehabilitation, the constricting and inviolable factors of prison rules and security have an over-riding influence. For this reason it is misleading to compare Grendon with a mental hospital. In a hospital there are only two fundamental considerations that limit what can be done; the welfare and health of the patients, and that of the outside community. If these were the only factors limiting what was done at Grendon, much more would become possible. Much of what the staff would like to introduce in the interests of rehabilitation cannot at present be done within the prison rules. In a sense this puts Grendon into an impossible position; on the one hand it is given the specific prison task of isolating its inmates and keeping them away from family, drink, children, banks, cars and all the other normal concomitants of life, while on the other hand it is criticised for failing to teach the prisoner how to handle the very problems and people from which he is being isolated. The difficulty is that Grendon is a prison, and as an instrument for rehabilitation, imprisonment lacks any rationale.

Grendon's staff are sensitive to the danger of habituating the inmates to an unreal existence and consciously seek for ways of reducing the isolation of prison life. Interested people such as magistrates, students and nurses are encouraged to visit the institution, and twice a week there are "Any Questions" sessions at which these visitors come onto the wings to take part in an hour's unsupervised discussion with the inmates. The prisoners, if they went to attend (normally about a third of them do), can then elicit and question the thinking of quite a wide variety of outsiders. Once every three months or so each wing also has a "social" to which visitors other than personal friends and relations are invited. Quite frequently too, students or visiting probation officers (often female) are attached to the wings for a month or two at a time, and this again is an opportunity for fresh outside views and persons to be experienced. Nevertheless, these measures, although they are designed to counterbalance the distortions and artificialities of the closed all-male society, cannot do more than to leaven the difficulties. Most of those who visit are by definition people with some special professional concern for prisoners, and come from different social backgrounds from the inmates; their visits are valuable but are not a substitute for ordinary social life. A prisoner made this clear when, at a wing meeting, he was pleading to be granted a day's parole; he said he wanted it in order to do something ordinary and to be with ordinary people. Other inmates echoed his feelings, and a life-prisoner said that he felt that he had lost the capacity ever again to do the ordinary things of life. Against these destructive effects of long-term imprisonment, Grendon, being a prison, can offer no immunity.

Prisoners in Grendon are allowed to be visited every two weeks, although visiting is naturally impeded by the remoteness of the prison, and the fact that the whole of England and Wales is its catchment area. The Prison Rules also provide for a very limited amount of home leave; at the time of our research, those serving two years or more were allowed two short periods of leave (not more than a week) in the last nine months of their sentence. Prisoners may, apart from home leave, apply for a day's parole, but this is rarely given to any who still have more than a year to serve.

The arrangements for leave, and indeed for release, underline again the basic fact that Grendon is a prison, not a hospital. In a hospital, if the staff feel that the time has come to move a patient out this will be done; if the patient does not do well, he can be re-admitted. At Grendon this is not possible. The amount of home leave allowed is rigidly pre-determined by the length of sentence, subject to parole. The advice of the prison is only one of many factors which the Parole Board take into account in their decisions; however much Grendon staff may think it in a prisoner's interest to be released, this is not a decision they can take.

Summary

The regime operating in Grendon during the period of our research (1971-3) was that of a therapeutic community, modified to the extent that prison rules require. Grendon was as much subject to these rules as any other prison, and therefore contacts with the outside world, although more carefully fostered probably than in any other security prison, remained strictly and artificially limited.

The adult part of the prison was divided into three wings, which functioned as separate communities. There were thirty to forty men on each wing, and a permanent staff which included ten uniformed officers, a psychologist and a psychiatrist. The latter's main function was the general management of the wing as a therapeutic community. He attended all staff and wing meetings, conducted groups, and gave guidance and support to the staff. The doctors did not as a rule give individual treatment. Nor did they often prescribe drugs — it was policy on all wings to avoid their use, save in exceptional circumstances.

The pattern of relationships amongst the staff was very different from the hierarchial one traditional in the prison service. The approach was democratic, and decisions were reached by consensus or vote. Great stress was laid on open communication and mutual support, and there were several staff meetings every day, at which problems could be discussed and difficulties shared.

Treatment was based upon group therapy, and most of these groups had prison officers as members. Within the group its members shared problems and experiences, and as a result there was considerable erosion of the barrier between staff and prisoners which is part of traditional prison sub-culture; the two sides interacted as individuals rather than as stereotypes. Relationships were relaxed, and officers generally handled behaviour problems with an understanding rather than a disciplinary approach. Regular meetings of the wing community all prisoners and all staff—enabled tensions and difficulties to be openly expressed and examined. Although over half the population had incurred convictions for violence, it was very rare in Grendon.

CARL A. RUDISILL LIBRARY
LENOIR RHYNE COLLEGE

CHAPTER 5

Changes During Treatment in Grendon

This chapter examines whether treatment in Grendon produces any measurable change in the men while they are there. Does all the talking which goes on in Grendon have any effect?

In order to seek an answer to this question, the men were seen periodically throughout their sentences and at release. On each of these occasions they were asked to complete the same series of tests and questionnaires which had been given at the initial assessment; the MMPI and the psychiatric examination were, however, repeated only at the final interview.

The re-interviews were arranged to take place three months after admission, nine months after it, and just before release. If a man was to be released within two months of the date at which the nine-month interview was due, then only the pre-release interview was held. For a minority of long-term men, interviews at fifteen months after admission were also arranged. Because of the time scale imposed upon the research by reason of its being also a post-release follow-up study, interviewing and re-testing ceased in the spring of 1973. The follow-up study required that the men should have been at liberty for at least two years, and since the research project was funded only until spring of 1975, it could therefore comprise only prisoners who were released by the spring of 1973.

Each time the men were re-interviewed they were asked whether they felt that treatment was helping them, and whether they thought they had learned anything about themselves. Details of the re-interview schedule and its reliability will be found at Appendix 9. The replies showed that they found treatment increasingly helpful as time went on. After three months, 85% of the men said that they were finding the treatment helpful, or very helpful, but 10% felt it was a waste of time. When the same men were seen nine months after admission, only one still regarded it as a waste of time (75 men, chi^2 = 4·25, 1 d.f. $p < 0·05$).

If Grendon is to be regarded as therapeutic in the broadest sense of the term, it would be expected that men would feel that they had gained insight and learned something about themselves during their period there: this is in fact what happened, and again it was a process related to the length of stay. After three months, two-thirds of the men said they had learned quite a bit, or a great deal, about themselves; at nine months, this proportion had increased to 85% (75 men, chi^2 = 8·76, 1 d.f. $p < 0·01$).

What evidence was there to support the men's opinions that treatment had been helpful? All the reassessments of mental state and personality which were made pointed in the same direction. Before going on to present this material, attention should be drawn to one factor which might be held to have influenced the changes which were recorded in symptomatology. This was the fact that at their initial psychiatric interviews, and when they first completed the MMPI, the men had been in Grendon for less than a month. If their anxiety and tension were heightened as a result of being in a new and unfamiliar environment, then some improvements in symptomatology could be expected simply because at their final assessment, they were no longer suffering from this initial tension. It was in order to avoid this difficulty that the men were not seen until they had been in Grendon for one or two weeks. Given the prison's relaxed and supportive atmosphere, it seemed unlikely that initial tension and anxiety would persist beyond this period. On the other hand, anxiety at the final interviews *was* likely to have been artificially heightened, for most of the men were then within a week or two of release, and a number of them commented on the increase in tension and anxiety they had been experiencing. This factor may have tended artificially to minimise reductions in symptomatology which were recorded between the initial and final interviews.

MMPI

Forty-eight men completed the MMPI on a second occasion, either just before their release (39 men) or after fifteen months in the prison (9 men). In order to establish whether these 48 men were representative of the whole population, they were compared with the men who were not retested. Comparisons were made on all the variables which had been collected at the initial assessment, and Table 20 shows those on which the two groups differed significantly. The 21 transferred "unsuitable" men were not included in the comparison.

Table 20　Differences between 48 Men who were Retested on the MMPI and 38 who were Not

Variables	Retested Group (48)		Not Retested (38)		
	Mean	s.d.	Mean	s.d.	t
Criminal					
1. Number of drug offences	0·65	1·6	0·05	0·21	2·24*
2. Length of present sentence (N = 47: one "lifer")	35·64	19·6	48·58	25·8	2·65**
3. Months served on previous sentences[1]	39·40	34·9	58·76	51·4	2·07*
4. Drug rating[2]	1·54	1·6	0·74	1·2	2·57*
Personality Characteristics (MMPI Scale Scores)					
7. Social introversion	65·87	14·5	59·68	14·3	2·33*
8. Ego strength	39·40	14·1	46·14	13·6	2·23*
9. Extraversion	42·62	9·2	48·35	12·9	2·39*
Social Characteristics	No	Yes	No	Yes	X^2
5. Removed by authorities as reason for paternal loss[3]	17	6	7	14	5·75**
6. Single status	21	27	26	12	4·27*

*p < 0·01　　[1] In prison, borstal or detention centre.
**p < 0·02　　[2] This 5-point scale is described in Appendix 3: the higher the score, the greater the involvement in illicit drug taking.
　　　　　　　[3] Omitting cases who did not suffer paternal loss.

That the retested men were serving shorter sentences than the others is to be attributed to the method of data collection. The retested prisoners were mainly those who were to be released by the spring of 1973, so the men with longer sentences automatically fell into the non-retested group. That they also had longer histories of previous incarceration reflects sentencing policy: the longer the previous record, the longer the current sentence is likely to be.

The most important differences between the groups are in the personality variables. Judged by the results of their initial completion of the MMPI, the retested prisoners were as a group less extraverted, more ill at ease in social situations, and generally less well adjusted than the other men. Their greater involvement in drug taking, and the higher proportion of single men among them fit in with this picture. These differences are important in the intepretation of the results of retesting. Given that the men who were to be retested showed more initial abnormality in personality characteristics, one would expect change in the direction of normality — i.e. towards the mean — to be more pronounced among them, than among those who were not retested.

The results of the final testing compared with the first, are shown in Table 21 for the four neuroticism scales.

All the neuroticism scales show a marked, and statistically significant change in the direction of "less pathology" between initial and final assessments. Although the essentially neurotic nature of the population remains — their scores for the first three scales in the table remain significantly higher than the American norms — the decrease in the amount of anxiety, tension and depression being reported is highly significant.

The largest change takes place in the manifest anxiety scale, which is perhaps the purest measure of the neuroticism dimension which was used. The ego-strength scale also demonstrates massive change: it is the only one of the four scales which at the second assessment showed no significant deviation from the (American) norm. The validity of the scale, as was noted earlier, was based on the principle that good "ego-strength" corresponded to good personality and was therefore indicative of a good prognosis for treatment by psychotherapy. The retested group, with their particularly low ego-strength scores at the first occasion of testing, thus represented the least hopeful end of the spectrum as regards prognosis. Their marked improvement on the neuroticism scales is therefore particularly encouraging.

The results for the extraversion scales at the final occasion of testing are presented in Table 22.

On all three scales there are substantial and significant changes. The social introversion scale, with its neurotic component, demonstrates the largest difference, with the men reporting a much greater degree of social participation. The purer extraversion scale changes in the same direction, reflecting an increase of ease in social functioning; on the second occasion of testing the sample no longer deviates

Table 21 Change in Neuroticism Scales between Initial and Final Assessment: 48 Men

MMPI Scale	Initial Assessment		Final Assessment		
	Mean	s.d.	Mean	s.d.	F
1. Hypochondriasis	63·2	14·5	58·7	13·9	4·77*
2. Depression	78·9	17·2	65·9	16·7	22·72**
3. Manifest anxiety	87·8	17·3	69·9	17·8	73·19**
4. Ego strength	39·4	14·1	49·8	12·2	35·84**

*p< 0·03 **p< 0·001

Table 22 Changes in Extraversion Scales between Initial and Final Assessments: 48 Men

MMPI Scale	Initial Assessment		Final Assessment		
	Mean	s.d.	Mean	s.d.	F
1. Social introversion	65·87	10·5	56·96	10·3	30·52**
2. Extraversion	42·62	9·2	47·71	8·4	13·91**
3. Manifest hostility	54·40	11·4	47·90	10·4	19·38**

**p< 0·001

significantly from the American norm (t = 1·26). And at the same time as they are reporting increased self-confidence in social situations, there is a fall in the amount of social hostility and antagonism being expressed.

These changes certainly present an encouraging picture. The first two extraversion scales reflect improvements in social participation, and a lessening of anxiety with regard to social functions, changes that can clearly be attributed to the emphasis Grendon places upon group interaction and communication. Concurrently, the men experience a decrease in the amount of hostility they feel towards others. Not only do they leave Grendon feeling less anxious, depressed and withdrawn, (as the neuroticism scales demonstrate), they have also improved their social functioning and attitude towards others.

In drawing attention to the magnitude of the changes evidenced by the MMPI, it should also be directed to two factors that have a bearing on it. One was the fact that the retested men were more introverted and less well-adjusted than the rest of the sample. Change in the direction of normality, i.e. towards the mean, would therefore be expected to be more pronounced in this group than in the men who were not retested. But the effect of any regression to the mean can only have been a small factor in the massive changes recorded, and is accounted for in the multivariate analysis of variance programme which has been used to measure change over time.

The second point relates to the possibility that at their first completion of the test, men were exaggerating their disturbance in order to call attention to their need for help. If by the time of the pre-release test this tendency had diminished, then a lower level of disturbance would be reported, and would reflect a changed attitude to the questionnaire rather than a change in psychological functioning.

There was a scale on the MMPI which threw light on this tendency. This was the F validity scale described by Meehl and Hathaway (1946). The scale is composed of 64 items, all of which were chosen by the authors because they were answered in a "deviant" direction by a relatively small proportion of the normal population. The authors suggested that the protocols of people who scored above a certain limit on the F scale should be regarded as invalid. This policy was not adopted in the present research, for the sample was not of "normal" men, and it is not valid to attribute invalidity to the answers given by an abnormal person on the basis of how normal persons respond. When dealing with a population of neurotic and recidivist men, it cannot be assumed that only a certain amount of deviation from the norm is acceptable, and that deviation beyond this norm implies untruthfulness. In the present research, therefore, the F scale has not been used to assess the validity of the replies. Instead it is regarded as a measure of the sample's tendency towards abnormal responding, and perhaps to some extent also, of its tendency to exaggerate problems as a means of calling attention to them. Interpreted in this way, the scale can be used to qualify the results of the other scales.

At both occasions of testing, the Grendon men's score on the F scale was far above that of the normal (American) population. Using standardised T scores, that population has a mean of 50 (s.d. 10) while the Grendon men at the first testing had a mean score of 83·7 (s.d. 17·3, t = 15·7, p < 0·001). By the second testing occasion, the Grendon mean had fallen to 69·7 (s.d. 17·1) a highly significant reduction (t = 30·12, p < 0·001), although the score remained much higher than the "normal" mean. The reduction represents a large drop in the tendency towards "abnormal reporting", but this decline was responsible for only part of the changes which were recorded on the seven selected scales. This was shown by analysing each of those scales in terms of change, after the effect of change in the "F" scale had been accounted for, by co-variance (Table 23).

Table 23   Changes on MMPI Scales between Initial and Final Assessments Before and After Covariance of the F Scale

		Univariate		With "F" scale covaried	
		F	p	F	p
Neuroticism Scales	Hypochondriasis	4·77	0·03	0·76	0·38
	Depression	22·43	0·001	3·22	0·07
	Ego strength	33·89	0·001	6·10	0·01
	Manifest anxiety	60·25	0·001	19·20	0·01
Extraversion Scales	Social introversion	28·71	0·001	5·92	0·01
	Extraversion	14·85	0·001	4·54	0·03
	Manifest hostility	17·98	0·001	2·09	0·15

As is clear from the table, the general effect of taking account of the "F" scale is to reduce the size of the statistical significance of the changes on all other scales. However, all but two continue to produce significant changes in score between initial and final testing and it can be concluded that the tendency for general abnormal reporting to diminish does not account for specific change in the neuroticism and extraversion scales. Two scales do lose their statistical significance, hypochondriasis and manifest hostility, but the former makes little independent contribution to the neuroticism dimension, and the reduction in the latter remains a strong trend. Thus, even when the changes in the "F" scale are taken into account, the general picture which emerges from the MMPI retesting remains: the men are reporting improved social functioning, a lessening of hostility towards others, and a reduction in neurotic symptomatology.

These changes relate to the group averages; obviously some men changed more than others. In order to see whether change on each of the MMPI scales was related to other variables, the retested men were divided into three groups; those who showed an average amount of change, those who showed an above average amount, and those who changed less than the average. Analyses were then carried out, for each scale, to see whether the degree of change was significantly related to the men's wing, their age, their degree of psychiatric disturbance, initial attitudes to psychiatry and to crime or to the length of their stay in Grendon. No significant findings of interest emerged.

Psychiatric Assessment

The psychiatric examination described in Chapter 3 was repeated for 67 men who by the spring of 1973 had either served fifteen months in Grendon (14), or were due for release (53).

Table 24 compares the results of the initial and final examinations of these men. On both occasions, reported symptoms were rated on a five-point severity scale (maximum 4, minimum 0). The table shows the mean rating for each symptom at each examination, and the proportion of men who reported its presence to a pathological degree (i.e. those with scores of 3 or 4).

The analysis shows that the main reductions in morbidity have been in somatic symptoms, fatigue, lack of concentration, depression, and anxiety; in other words in affective symptoms. The overall drop in symptomatology as reflected in the total symptom score, is highly significant. It should, however, be noted that two important symptoms, irritability and sleep disturbance, showed little change.

The psychiatric interview also included an assessment of the manifest abnormalities observed, and these, like the reported symptoms, showed a marked decline between the two occasions. Twelve abnormalities (slowness, suspiciousness, hysteria, depression, tension, elation, incongruity, hypochondriasis, delusional thinking, hallucinations, intellectual impairment and depressive thoughts), were each rated on a five-point severity scale, and a total score was arrived at by adding all the scores together. The mean total score of the 67 men had been 6·40 (s.d. 3·9) at the initial examination; by the second it had dropped to 4·21 (s.d. 3·6), $t = 4·74$, $p < 0·01$.

As an overall indication of the men's condition at the two examinations, the psychiatrist's rating of "overall severity" is probably the best measure. It is based on both reported symptoms and observed abnormalities. It should be remembered that at the final examination, which usually took place shortly before the men's discharge, their anxiety and tension was liable to be artificially heightened by the symptoms of "gate fever"; a number of the men commented on the recent increase of anxiety they had been experiencing, as their release date drew near.

Table 24   Changes in Symptomatology between Initial and Final Assessment: 67 men

Reported Symptom	Mean Severity Score				t	p	Proportion of Men with Significant Pathology	
	Initially		Finally				Initial	Final
	Mean	s.d.	Mean	s.d.			Percentage	Percentage
Somatic symptoms	0·93	1·29	0·46	0·85	2·52	0·05	14	9
Fatigue	0·96	1·26	0·48	0·88	2·71	0·01	16	8
Sleep disturbance	1·43	1·59	1·22	1·53	0·93	NS	33	24
Irritability	1·13	1·21	1·03	1·18	0·60	NS	16	16
Lack of concentration	1·63	1·38	0·78	1·06	4·52	0·01	33	8
Depression	1·22	1·32	0·73	1·18	2·48	0·05	21	14
Anxiety	2·00	1·41	1·61	1·19	2·30	0·05	35	24
Phobias	0·69	0·98	0·70	0·90	0·11	NS	8	6
Obsessions and compulsions	0·93	1·05	0·94	1·01	0·11	NS	11	9
Depersonalisation	0·39	0·71	0·27	0·58	1·27	NS	—	2
Total: All symptoms	11·36	7·34	8·30	6·22	3·31	0·01		

Table 25 shows that the proportion of men rated as undisturbed or with only sub-clinical degrees of disturbance rose from one-third at initial interview to two-thirds by the time of release (chi^2 = 11·94, 1 d.f., p < 0·001). At the same time the proportion regarded as moderately or severely disturbed dropped from 37% to 18%. Like the MMPI, the findings of the psychiatric interviews demonstrate Grendon's efficacy as a therapeutic institution: it made its patients feel better.

Table 25   Overall Severity of Psychiatric Disturbance: Initial and Final Examination of 67 Men

	Initial		Final	
	No.	%	No.	%
No disturbance	12	18	8	12
Sub-clinical degree of emotional disturbance	11	16	36	54
Mild disturbance, just clinically significant	19	29	11	16
Disturbance of moderate degree	15	22	9	13
Marked or severe degree of disturbance	10	15	3	5
	67	100	67	100

General Health Questionnaire

Substantial reduction in symptomatology was confirmed by the other assessment method that was used. This was the "General Health Questionnaire" (see p. 49). The men were asked to complete the questionnaire initially, and again after every subsequent re-interview. After three months, the drop in the level of symptomatology reported was marked and highly significant: the mean score of the 76 men who completed the questionnaire initially and at three months fell from 16·4 (s.d. = 13·7) to 11·1 (s.d. = 11·2) F = 6·82, p < 0·01. Between three months and nine months, there was a trend for the score to reduce further, but this reduction was not statistically significant.

Since it is in the nature of neurotic disorder to abate with time, it could perhaps be argued that the changes at Grendon were no more than what might occur among similar populations in any prison. Information available from the census in the South-East Region showed that this was not the case. Prisoners taking part in the census completed the General Health Questionnaire, and those who were still in prison nine months later were asked to repeat the exercise. It thus became possible to see whether, over nine months, the Grendon men evidenced more changes on the questionnaire than did a random sample of prisoners; and the results showed that they did so to a significant extent.

Table 26　General Health Questionnaire: Mean Scores after Nine Months

	Occasion 1		Occasion 2 (9 months later)		F 2 way An. of V	p
	Mean	s.d.	Mean	s.d.		
Census 137 men	17·7	16·1	15·2	16·1		
					5·05	0·03
Grendon 70 men	17·6	13·1	10·7	13·2		

It is clear from Table 26 that although the level of symptoms was initially very similar in the two groups, the Grendon men reported much more improvement after nine months than did the census men, and the difference became still greater when another factor was taken into account. It was found — the work is reported in Chapter 11 — that such improvement as occurred on the General Health Questionnaire among the retested census population occurred only among those who were in the early stages of their sentence when they first completed the questionnaire. The questionnaire asks about symptoms in terms of how a person normally or usually feels, and it is natural that men should report feeling more anxious, tense and depressed than usual during the first months of imprisonment, and that nine months later such symptoms will either have become chronic — and therefore not unusual — or will have dissipated with adjustment to prison conditions. Since the census respondents included many more men in the early stages of sentence than the Grendon sample (40% against 24%), a comparison of the two populations was made which included only men who had been imprisoned for more than six months when they first completed the questionnaire. Table 27 presents the results, and shows that while there was a large fall in the level of symptoms reported by the Grendon men, no reduction at all occurred among the census sample: in fact their symptoms showed a slight, though not statistically significant, increase.

Table 27   General Health Questionnaire: Mean Scores Initially
and After 9 Months for Men Who had Served more than 6 Months
at Initial Testing

No. of men	Initial Occasion Mean	s.d.	9 months later Mean	s.d.	F	p
Census 82	14·7	15·6	17·0	22·6		
					8·18	0·005
Grendon 53	17·40	13·0	11·4	14·1		

Tables 26 and 27 demonstrate that the massive improvement in neurotic symptoms reported by the Grendon men was not a natural phenomenon that could have been expected to occur spontaneously: no such improvement occurred among the ordinary prison population.

Attitude Changes as Measured by the Semantic Differential

Table 28 shows the results of the semantic differential when it was completed by the Grendon men three months after the initial occasion; seventy-five completed their forms each time.

The men's evaluation of prison officers and doctors rose dramatically between occasions; governors and police also improved their ratings significantly. From the clinical standpoint, the most important result is the increase in the rating of the "myself" element: after three months in Grendon, the men's self-esteem had risen significantly. That the

Table 28   Changes in Attitude after 3 Months, towards Figures
in the Semantic Differential: 75 men

	Initial Rating Mean	s.d.	3-Month Rating Mean	s.d.	F
Social Workers	55·0	10·8	55·7	10·9	0·33
Prison Officers	37·4	15·4	47·3	15·8	27·25**
Magistrates	40·8	13·4	43·6	13·9	3·33
Governors	43·4	14·7	47·2	13·9	4·33*
Psychiatrists	60·3	7·9	61·1	6·9	0·81
Myself	52·6	9·2	56·5	7·1	11·98**
Prison Doctors	40·5	15·3	49·5	15·0	21·95**
Police	39·1	14·1	41·8	14·1	3·70*

*p< 0·05 **p< 0·01

police should have improved their standing was an interesting finding, since the men were not likely to have had any contact with them during the course of treatment. The change seems to reflect the general modification of attitudes that occurred; as the MMPI results showed, feelings of hostility and resentment decreased while the men were in Grendon, and the police, traditional scapegoats of prisoners, could be expected to benefit from this change.

Fifty-four men completed the test three times, initially, at three months and at nine months. The results showed that the substantial improvements in the standing of prison staff—doctors, officers and governors—was maintained, i.e. it was significantly higher at nine months than it had been initially. Table 29 shows how the men rated the various figures on the semantic differential at each occasion.

The movement of opinion among the 54 men can be traced from the table. The rating of magistrates and of social workers remains stable over the three occasions. There is a trend for police and prison governors to increase their standing each time the test is repeated. Prison officers rise dramatically in popularity during the first three months, and then suffer a fall back. The "myself" element shows a big increase at three months, and remains at the same level thereafter.

The rating of psychiatrists shows a pattern different from all the other elements; their very high initial rating is maintained at three months, and then drops significantly at nine months. The trend is an interesting one. On the first two occasions, psychiatrists seem to enjoy unrealistically high ratings, towering in popularity above all other figures in the differential. By nine months the men have acquired a more realistic appreciation of what psychiatrists, particularly psychiatrists in Grendon, have to offer. The regime constantly emphasises that there are no easy psychiatric "cures" and that if a man is hoping for change, then it is to himself, rather than to his doctor, that he has to look. The drop in what can be regarded as an unrealistic degree of confidence expressed in psychiatrists is thus not a surprising development, and together with the increase in self-esteem it is, from the therapeutic point of view, one of the most encouraging results to come from the study. Less faith in the all-powerful witch-doctor, and more confidence in one's own ability to control the future, constitute hopeful prognostic signs.

Prison doctors increased their standing markedly at three months; six months later their popularity had declined significantly, although it remained higher than it had been initially. The reasons involved in the drop between three and nine months are likely to have been the

Table 29   Attitudes towards Figures in the Semantic Differential on Three Occasions: 54 men

	Initial Testing		3 Months		9 Months		Initial v. 9 Months		3 Months v. 9 Months	
	Mean	s.d.	Mean	s.d.	Mean	s.d.	F	p<	F	p<
Social Workers	55·4	10·1	56·0	11·0	56·1	8·9	0·46	NS	0·00	NS
Prison Officers	38·9	13·9	48·3	15·0	45·4	15·7	15·68	0·01	2·86	0·09
Magistrates	42·0	12·8	42·5	13·4	41·4	13·5	0·01	NS	0·56	NS
Governors	43·2	14·4	47·2	13·7	48·0	15·7	5·24	0·02	0·20	NS
Psychiatrists	60·4	7·3	61·4	6·3	57·4	10·2	1·14	NS	8·04	0·01
Myself	52·4	8·9	56·5	6·6	56·3	6·7	10·38	0·01	0·07	NS
Prison Doctors	41·4	14·9	49·5	14·2	45·2	16·1	9·82	0·01	3·98	0·05
Police	39·6	14·0	41·9	13·3	43·0	13·6	3·74	0·05	0·45	NS

same as those which caused the decline in the rating of psychiatrists. When the men arrived in Grendon and made their initial assessments in the semantic differential, they were rating the 'prison doctors' they had known elsewhere. After three months, it is the Grendon doctors — whom they have got to know well — who are being assessed under this heading, and their rating rises sharply. But after a time in Grendon, the distinction between prison doctors and psychiatrists would be less clear than it had been initially, since Grendon's doctors, unlike ordinary 'prison doctors', are also psychiatrists. By nine months, it is in fact, difficult to know the extent to which the two elements "prison doctors" and "psychiatrists" are regarded by the men as being separate. The decreased rating given to both appears to reflect the same kind of disillusionment — a recognition that these figures are not miracle workers — which from the clinical point of view is a promising development.

In order to see whether changes in attitude as expressed in the semantic differential, were related to other factors, the sample was divided into three groups: those whose attitudes changed to an average extent, those who changed more and those who changed less than average. The degree of change was then examined in relation to a number of other variables — age, length of time spent in Grendon, wing, initial attitudes to crime and psychiatry, and initial degree of disturbance as assessed by the psychiatric interview. No significant findings of interest emerged.

Discussion of Semantic Differential Results

The results showed that substantial changes take place in the men's attitudes whilst they are in Grendon. Since these changes are in what might be called a generally desirable direction — hostile attitudes diminished, and more favourable ratings were given to most of the authority figures — was there any reason to question their validity? Is it possible that the men were deceiving the investigators by answering in the "desirable" direction? Could they, either in the mistaken hope of obtaining some advantage, or simply for the pleasure of pleasing, have given the responses which they thought were "right"?

The facts do not suggest that this occurred. The men did not give "desirable" answers at the beginning of their time in Grendon, a time when, if they were hoping to secure advantage from the research workers, such answers might have been expected. Instead they gave the standard kind of responses to be expected from men with long exposure to the prison subculture. And had they been responding with the object of pleasing the Institute of Psychiatry, they would hardly have arranged for the rating of most elements to increase over time, but for that of psychiatrists to fall.

Can the changes in attitude which occurred be attributed to Grendon's effect, or could they have been expected to occur in the natural order of things?

Stanton Wheeler (1961) in an often quoted study, attempted to look at the way in which certain attitudes among prisoners change in the course of sentence. His interest was in the "prisonisation" process described by Clemmer (1940) whereby prisoners come to adopt the "folkways, mores, customs and general culture of the penitentiary". Wheeler devised a series of hypothetical prison situations of which the prisoners could be expected to take a different view from the staff: for example, he described two prisoners who are friends, one of whom has succeeded in smuggling money into the prison; feeling that the staff suspect him, he gets his friend to hide the money for him. Wheeler asked three samples of prisoners, each at a different stage of their sentences, whether they approved or disapproved of this and four similar hypothetical forms of inmate behaviour. He categorised the replies by the degree of conformity they showed to the views of the staff. He found that the proportion of responses with low conformity to staff views was lowest among the recently imprisoned sample, was higher among the sample in the middle phase of imprisonment, and highest of all among the sample in the last six months of their sentences. The proportion of responses showing high conformity to staff views took a different, U-shaped form, when the three samples were compared; it was highest among the recently imprisoned men, slightly lower among those in the last six months and lowest of all among men in the middle phase of sentence. The distribution of "medium conformity" responses among the three samples took the opposite shape, that of an inverted U.

Wheeler's work is sometimes quoted as evidence of a tendency for prisoners' attitudes in general to display a U-shaped form, but his data do not warrant (or claim to warrant) this. His study is mentioned here only lest it should be suggested that the changes in attitude evidenced by the Grendon men reflect some natural "Wheeler-type" trend for prisoners' attitudes to change in socially desirable directions as their sentences come to an end. Wheeler's study did not show the existence of any such general trend nor indeed did it show — as Wheeler himself emphasised — that men changed their attitudes over time, for he did not interview the same men at different points of their sentences. There is nothing in Wheeler's study to suggest that the changes evidenced by the Grendon men on the semantic differential could have been expected to occur in the natural order of events, and it will be seen in Chapter 7 that no such changes occurred among Wormwood Scrubs men, when they were retested.

As far as the semantic differential was concerned, there was, in fact, no evidence in our research to suggest that prisoners at different stages of their sentences had different attitudes. Data on this were available from the control study which is reported in Chapter 9. For the purpose of comparing re-conviction rates, the Grendon men were matched on a series of social and criminal variables with a control group of untreated prisoners. The matching ensured that the controls were a similarly recidivist group, with the same previous experience of imprisonment. They were interviewed, and asked to complete the questionnaires and tests which had been given to the Grendon men, including the semantic differential. The controls were seen once only, on average four months before their release. Their scores on the semantic differential were compared with those obtained from the Grendon men when first tested on arrival in Grendon, and when on average they still had sixteen months to serve. The test results of the two groups were almost identical; there was no trend at all for the controls to have more favourable attitudes towards any of the listed figures, including "myself". The attitudes of the Grendon men when they first arrived there, and of the controls as they neared their discharge date, evidently represented perceptions and values common to much imprisoned men; both groups gave hostile and negative ratings to the authority figures, and both reported the same low levels of self esteem. But after three months, the Grendon men had diverted significantly from these attitudes.

Wheeler's study did not look at prisoners' self-esteem, but Bennett (1974) attempted to see whether this would show a U-shaped pattern over time. He saw a sample of prisoners at Vaccaville Medical Facility within a month of being sentenced, and saw them again, in the various prisons to which they were allocated, at six-monthly intervals for two years. He found that the mean level of self-esteem rose significantly within the first six months, presumably because immediately after sentencing, when they had just been publicly condemned and degraded, the self-esteem of new inmates is at its lowest. After this initial rise, Bennett found that mean scores for self-esteem remained level; when changes among individuals were examined, he found no evidence of a U-shaped curve or of any other consistent trend.

The Grendon findings show a very different pattern from Bennett's. When they first completed the semantic differential the Grendon men had on average already been in prison 12·9 months (s.d. 13·9). Had Bennett's pattern obtained, no significant changes in the mean level of self-esteem thereafter would have been expected. Indeed, there is evidence from other parts of our research that self-esteem can be expected to fall as time in prison increases.

The changes recorded on the semantic differential thus appear to represent real changes in attitude. They have two aspects, social and therapeutic. From both points of view, the results obtained were encouraging.

The change in attitude towards prison staff and police reflects what Grendon achieved in its capacity as a social agency. It was not "taught" at Grendon that prison officers are "nice". Indeed, it would be impossible to teach such a thing to a group of men with so much experience of imprisonment. They had on average already served over three years on previous sentences, and before their transfer to Grendon, had spent at least six months of the current sentence in conventional prisons. The way they initially rated prison staff on the semantic differential therefore reflected the men's previous prison experience. Opinion changed because of two factors. First, the behaviour of the officers, and their role, was different in Grendon from what it was in other prisons. Secondly, the traditional values of the inmate sub-culture, in which "screws" are always the enemy, did not pervade Grendon as they pervade other prisons: consequently it became possible for the men to react to the officers' changed role. Open communications, and especially the interaction within the small groups, demonstrated that the staff were also human, and even not unlike themselves in some respects. (The same process, as was seen in Chapter 4, also occurred among the staff). In this way Grendon achieved a partial reconciliation between two traditionally opposed social groups, prisoners and prison authorities; that this degree of reconciliation generalises to some degree and extends towards other members of society was suggested by the changed attitude to the police, and also by the decline in social hostility reported on the MMPI.

These changes in social attitude towards authority elements are significant, but it is important to distinguish them from the therapeutic or psychiatric aspects of the Grendon regime. A person cannot be regarded as "ill" because he has a low opinion of police or prison officers. Nor can he be regarded as having improved in health because he has a somewhat higher opinion of police and prison officers than he had before. Grendon's psychiatrists do not regard it as part of their job to make inmates think well of prison officers: the changes in attitude that occur are a by-product of the psychiatric and humanitarian orientation of the regime.

The changes in attitude which can be regarded as therapeutic, rather than social, were those which occurred in the evaluation of "myself" and of psychiatrists. The extraordinarily high esteem in which the latter were initially held, drops by nine months; they ceased to be given full marks on every count, and started to be assessed rather more realistically. The change is likely in part to reflect the men's realisation that psychiatrists cannot, and do not, solve their patients' problems for them. A constant theme in Grendon, and one that is basic to the concept of a therapeutic community, is that people should look to themselves for help, rather than doctors, drugs or hospitals. The regime itself demonstrates this: treatment largely consists of the patients learning from each other. The semantic differential appears to reflect what is happening in the institution: the standing of "myself" rises, and that of psychiatrists' falls. The increase in self-esteem is the most significant of all the findings, and the most encouraging. Imprisonment can be expected to have a degrading effect on a man's self-evaluation, and there is data, both from this study and from others (Heskin *et al.*, 1974) to suggest the self-esteem of the prisoners is inversely related to the amount of time they have spent in prison. By treating its prisoners as individuals, and by giving them the opportunity, in group therapy, to help others as well as themselves, Grendon goes some way towards repairing this damage, and redressing the balance of the years.

Changes in Attitudes to Crime and Psychiatry

The questionnaire relating to attitudes to crime was given to the men each time they were re-interviewed. There was a trend for motivation against crime to increase, but it did not reach statistical significance.

The questionnaire on attitudes to psychiatry showed no differences between occasions. However, the interviewers' ratings on motivation for psychiatric treatment showed a small but consistent increase in motivation when the ratings made at nine months were compared with those made initially (60 men; initial mean 3·1, s.d. 1·0; 9 months mean 3·4, s.d. 0·9, F = 6·83, p < 0·01).

These findings relate to group averages, and some men obviously changed more than others. The sample was divided into those whose degree of change on each of the two questionnaires was average, above average and below average, and analyses were then carried out to establish whether the degree of change on the two scales was significantly related to one another, or to other variables such as age, wing, length of time spent in Grendon, and initial severity of psychiatric disturbance. No features of significant interest emerged.

Summary

In all the main areas that were measured — psychiatric state, symptomatology, personality and attitudes to authority figures and to self — large changes were recorded between the first and subsequent assessments. Some part of these changes may be due to factors other than Grendon's treatment effect: e.g. to regression to the mean, and to a decrease in the men's tendency towards "abnormal responding", but it was clear that these factors can have made only a minor contribution to the massive changes which were recorded.

The changes which occurred whilst the men were in Grendon can best be summarised under two headings; therapeutic changes and social changes.

As far as therapeutic changes were concerned, the psychiatric interviews and the General Health Questionnaire both showed a highly significant reduction in neurotic symptoms — anxiety, tension, depression, etc. Whereas at the initial psychiatric examination two-thirds of the sample were regarded as suffering from a clinically significant degree of psychiatric disturbance, by the time of the final assessment this proportion had dropped to one-third, and cases of moderate or marked severity had dropped from 37% of the total group to 18%.

These results were confirmed by the MMPI. The four neuroticism scales showed a marked change in the direction of less pathology, with the men reporting fewer feelings of anxiety, depression and tension. The selected extraversion scales also showed significant changes, with the men reporting a greater degree of social participation, and a lessening of anxiety about social interaction: moreover, at the same time as their social self-confidence improved, they were reporting a decrease in their feelings of antagonism towards others.

The attitude changes recorded in the semantic differential largely concern Grendon's social function, but two of the changes can be regarded as having therapeutic significance; these were the rise in esteem for the "myself" element, and the fall in the unrealistically high estimation of psychiatrists. The changes show the men gain increasing self-confidence in their own worth, and at the same time coming to realise that psychiatrists do not have the superhuman attributes with which they were initially credited. The result reflects the orientation of Grendon's therapeutic regime, where the primary emphasis is laid on people's own ability to help themselves.

All these changes point to Grendon's efficacy as a therapeutic institution; its inmates left feeling less anxious and depressed, more self confident, and better able to relate to others. And at the same time as these therapeutic changes took place, the men's social attitudes also altered. In the semantic differential there was a large and significant increase in the ratings given to prison staff — officers, doctors, governors — and in the MMPI the men reported a decrease in the amount of hostility felt towards other people and to society in general.

The research showed that most of the changes, both social and therapeutic, took place within the first three months of the men's stay in Grendon; the General Health Questionnaire and the semantic differential both produced dramatic changes during that period. This suggests that men with short sentences should not necessarily be excluded from the regime, but it is of course no reason for suggesting that prisoners need only spend three months in Grendon. If such a policy were to be adopted, the stability of the therapeutic subculture within the prison, the pre-requisite for Grendon's efficacy, would be destroyed, as prisoners were whisked in and out. Moreover, it is likely that some changes, whilst they occur quickly, require more time for consolidation and reinforcement, although these were aspects of change which the research did not attempt to measure. There was, however, evidence from the study that certain changes or learning processes do need more than a few months to occur; for example, the drop in the unrealistically high rating given to psychiatrists, which is a useful change from the therapeutic point of view, had not occurred within the first three months. The men themselves also reported that they found the treatment more useful as time went on, and the proportion who felt they had learned a considerable amount about themselves rose from 66% at three months to 85% at nine months.

Those who regard Grendon's chief function as that of reducing future offending behaviour will perhaps not be interested in what this chapter relates, but in our view, the appropriate criterion by which Grendon should be judged is whether or not it serves a useful therapeutic function. It is, after all, a prison. Its inmates, had they not been transferred to Grendon, would have served out their time in ordinary prisons. If its re-conviction rate is no worse than that of other prisons, and it is also performing an effective therapeutic function, then Grendon can claim success. The findings presented in this chapter show that in addition to fulfilling its statutory custodial role (and no-one has ever escaped from Grendon) Grendon was functioning both as an effective therapeutic community and as an agency that dissolved at least some of the social hostility with which the recidivist prisoner becomes imbued.

CHAPTER 6

Wormwood Scrubs and Its Treatment Population

Grendon is a unique and special institution within the prison system: this chapter looks at prison psychiatry in its ordinary guise. Whereas Grendon was set up for a particular purpose, psychiatric work in the rest of the prison system had developed and grown gradually. This chapter examines the result, and tries to answer some of the following questions: What does psychiatry consist of in an ordinary prison? Who gets it? And by what process?

The prison chosen for this part of the study was Wormwood Scrubs. It was particularly suitable for a number of reasons. It was the establishment where Dr. de Hubert began his work 40 years ago, and, Grendon apart, it probably remains the largest and most important centre for the psychiatric treatment of sentenced prisoners. Moreover, because of its seminal role in the development of prison psychiatry, the pattern of treatment evolved at Wormwood Scrubs became the model for other establishments. Whereas what happens in Grendon is unique, the psychiatric arrangements at Wormwood Scrubs represent, broadly speaking, the kind of psychiatric treatment system ordinarily used in the prison service.

Wormwood Scrubs Prison

The following account of the treatment arrangements in Wormwood Scrubs relates to the period of our research: 1971-2. Changes have, of course, been introduced since then, and some of them are referred to in the course of Chapter 7.

Wormwood Scrubs is one of the largest prisons in the country: in 1971 its average population was 1300. The enormous complex of buildings houses what are in fact a number of quite different establishments. In 1971 there was a borstal allocation centre (a transit location for men on their way to borstal institutions) and a small centre for prisoners under the age of 21 years. But most of the population was adult, consisting of long term prisoners (those serving four years or more), and of "stars" serving less than four years. A "star" is a man who has not previously been imprisoned as an adult.

The newly sentenced adult usually started his prison life on the allocation wing, where decisions about his future location were made. In 1971-2, the shorter term men left this wing within a few weeks, but those with long sentences were liable to remain there for several months. There were some 150-200 men on this wing at a time, and most of them were kept locked up in their cells for some twenty-two hours of the day.

After this the majority of the men were transferred to the "local" wing. Here those who had been allocated to other prisons, or to other wings in Wormwood Scrubs, would wait until they could be moved — sometimes for weeks, sometimes for months. The rest of the population on the local wing were those who were to complete their sentences there, mainly stars with sentences of less than four years. The local wing housed some 600 prisoners, many of them having to share cells. The men worked for five-and-a-half hours a day. Apart from an hour's daily exercise and some evening classes, they were locked into their cells for the rest of the time.

Long term prisoners (i.e. those serving four years or more) were transferred, usually after a few months of waiting on the local wing, to the long term wing. This housed some 300 men, a third of them life prisoners. Conditions were somewhat more liberal and relaxed. The men were not locked into their cells except at night, and in the evenings they could associate with each other. Cells were not shared on this wing.

One other part of the prison that should be mentioned is the segregation block. Here were confined not only the men who had been given solitary confinement as a punishment, but also those who felt themselves so threatened by their fellow prisoners, that they had asked to be segregated (under Prison Rule 43) for their own protection. Men who have committed offences against children, who are regarded as pariahs by the rest of the prison community, are normally forced to make use of this facility. At the time of the research these men were kept confined to their own cells for the whole day, except for one hour's exercise. A shop in which they can work together has since been introduced.

Arrangements for Psychiatric Treatment

How do psychiatric problems come to light in this large and mixed population? One of a prisoner's rights is to see a doctor; and every morning the medical officer on duty will make the rounds of each wing, seeing men who have reported sick. This work is usually done by local general practitioners who are employed as prison medical officers on a part-time basis.

If a man's complaints appear to have a psychiatric component, the doctor will deal with it as he thinks appropriate. He may prescribe drugs, he may reassure the patient, or if he thinks the problem warrants further investigation, he may refer the man for an appointment in the prison hospital. In all these respects, the GP acts very much as he would do in his outside practice; indeed, the greater part of psychiatric work in prison, as outside, is dealt with by the GP without further referral.

A prisoner's own decision to "report sick" is of course not the only way in which his psychiatric problems may come to attention. Men held in segregation are automatically seen by a doctor every day, and their problems are thereby likely to be noticed. Prison staff on the various wings may feel concerned about a man's condition and refer him for a hospital appointment. Probation Officers or doctors who have known the patient outside may also press for treatment to be tried, and, of course, judges, in sentencing, may make recommendations for psychiatric treatment.

By any of these means, a prisoner may come to be referred to a full-time medical officer for psychiatric assessment. He will then be seen in the prison hospital. If he is found to be seriously disordered, e.g. psychotic or suicidal, he will stay in the hospital as an in-patient. Some 28 psychiatric beds are available, and in 1972 there was an average bed occupancy of 21 patients (range 14-26). A few of the hospitalised men (17 out of a total of 330 admissions in 1972) will eventually be transferred to mental hospitals under S.72 of the Mental Health Act 1959, but the great majority will be returned to their ordinary location in the prison after being treated. In 1972 the average length of stay in the hospital for psychiatric patients was 25 days.

If a man's condition does not warrant hospitalisation, but some treatment is considered to be necessary, the medical officer can choose between two alternatives. He may prescribe drugs, and arrange to see the man again to assess his progress: or he may ask one of the visiting psychotherapists to interview the patient and assess his suitability for psychotherapy. If the psychotherapist recommends treatment — and the prisoner's interest in receiving it is of course an important factor in the decision — the medical officer will pass the recommendation onto the regional office. No psychotherapist can start treating a patient until this office has given its consent; and though refusal is unlikely, there may be considerable delay before consent is given and treatment can begin. Once treatment has started the patient will not be transferred to another prison until the psychotherapist closes the case.

Prisoners who have been recommended for treatment by judges are dealt with in the same way as other referrals. They are assessed by a full-time medical officer who may, or may not, endorse the judge's recommendation. Obviously the man's own attitude is an important factor here; if he is unwilling to have treatment, it is unlikely that the judge's recommendation can be acted upon.

Thus there were in 1971-2 three levels, or tiers, at which psychiatric treatment could be given in Wormwood Scrubs. The first was the GP level, and by far the largest volume of work came under this heading; for the most part, it was dealt with by reassurance, by sedation and tranquillisation. Secondly, there were the specialist services of the visiting psychotherapists; and lastly, there was the in-patient facility of the prison hospital. For the purposes of the present research it is the second treatment tier — psychotherapy — which has been selected for study. This is the type of treatment which courts usually have in mind when they recommend that a prisoner should receive psychiatric treatment. It is also the type of therapy which lends itself to comparison with Grendon's treatment, since it is used for a similar type of population — a population that is not psychotic or subnormal, but which is regarded as needing more than the GP-type of psychiatric attention.

When the research began at Wormwood Scrubs in 1971, there were seven visiting psychotherapists. Most were consultant psychiatrists in the National Health Service and they normally worked two half-day sessions a week in the prison. Five of the doctors practiced psychotherapy on an individual basis; one specialised in the group treatment of men addicted to drugs and alcohol. The seventh doctor ran a clinic for men with sexual problems; the treatment consisted mainly of hormone implants being given to the men shortly before discharge.

Research Design

Obviously there was a severe limit to the amount of treatment which seven psychotherapists, each working one day a week, could offer to a population of 1300 prisoners. The object of the research was to see how this treatment resource was used, for what patients and to what effect. The method used, was to study all new cases that psychotherapists took on for treatment in the course of the year, August 1971-August 1972. As in the case of the Grendon sample, the men were interviewed and tested when they began treatment and were seen periodically thereafter. The same interviews, tests and questionnaires were used as had been used in Grendon.

In the event, it was the patients of only four of the psychotherapists who became the focus of the study. This was because one of the doctors died shortly after the research began, and another, who specialised in giving long-term psychotherapy to murderers, took on no new patients during the research period. The third doctor to be excluded was the one who specialised in giving hormone treatment to men with sexual problems; the treatment given did not lend itself to the methods we had adopted, and in any case he was already conducting his own research programme.

Out of the many men sent to them for assessment during the year of study, our four doctors took on, between them, 44 new patients for treatment. Two of these refused to take part in the research project, so our sample comprised 42 men. Who were they? Why were they selected for treatment? Did they differ from men chosen for treatment at Grendon?

Source of Referral, Age, and Sentence Length

The men were asked how they had come to receive treatment, and their files were also searched for this information. Prison medical officers were solely responsible for the referral of almost half the cases (19 men, 45 per cent); in another third (15) courts had recommended treatment. Other pressures — e.g. from probation officers — were a factor in the referrals of the remaining eight men. Two of the sample had been transferred from other prisons in the south-east region specifically so that they could receive treatment, but all the other men were prisoners serving their sentences in Wormwood Scrubs. In the past, a substantial proportion of the men treated at Wormwood Scrubs were transfers from other prisons, but with the spread of psychiatric facilities throughout the service, the prison now caters primarily for its own men.

Seven of the sample came from the Young Prisoners Centre and were aged 20. Of the adults, 22 were aged 21-4; five were aged 25-9; seven were in their thirties and one in his forties. The average age of the sample was 25 (s.d. 6·9) compared with the Grendon average of 27·3 (s.d. 6·1) (t 2·032 p < 0·05). The differences arises from the presence of the 20 year-olds in the Wormwood Scrubs group; the adults of the two samples did not differ significantly in age and were considerably younger than the general population of adult prisoners (see Table 1, p. 54). The sentences imposed on the men are shown in Table 30.

Table 30   Length of Sentence—42 men

Months	No. of men	%
6-12 months	9	21
13-18 months	9	21
19-23 months	2	5
24-36 months	8	19
48 +	10	24
Life	4	10
	—	——
	42	100

Range 6 to 84 (and Life). Mean 30·9 (s.d. 25·6).

Over 40% of the men were serving 18 months or less (in Grendon this proportion was 10%), but there was a substantial group of prisoners with sentences of 4 years or more. The average length of sentence was considerably lower than Grendon's average of 42·3 months (s.d. 22·9) (t 2·564 p < 0·05).

The men were normally referred for treatment early on in their sentences. Table 31 shows how long they had served before treatment began. Almost three-quarters of the men (30) started treatment within their first six months, and only two had served more than a year. The Grendon sample (Table 15, p. 70) presented a different picture in this respect, three-quarters of them having already served more than 6 months when they were transferred.

Table 31   Length of Time Served on Present Sentence
before Treatment Began

Months	No. of Men	%
0- 3	15	36
4- 6	15	36
7- 9	8	19
10-12	2	5
Over 12	2	5

Psychiatric Characteristics

Shortly after they had been accepted for treatment, the men were psychiatrically examined. The same standardised interview and assessment methods that had been used on the Grendon sample were employed: current neurotic symptoms and manifest abnormalities were rated on a severity scale for each man, and taking both into account, the overall severity of his disturbance was assessed. On all these indices, the level of disorder found among the Wormwood Scrubs men was considerably greater than that in the Grendon sample. Table 32 shows for both groups the psychiatric rating of the overall severity of disturbance.

Table 32   Overall Severity of Psychiatric Disturbance
at Initial Interview

	Grendon		Wormwood Scrubs	
	No.	%	No.	%
0 No disturbance	19	18	1	2
1 Subclinical degree of disturbance	25	23	7	17
2 Mild psychiatric disturbance	30	28	16	38
3 Moderate psychiatric disturbance	20	19	9	21
4 Marked or severe psychiatric disturbance	13	12	9	21
	107	100	42	100

One in five of the Wormwood Scrubs men were regarded as suffering from a marked or severe degree of disturbance, and 80% of the population, compared with 59% in Grendon, was rated as pathologically disturbed (chi² 5·53 p < 0·05).

When current neurotic symptoms were enquired about, depression, sleep disturbance, irritability, anxiety, and obsessions were the most serious problems; at least a quarter of the men complained of pathological severity in respect of these symptoms. Table 33 shows the reported symptoms in order of frequency.

Table 33   Reported Neurotic Symptoms—42 Men

Symptom*	Men with Significant Pathology	
	No.	%
Depression	18	43
Sleep disturbance	17	41
Irritability	14	33
Anxiety	13	31
Obsessions and compulsions	11	26
Fatigue	10	24
Somatic symptoms	8	19
Lack of concentration	8	19
Phobias	4	10
Depersonalisation	2	5

*Not mutually exclusive.

A comparison of the above table with the corresponding one for Grendon (p. 59, Table 7) shows the Wormwood Scrubs men reporting more pathology in respect of almost every symptom enquired about. The largest differences were in respect of obsessions and compulsions (26% in Wormwood Scrubs, 7% in Grendon p < 0·01), depression (43% in Wormwood Scrubs, 23% in Grendon p < 0·05), and irritability (33% in Wormwood Scrubs, 17% in Grendon p < 0·05).

Reporting, as they did, more pathology in respect of almost all the neurotic symptoms, the Wormwood Scrubs men had a significantly higher mean total symptom score than the Grendon men (13·24 s.d. 6·56, compared with the Grendon mean of 10·56 s.d. 7·21, t 2·09 p < 0·05). The rating of manifest abnormalities was also higher for the Wormwood Scrubs group: their mean total score for the twelve abnormalities was 7·55 (s.d. 4·06) compared with the Grendon mean of 5·87 (s.d. 3·77) t 2·39 p < 0·05. From all the clinical assessments that were made, it was apparent that the current level of psychiatric disturbance in the sample was high, and certainly higher than had been found among the Grendon men at their first interview. The same picture emerged from the responses of the two groups to the General Health Questionnaire: there was a strong trend for the Wormwood Scrubs prisoners to have higher (i.e. more disturbed) scores. (The mean score for 40 Wormwood Scrubs men was 21·88, s.d. 14·32, whilst that for the 107 Grendon men was 17·05, s.d. 13·28 t 1·912 p <0·06.)

The diagnostic classification of the Wormwood Scrubs men is shown in Table 34. It is based on the "International Classification of Diseases" (General Register Office, 1968), but for the reasons explained earlier the diagnosis of "personality disorder" has not been used.

Table 34   Summary of Psychiatric Diagnoses Used:
42 Wormwood Scrubs Men

Diagnosis*	No.	%
Subnormality	1	2
Epilepsy	3	7
Alcoholism	6	14
Sexual deviants	8	19
Drug abusers	18	43
Paranoid state	1	2
Pathological gambling	6	14
Explosive irritability	6	14
Depression	18	43
Anxiety states	13	31
Obsessive/compulsive states	5	12
Depersonalisation syndrome	1	2

*These are not mutually exclusive categories.

Depression and drug abuse were the most common diagnoses, each being applied to 43 per cent of the sample (in Grendon as Table 8, p. 61 showed the proportions so diagnosed were 8% and 13% respectively, p<0·001). Almost a third of the men were diagnosed as anxiety states (in Grendon the proportion was 15 per cent p < 0·05).

The drug takers were all past the withdrawal stage when they were interviewed, but it may be that the generally higher level of neurotic symptomatology among the Wormwood Scrubs men was connected with the higher proportion of drug abusers among them. Two other factors are, however, probably more relevant to the different levels of disturbance found in the two samples. In the first place, men were not sent to Grendon in order to have treatment for symptom relief, but referrals for psychotherapy in Wormwood Scrubs were frequently made for this purpose (though other purposes may also have been present). The medical records showed many of the Wormwood Scrubs men were referred for the treatment of symptoms of one kind or another: e.g. "acute depression", "acute anxiety reaction", "depressive reaction to homicide". Secondly, there was an important difference between the samples as regards the stage of sentence they had reached when they were first interviewed. Unlike the Grendon prisoners, the Wormwood Scrubs men were recently sentenced, and the early part of a man's sentence tends to be associated with particularly high levels of neurotic symptomatology. To find himself in prison, suddenly deprived of family, friends, comforts and self-determination must have a severe effect on a man's mental state, particularly if he has not been in prison before. This would be exacerbated in Wormwood Scrubs by the conditions in which the men were held, with many of them experiencing very considerable periods of cellular confinement. Men can be expected to react symptomatically to such conditions, unless they get used to them.

Although the stresses and distresses of their recent imprisonment were likely to have been important factors in the high level of disturbance displayed by the Wormwood Scrubs sample, they obviously did not account for all the referrals, or all the men's problems. Psychiatric difficulties were often long standing, and apart from more previous involvement with drugs, the Wormwood Scrubs men did not differ from their Grendon counterparts in the extent to which they reported histories of such difficulties.

Almost half of each sample had been in-patients in mental hospitals, a third of each had histories of alcoholic symptoms, and over 40% of each had histories of suicidal behaviour.

Criminal Histories

Just over half the sample (55%, 23 men) had never served a previous custodial sentence. Of those who had, none had spent more than three years inside: 7 men had served up to a year, 9 had served between 13 months and 2 years, and 3 men had served between 2 and 3 years. The

Table 35 Reported Pre-prison Psychiatric Histories

	Wormwood Scrubs (42)		Grendon (107)		P
	No.	%	No.	%	
Epilepsy	3	7	3	3	n.s.
Suicide attempts	20	48	44	41	n.s.
Alcoholic symptoms*	16	38	35	33	n.s.
Drug problems†	18	44	28	26	0·05
In-patient psychiatric treatment	19	46	48	45	n.s.

*Tremors, amnesia, delirium or withdrawal symptoms.
†Moderate or severe problems together with withdrawal symptoms.

picture was very different from that obtaining among the Grendon sample, the majority of whom had served more than 2 years on previous sentences (Table 6, p. 59). The average time served on previous sentences was 7·8 months (s.d. 10·7) in Wormwood Scrubs, compared with 36·7 months (s.d. 37·5) in Grendon (t = 4·9 p <0·001).

Although over half the 42 men had not been in prison before, the sample was not one of first offenders: some 80% had previous convictions. Using the counting method described earlier (p. 56) which includes the offence for which they were currently imprisoned, the average number of convictions for the sample was 11·4 (s.d. 7·6, range 1-32). Again this was much lower than the Grendon average of 21 (s.d. 12·5 range 1-62, t = 4·6 p <0·01).

Just under half of the Wormwood Scrubs men (20) had started to come before the courts for offences as juveniles; 9 had their first conviction between the ages of 17 and 20, and all but 3 of the remainder were first convicted in their twenties. The mean age at first conviction was 18·2 (s.d. 6·39), significantly higher than the Grendon mean of 15·7 (s.d. 4·47, t = 2·699 p< 0·01). Only 10% (4) of the Wormwood Scrubs men had been to Approved School: in Grendon the proportion was 28% (p < 0·05).

Whilst the Wormwood Scrubs men lagged well behind their Grendon counterparts as regards the length and density of their criminal careers, the pattern of their offending was not dissimilar. As in Grendon, the three most common offences were, in descending order, larceny, motoring and violence. Almost 70% of the sample had larceny convictions; 55% had motoring convictions, usually incurred in connection with "taking and driving away" vehicle thefts; and 47% had convictions for violence, including 5 men who were serving sentences for homicide.

Although most of the Wormwood Scrubs men had been involved in offences of dishonesty, only 8 (19%) were rated as having been financially dependent upon crime to a large extent. It was interesting to find that in the Grendon sample this "professional" element was no bigger (it was 16 per cent), even though the Grendon men had been convicted of theft much more often. (Their mean number of such convictions was 10·83 (s.d. 8·7) compared with the Wormwood Scrubs mean of 4·79 (s.d. 5·6) t = 4·16 p < 0·01.)

A summary of the convictions incurred by the Wormwood Scrubs men is shown in Table 36.

Table 36 Type and Number of Convictions
(Current conviction included) 42 men

Offence	Men with Convictions		No. of Convictions	
	No.	%	Range	Mean
Theft (includes taking and driving away)	29	69	0-24	4·8
Motoring	23	55	0-11	2·3
Violence	20	47	0- 8	1·00
Drugs	13	31	0- 7	
Fraud	13	31	0-12	
Sex	12	29	0-11	
Drink	7	17	0- 3	
Robbery	5	12	0- 2	

When the above table is compared with the corresponding one for Grendon (p. 58. Table 5) the main difference is the presence of more men with sex (p < 0·10) and drug (p < 0·01) offences in the Wormwood Scrubs sample. Several factors probably account for this. One is that Grendon operates a selection policy which aims at maintaining a balanced population; care would be taken to avoid an unduly large intake of men—like sex or drug offenders—who could not easily be absorbed. Secondly, the presence in Wormwood Scrubs of a psycho-therapist who specialised in the treatment of addicts meant that drug takers were particularly likely to be selected for treatment. Thirdly, sex offenders have traditionally been a focus of interest to psychiatrists: and if they are segregated for their own protection under Rule 43, and therefore seen daily by a doctor, their problems are particularly likely to attract medical attention. One man in the sample certainly fell into this last category. He was subnormal, and had a four-year sentence for sexual assaults on children; he had always denied these and he could not reconcile himself to his sentence. He was kept in isolation·under Rule 43. Although subnormal patients were never as a rule considered for psychotherapy, in this case the therapist took the man on to his list, suggesting that "he be seen from time to time for supportive psychotherapy".

Social and Demographic Data

Just over half of the sample (22 men) were unmarried; and of the 20 married men, 5 were separated or divorced. When asked whether, after they were released, they would have financial responsibility towards anyone other than themselves, over half the men (23) answered in the negative. The general picture was not significantly different from that obtained in Grendon.

Asked about separation from their natural parents in early life, almost half (48%) of the men said they had been separated from their father for at least a year before they were 15; and over a third (38%) had been separated from their mothers to this extent. In these respects again the Grendon men were very similar.

Most of the sample had left school at the earliest possible opportunity, but 11 had at least one "O" level and 5 men had some "A" levels. Intellectual ability was tested by means of the AH4 intelligence test but eight men could not be assessed, five because English was not their first language, one—known to be subnormal—because he was illiterate, and two because they failed to complete the test. For the 34 men who were assessed, intelligence was normally distributed when compared with Heim's normative population and there was no difference between the mean score of the Wormwood Scrubs men and that of the Grendon men.

Asked about employment at the time of their current offence, a quarter of the men said they had been unemployed for several months. The rest were asked to describe their work in sufficient detail to enable it to be classified into the census social categories. As Table 37 shows, the distribution of occupations in the sample corresponded broadly to that in the ordinary working population.

A comparison between Table 37 and the corresponding one for Grendon (p. 55, Table 3) shows rather more of the Grendon men in the two lowest social classes (57% compared with 38% chi^2 $2 \cdot 28 < 0 \cdot 20$).

Table 37   Social Class of 31 Employed Men

	No.	%	Percentage of Male Working Population*
1 Professional, etc.	1	3	4
2 Intermediate occupations	3	10	16
3 Skilled occupations	15	48	50
4 Partly skilled occupations	4	13	21
5 Unskilled occupations	8	25	9
	31	100	100

*From 1966 *Sample Census, Economic Activity Tables No. 29.*

The point is worth a brief mention, because when the two samples were asked about the social class of their fathers, no differences emerged: fathers were reported as being of comparable occupational status, although the sons were not. The difference is likely to reflect the longer criminal records of the Grendon sample: years in approved schools, borstals and prisons must have detrimental effects upon patterns and prospects of employment.

Personality Characteristics

Except for the illiterate man, all the prisoners completed the MMPI; and their mean scores on the seven scales selected for use in the research are shown in Table 38. The scores are presented as standardised T scores in which the (American) normative population has a mean of 50, and a standard deviation of 10. The last column shows for each scale, the significance of the difference between the mean score of the Wormwood Scrubs men and that of the American normative population.

On all the neuroticism scales, and on the social introversion scale, which has a strong neurotic component, very abnormal mean scores were recorded. But the extraversion and manifest hostility scales show

Table 38   MMPI Scale Results: T scores of 41 men

	Mean	s.d.	t	p<
Neuroticism Scales				
Manifest anxiety	81·85	16·5	12·53	0·001
Ego strength	42·75	12·2	3·85	0·001
Hypochondriasis	63·78	16·6	5·38	0·001
Depression	73·73	16·9	8·98	0·001
Extraversion Scales				
Social introversion	58·83	13·2	4·28	0·001
Extraversion	48·87	11·5	0·63	N.S.
Manifest hostility	52·26	11·5	1·26	N.S.

that this neurotic maladjustment was not accompanied by severe social malfunctioning or abnormal feelings of social hostility. When the scores were compared with those initially recorded by the Grendon men, there were no statistically significant differences, but there was a trend for the Grendon men to score more abnormally on the extra-version scales — i.e. to report more alienation from normal social contacts.

Attitudes to Authority and to Self

The men were asked to rate the various authority figures, and "myself" on the semantic differential. When their mean scores were compared with the initial scores of the Grendon men, there was a consistent trend for the prison authority figures — governors, prison doctors, and officers — to be rated more favourably by the Wormwood Scrubs men, although the differences were not significant at the 5% level. Since the Grendon men had had much more prison experience, the results suggest that familiarity breeds contempt and "prisonised" anti-staff attitudes of the kind to which Clemmer (1940) has drawn attention. In attitudes towards police, psychiatrists and magistrates there were no differences between the groups. But there was an interesting difference in the way the two samples rated "myself", the self esteem of the Wormwood Scrubs men being significantly higher: the mean of the 34 Wormwood Scrubs men who completed the test was 56·9 s.d. 9·7, while the mean of the 93 Grendon men was 52·3 s.d. 9·4 t 2·723 p <0·01. In order to seek an explanation for this finding, all the other differences between the two samples were examined. The only variable found both to differentiate between the samples and to relate to the "myself" rating, was "months served before the present sentence" (r = −0·20 p < 0·05). Although the relationship is small, it is the only clue in the data which might explain the difference between the groups on the factor of self-esteem. It suggests that self-esteem is inversely related to the amount of previous imprisonment, a finding consistent with that made by Heskin *et al.* (1974). The relationship may well be one of cause and effect.*

Attitudes to Treatment and to Crime

The attitude of the Wormwood Scrubs sample towards psychiatric treatment was assessed both by interview, and by the Attitude to Psychiatry questionnaire. The questionnaires showed — as did those of the Grendon men — more favourable attitudes towards psychiatry than were evidenced by the general prison population who took part in the south-eastern census. (The mean score of the 42 Wormwood Scrubs men on the questionnaire was 18·71, s.d. 3·33, while the mean for the 613 respondents in the census was 16·36, s.d. 5·18, t = 2·76 p < 0·01). This finding was of course expected, since both the Wormwood Scrubs and Grendon men had agreed to accept treatment; between the two samples themselves there was no significant difference.

When the interviewers assessed the men's attitudes towards treatment, they regarded 41% as being strongly motivated, 21% as ambivalent, and 12% as having little or no interest. Another 26% were regarded as being interested in treatment partly for its own sake, but partly for other reasons — e.g. a hope of peripheral benefits, or a wish of keeping on the right side of the prison authorities. This

---

*After the first draft of this book was prepared some further work by the Durham team — Bolton *et al.* (1976) — was reported throwing doubt on their earlier findings. In this fourth paper they followed a group of prisoners over time and found that there were significant reductions in hostility, including self-directed hostility, which occurred during a 19 month period of imprisonment, and which were associated with increasing emotional maturity. Unfortunately, however, the changes in attitudinal variables which are of most direct relevance to our study are not given. Nevertheless it is clear that the measurement of psychological factors such as we were interested in is a complex affair. We are inclined to place more emphasis on the direct comparison we were able to make between the Grendon men and the Wormwood Scrubs men (Table 45, p. 161).

distribution of initial attitudes towards treatment was virtually identical to that found among the Grendon sample (p. 67, Table 11).

Finally, the men were asked to complete the Attitude to Crime questionnaire. Their replies were compared both with those of the Grendon men, and with those of the census respondents: no differences emerged. In so far as the questionnaire was measuring it, the wish to abandon crime was no stronger among the Wormwood Scrubs men than it was among the general prison population.

Summary and Discussion

During the 12-month research period, the four visiting psychotherapists took on 44 new patients out of Wormwood Scrubs' population of 1300 prisoners. All but two of the men agreed to take part in the study.

The men were mainly in their early twenties; just over half were unmarried. Intelligence was normal. The majority had been working at the time of their arrest, and their occupational status corresponded to that of the ordinary working population. Responses to the MMPI showed that, as a whole, the group functioned "normally" in their social relationships. Attitudes to crime among the sample, as measured by our questionnaire, were not different from those of the general prison population, but attitudes to psychiatric treatment were more positive.

The average length of sentence being served was 31 months (s.d. 26). Most of the men were beginning their sentences; three-quarters had not served more than six months and over a third were within their first three months. Just over half (55%) had never served a prison or borstal sentence before, but the great majority (80%) had previous convictions. As a group the Wormwood Scrubs men were markedly less criminal than the Grendon sample: they incurred their first conviction at a later age (18·2, as compared with 15·7); had fewer offences to their name (11 on average, compared with 21) and had before the present sentence spent much less of their lives in custody (8 months, compared with Grendon's average of 37 months). However, the pattern of offending within the two groups was not dissimilar, although there were rather fewer drug and sex offenders in Grendon. Taking past and present convictions into account, the most common offences for the Wormwood Scrubs men were larceny (of which 69% of them had been convicted), motoring (55%), violence (47%), drugs (31%), fraud (31%) and sex (29%).

Psychotherapy in Wormwood Scrubs was authorised only when a recommendation for it had been made both by a prison doctor and by the psychotherapist himself. Men came to be referred in three main ways. Over a third of the sample had been recommended for treatment by a sentencing judge. (Such recommendations were not automatically acted upon, but the proportion of cases in which a judge's recommendation was not followed could not be ascertained from the present research, since the sample consisted only of men who were being treated). Another 20% of cases had been the subject of requests or pressures for treatment from other outside sources—e.g. probation officers. But the most common way in which men came to receive psychotherapy was through the prison's own internal referral machinery: 45 per cent of the sample were receiving treatment as a result of this process.

The overall level of current psychiatric disorder in the sample was high, and certainly higher than that found in Grendon. Taking reported neurotic symptoms and manifest abnormalities into account, 80% of the men were assessed as being pathologically disturbed, 21% as seriously so. Over 40% were diagnosed as suffering from depression and 31% as anxiety states. This high level of neurotic symptomatology was confirmed by very abnormal scores on the neuroticism scales of the MMPI.

As the men were mainly recent arrivals in Wormwood Scrubs, their symptoms could to some extent be regarded as a reaction to the conditions of their imprisonment. Reaction to the offence itself, e.g. depression in the case of murderers, was also a cause of disturbance in some cases. But the men's previous histories often demonstrated psychiatric problems of long standing: almost half had been in-patients in mental hospitals and the same proportion had a history of suicidal behaviour. Although the distress of their recent imprisonment was an important factor in the high level of current disturbance found in the sample, it did not account for the totality of the men's psychiatric difficulties.

From the great number of problems which Wormwood Scrubs contains—and generates—the psychotherapists could select only a few cases for treatment: they were only part-time workers and the time all of them together spent in the prison, when totalled, amounted to no more than one full-time consultant's week. This chapter has described the population selected for treatment. Since the research did not include a study of the general Wormwood Scrubs population, it was not possible to compare cases that were chosen for psychotherapy with those that were not. But from what is known about those who were selected, some comments can be made about the selection process.

First, there is the fact that almost all the 42 men in the sample were recent arrivals in the prison. In their selection of new cases, the psychotherapists clearly concentrated on the newcomers. The next chapter looks at the question of how long these men remained in treatment, and from the evidence discussed there, it is clear that newcomers were not only the mainstay of the psychotherapists' new intake, but of their work altogether, for as a rule these patients did not remain in treatment for very long. Newcomers are obvious candidates for psychiatric attention for several reasons, but probably the most important is that they are likely, simply because they are newly imprisoned, to be upset and disturbed.

Secondly, it appeared that certain groups of prisoners were almost certainly over represented in the treatment sample; sex, drugs and violence offenders are unlikely to have been as numerous in the general Wormwood Scrubs population as they were among the psycho-therapists' patients. Whether such offenders are more likely than others to react symptomatically to imprisonment was something that the research was not designed to ascertain; but it may be that certain violent offenders — e.g. murderers — are particularly prone to depressive reactions to their offences. However, the high proportion of drugs, sex and violence offenders in the treatment sample probably chiefly reflects the fact that it is upon such men — rather than upon the thieves who make up the mass of the prison population — that psychiatrists have traditionally focused their interest.

The Wormwood Scrubs sample, when compared to the Grendon one, was more varied and less homogeneous, but it seemed to comprise two main elements. One of these elements was that of severe symptom-atology, e.g. the prisoner suffering from depression, or an anxiety state, who was referred for psychotherapy in the hope that treatment would alleviate the distressing symptoms. The second element was that of the long standing behavioural or personality problem — e.g. drug addiction, or sexual deviance. A prisoner with such problems may be referred for psychotherapy in the hope that it will help him to understand and overcome them. In many cases, of course, these two elements exist in the same person; for example, a drug addict might initially be referred for treatment because of his severe depression. The task for the prison psychotherapist is to try to help his patients with both these elements in their problems and the next chapter looks at his work, and its results.

CHAPTER 7

Treatment in Wormwood Scrubs and Changes during Treatment

The previous chapter described the population selected for psychotherapy. What happened to them? What treatment did they receive and with what results?

The first point to be made is that, unlike the Grendon men, the Wormwood Scrubs prisoners were treated on an out-patient basis; they went to the prison hospital to see their psychotherapists periodically, but for the rest of the time they lived on their respective wings, and were subjected to the ordinary routine of prison life. At the most they were "patients" for one hour a week: the rest of the time they were prisoners, no different from the hundreds around them, exposed to the same pressures and influences and subjected to the identical regimes.

Given this background, what were the objectives of the psychotherapists? All were highly conscious of the difficulty of exercising beneficial effects upon patients living in far from therapeutic conditions, and regretted that they could not exercise more control over those conditions. The doctor who specialised in group treatment has made his views publicly known: "I felt frustrated because the little that could be attempted in individual or group sessions once or twice weekly seemed to become lost during the 24 hour day in a custodial, non-therapeutic atmosphere. This environment often engendered . . . reactions of tension, depression and frustration, with continual demand for tranquillisers and similar drugs" (Glatt, 1974). The other doctors echoed these feelings. They said that they did not expect that their treatment could, as a rule, lead to significant changes of attitudes or

behaviour in their patients. They had become disillusioned about the
prospect of carrying out effective long-term individual psychotherapy
in the current prison setting, and had come to regard their work as
largely palliative, concerned with relieving the distress caused by
imprisonment. This was illustrated when one of the doctors was asked
about his policy regarding transfers to other prisons. As was noted
earlier, a man receiving treatment will not be transferred elsewhere
unless his therapist closes the case. The doctor said that he felt that the
humanitarian value of getting a patient transferred to a more suitable
prison was almost invariably greater than any benefit he could be
receiving from his treatment.

One doctor we interviewed summed up his work in Wormwood
Scrubs in a single phrase: "Too many cases, too little time." In such a
situation priority will always be given to the most immediately pressing
cases. A therapist who attends Wormwood Scrubs for four hours
weekly, could give four patients an hour's intensive psychotherapy; or
he could use the same amount of time to treat perhaps twelve men on a
different basis — concentrating on their current symptoms and distress,
rather than making any attempt to examine their underlying personality or behaviour problems. Given the prevailing prison conditions
and the large numbers of seriously disturbed men, it was this latter
type of treatment which was most common. The doctors themselves
were the first to point out to the research workers how unsatisfactory
this was; and some of their suggestions for remedying it, together with
changes which have been made since the research was carried out, are
discussed later.

The Treatment

What did treatment consist of? A distinction has first to be drawn
between the individually- and group-treated men. Thirteen men in the
sample were treated on a group basis, two of them also receiving
individual treatment from the group therapist. Except for one compulsive gambler, all the group-treated men were drug or alcohol
addicts. They tended to be men with shorter sentences: none was
serving more than 2 years, and the average length of sentence was 13
months. The groups met weekly and with two exceptions the men
continued attending either until they were released, or until the end of
the research period. The exceptions were one man who got "fed up"
after eight months and opted out, and another who was dropped by his

group because he made clear his determination to return to drugs. Group sessions centred on the underlying problem — addiction — which had brought the men to prison, and behavioural and personality difficulties, rather than current symptoms, were the focus of concern.

The pattern of treatment among the men receiving individual therapy was more varied. "Psychotherapy" is a very broad term, used to describe a spectrum of treatments which ranges from regular long-term sessions of intensive psychotherapy to brief consultations centred around the events of the previous week or month. Only one man in the present sample received anything like the former type of treatment. The treatment received by the rest of the individually treated men was of the latter type, and is most appropriately described as "supportive psychotherapy". The usual pattern was for the patient to be seen fairly regularly at the beginning of treatment, when he would often be complaining of severe symptoms; then, as the symptoms abated (often with the use of psychotropic drugs), sessions would become shorter and less frequent. Eventually the man might be seen at fortnightly or monthly intervals for a ten-minute interview, the purpose of which could be regarded as much humanitarian as therapeutic. The doctors were well aware that one of their most valuable functions was to offer a helpful relationship to people experiencing an exceptionally stressful environment. Some of their patients took the same view: when asked what aspects of treatment they had found most helpful, their replies included remarks such as "the best thing is talking to someone who will listen" and "it makes you feel you're not forgotten, and helps you feel that someone is interested in you".

The men were asked after three months and nine months how frequently they had seen their therapists: the average number of visits per month was 2-3. There was however, a wide distribution, as Table 39, which refers to the first three months, shows.

The duration of treatment among the 29 men receiving individual therapy varied considerably: just over half of them — 16 — terminated their treatment within the first four months; the rest went on seeing their therapists until they were released, or were still seeing them when data collection stopped. The pattern of treatment among those who continued after the first few months was very varied. Some were "called up" every four or five weeks, and some had weekly appointments; some were seen for no more than five or ten minutes, but one man at least continued with hourly sessions.

Comparison of the individually treated men with the group treated,

Table 39   How Many Times have You seen Your Psychiatrist?
First Three Months of Treatment: 31 Individually Treated Men*

Response	Number	Percentage
1- 2	2	6
3- 4	5	16
5- 6	7	23
7- 8	7	23
9-10	1	3
11-12	7	23
13	1	3
18	1	3

Mean 7·74. *The number includes two group-treated men who also saw their group therapist on an individual basis.

showed both that the latter remained in treatment longer, and that they met on a more regular basis. This was because of the different approach which characterised each form of treatment: group therapy centred on the discussion of the men's underlying problems, and individual treatment was usually directed at the relief of symptoms such as anxiety and depression. Thus when their symptoms abated, the individually treated men were likely to be seen with diminishing frequency, or to be taken off the psychotherapist's list, whereas group treatment normally continued until the men were released.

Changes during Treatment

What effect did the treatment have? As with the Grendon men, the research design was to re-interview the men after three months, and then again (unless treatment had ceased at three months) nine months after the initial interview. For men who were to be released within a year of the first interview, a pre-release interview was also sought; this was substituted for the nine month interview if the dates fell within two months of each other. At each re-interview, the men were asked about the treatment they were receiving, and they were asked once more to complete the semantic differential, the General Health Questionnaire and the questionnaires about their attitudes to psychiatry and crime. A final psychiatric assessment was made at the last interview. The MMPI could not, unfortunately, be repeated.

The proportion of cases which were re-assessed by all these measures was not as high as we had hoped: some men were transferred before it was possible to see them again, and a number of others failed to complete questionnaires in full. At three months, 34 men were re-interviewed, but only 26 of them returned a complete set of questionnaires. By nine months the drop-out rate had inevitably become much higher, with discharges, transfers, and cessation of treatment in some cases. Twenty-three of the men were re-interviewed at nine months, but only 12 of them completed the questionnaires.

Each time the men were seen, they were asked whether they felt treatment was helping them, and both at three months and at nine months, three-quarters said they were finding it helpful or very helpful. They were mainly referring to the value of being able to talk to someone about current problems, and to improvements in symptomatology. Only a minority felt that they were gaining insight into their problems. At three months 79% of the men, and at nine months 61%, said that they had learned little or nothing about themselves in the course of the treatment. In so far as psychotherapy is intended to improve the patient's insight and thereby help him with his behaviour or personality problems, these responses were disappointing, and very different from those achieved in Grendon, where the great majority of men felt that they were learning a substantial amount about themselves.

General Health Questionnaire and Psychiatric Reassessment

Both these indices showed that, with time, the sample as a whole began to feel much better. Twenty-seven men completed the general health questionnaire both initially and at three months, and they reported a highly significant reduction in symptomatology, their mean score falling from 19·5 (s.d. 14·3) to 13·1 (s.d. 15·6) $t = 3·38$ $p < 0·01$.

The reduction cannot necessarily be attributed in full to the treatment the men received, for it is in the nature of neurotic disorders to abate with time. It is also likely that to some extent the decrease in symptomatology simply reflected the men's increasing habituation to prison life. Distress and anxiety will, especially for the first timer, be at their height at the start of the sentence, and with time the prisoner will begin to adjust himself to his new setting. This tendency was demonstrated by the general health questionnaire responses from a random, non-treatment sample of ordinary prisoners who took part in the South Eastern Census, and who were asked to complete the questionnaire again nine months after they had first done so. The results given in Chapter 11, p. 211 showed that recently imprisoned men reported more neurotic symptomatology than other prisoners, and that their reported symptoms reduced significantly with time and without treatment.

It is against this background that the fall in general health questionnaire scores of the Wormwood Scrubs men has to be considered. In order to see whether the reduction was likely to have been caused by a treatment effect, a comparison was made between the Wormwood Scrubs men who had not served more than six months when they initially completed the questionnaire, and the corresponding men in the census. Table 40 shows the scores of the two groups both initially and nine months later, and it will be seen that the reduction in symptom reporting is not significantly higher among the Wormwood Scrubs treatment sample than it is among the untreated men of the census.

Table 40   General Health Questionnaire. Men Who had not Served More than 6 Months at Initial Testing: Mean Score Initially and 9 Months Later

	No. of Men	Initial Score		9 Months Later		F	p<
		Mean	s.d.	Mean	s.d.		
Wormwood Scrubs	13	20·7	15·9	10·4	15·1	0·04	0·83
Census	41	21·4	15·5	15·5	15·2		n.s.

The reduction in symptomatology reported by the Wormwood Scrubs men cannot, therefore, be clearly attributed to the treatment they received, for a similar reduction occurred in a random sample of newly imprisoned men. But whatever its cause, there was no doubt that the improvement was real, and it was confirmed when the men were re-examined psychiatrically, usually just before their release. Twenty-five of the sample were re-examined; the mean length of time between their two assessments was 6·8 months. Table 41 shows, for both the initial and the final examination, the mean rating for each neurotic symptom, and the proportion of men who reported its presence to a pathological degree.

Table 41 Changes in Reported Neurotic Symptomatology between Initial and Final Assessments: 25 Wormwood Scrubs Men

Reported Symptoms	Mean Severity Score						Proportion of Men with Sign. Pathology	
	Initial Mean	s.d.	Final Mean	s.d.	F	p	Inital %	Final %
Somatic symptoms	1·04	1·3	0·84	1·1	0·78	NS	16	12
Fatigue	1·32	1·3	0·56	0·9	2·85	0·01	28	24
Sleep disturbance	1·48	1·7	1·00	1·4	1·38	NS	32	20
Irritability	1·60	1·4	0·92	1·2	2·41	0·05	32	12
Lack of concentration	1·44	1·1	1·08	1·2	1·30	NS	16	16
Depression	1·76	1·6	1·08	1·4	2·09	0·05	36	24
Anxiety	1·28	1·2	1·40	1·5	0·45	NS	20	24
Phobias	0·64	0·8	0·56	0·8	0·57	NS	4	4
Obsessions and Compulsions	0·80	0·9	0·60	0·9	1·16	NS	4	8
Depersonalisation	0·40	0·8	0·32	1·0	0·44	NS	4	8
Total all symptoms	11·96	5·9	8·64	7·3	2·31	0·05		

The mean total symptom score for the sample shows a significant reduction, reflecting that the scores for most symptoms had fallen; the biggest reductions were in fatigue, irritability, and depression. The men's improved mental state was also reflected in the rating of the twelve manifest abnormalities (see p. 49): at the initial interview, the mean score of the 25 men had been 7·44 (s.d. 3·9); by the second it had dropped to 5·00 (s.d. 5·3) $F = 2·52$ $p < 0·05$.

Both the psychiatric interview and the general health questionnaire thus showed that after a few months the Wormwood Scrubs sample as a whole were feeling markedly better. Group-treated men were compared with those treated on an individual basis to see if there was any difference in the extent to which they improved: they showed an equal amount of improvement both on the general health questionnaire, and at the psychiatric examination.

Motivation and Attitudes

No significant changes occurred in the men's motivation, as assessed by the interviews and by the questionnaires on attitudes to psychiatry and crime. In this respect the sample were not different from the Grendon men. But there was a big difference between the two groups in the way they re-rated the various figures in the semantic differential. In Grendon, markedly higher ratings of prison staff, and of "myself" were given after three and nine months. But in Wormwood Scrubs there was no change in attitude to these, or to any other elements in the semantic differential.

Did the men who had received group treatment show a different pattern of response from those who were individually treated? To see if this was the case, data from the initial and final testing of 26 men was analysed: the mean length of time between the two testing occasions was 5·4 months. Eight of the 26 men had been treated in groups: they were first compared with the 18 individually treated men in order to see whether they were comparable as regards the information that had initially been collected about them. A few differences emerged, of which only one was significant at the 5% level: this was the length of sentence, which was shorter for the group treated men, who on average were serving 16·5 months (s.d. 6·41) compared with the 36·4 months (s.d. 24·4) being served by the individually treated men. Another difference between the two samples (significant at the 10 per cent level) was a trend for the group-treated men to have higher scores on the drugs rating scale (see Appendix 3) a finding which reflected the fact that group treatment was mainly used for men with addiction problems. A third difference was the tendency of the group-treated men to give more unfavourable initial ratings to three authority figures on the semantic differential: magistrates, police and prison doctors. It may be that members of the drug sub-culture believe these figures to have a particularly unsympathetic attitude to drug takers.

Having established the extent to which they differed initially, the groups were then compared on the degree to which they changed in attitude between the initial and final assessment. Attitudes to crime and psychiatry, as measured by the questionnaires, showed no change by either group. But when the interviewers rated the men's motivation for treatment, they tended to give the group-treated men higher scores finally than they had done initially, whereas their ratings of the individually treated men remained stable; the difference between the groups was significant at the 8% level (F = 3·42).

When the two groups were compared on their responses to the semantic differential, several differences emerged. Table 42 shows the position.

The group treated men had tended initially to express particularly unfavourable attitudes to magistrates, police and prison doctors. By the time of the second testing, their assessment of the first two of these figures had risen considerably, and had, in fact, come into line with the ratings that were initially given by the individually treated men. It is not easy to evaluate this change; it cannot with any certainty be attributed to the group-treatment process, since it is possible that the group-treated men just gradually came to adopt the same sort of view of police and magistrates as prevailed among the general Wormwood Scrubs population. But it could be that as a result of group therapy, the men had become less ready to attribute their difficulties to the unreasonable behaviour of police and magistrates. Whatever the explanation, the change is interesting, particularly as no change at all occurred in the attitudes of the individually treated men towards the police or magistrates.

The most significant difference—clinically and statistically—between the groups is the way in which their rating of "myself" changed. Whilst their initial rating of this element was almost identical, the individually treated men showed a decrease in self-esteem over time, whilst the group treated men reported an increase. The difference suggests that group treatment may in some way counteract the fall in self-esteem which imprisonment induces. Why group

Table 42   Changes in Attitude on the Semantic Differential: Comparison of Group and Individually Treated Men

| | 8 Group Treated Men | | | | 18 Individually Treated Men | | | | F |
| | Initially | | Finally | | Initially | | Finally | | |
	Mean	s.d.	Mean	s.d.	Mean	s.d.	Mean	s.d.	
Social workers	60·2	5·5	59·1	6·4	56·3	11·6	52·4	11·9	0·33
Psychiatrists	59·5	10·9	62·9	6·8	59·2	9·4	59·2	9·0	1·47
Police	29·5	18·6	39·2	16·6	40·3	17·0	39·7	14·6	4·23**
Magistrates	30·7	19·1	39·0	22·5	41·2	9·9	42·4	14·4	3·14*
Prison officers	37·0	13·1	41·0	17·3	41·9	11·0	41·8	11·8	1·05
Prison doctors	34·4	20·1	38·0	19·7	46·6	13·5	46·1	13·4	0·37
Prison governors	44·0	11·5	45·6	15·9	47·2	12·6	50·9	10·7	0·17
Myself	56·5	5·2	59·7	8·8	57·1	6·9	55·1	8·8	5·09***

*   p < 0·08
**   p < 0·05
*** p < 0·03

treatment should have this effect is an important question; on the basis of the present research it is possible to point to at least two factors which may be relevant. One is that the group-treated men met on a more regular basis and for longer periods, than did most of the individually treated men. The other is that group-treatment provides the prisoner with an opportunity to give support and help to others, and to feel that he is part of a worthwhile human group. However degraded imprisonment may make a man feel, these are substantial aids to the maintenance of self-respect.

Summary and Discussion

The changes which the research was attempting to measure can be summarised under two headings: therapeutic changes and attitude changes.

The findings about self-esteem properly belong under the therapeutic heading, for self-image is fundamental in psychotherapy, and the "myself" element was included in the semantic differential so that any changes in its rating could be examined over time. In the Wormwood Scrubs sample as a whole, no change in the mean level of self-esteem occurred over time, but analysis showed that this overall lack of change concealed opposing trends within the sample: group-treated men increased their rating of the "myself" element, whilst the other men decreased theirs. The finding is of some importance, suggesting as it does that the support afforded by group-treatment may help to counteract the ordinarily demeaning experience of imprisonment. Individual psychotherapy — at least, as practised in the far from ideal conditions prevailing in Wormwood Scrubs — does not have this effect.

As far as other therapeutic changes were concerned, the psychiatric re-examination, and the repetition of the general health questionnaire both showed a significant reduction in psychiatric pathology. Group-treated and individually treated men improved to the same extent.

The reduction in symptomatology has to be considered in the light of two relevant factors. First, most of the men had never been in prison before and the great majority, when they were first interviewed, were in the early stages of their sentences and had not had time to acclimatise themselves to prison life. The anxiety and depression which many of them were experiencing, and which was often the reason they were referred for psychotherapy, has to be seen as an initial reaction to the conditions of imprisonment, and would therefore be expected to reduce with time. This is the normal pattern which obtains among newly imprisoned men, and the census data suggested that neither the high level of initial disturbance, nor its reduction after nine months, was different in the Wormwood Scrubs treatment sample than it was in a random sample of newly imprisoned men.

A second consideration relates to the type of disturbance which characterised the sample: it is in the nature of neurotic symptoms and disorders to abate with time of their own accord, and some spontaneous improvement would therefore have occurred irrespective of other factors. Moreover, in a group suffering from severe and acute symptoms, as the sample did, this change in the direction of normality would be more pronounced than in a group with a less severe degree of neurotic disturbance (such as, e.g. the Grendon group).

These factors make it difficult to gauge the contribution which psychotherapy made to the improvement in the men's mental state. But there was no doubt that very substantial improvements in symptomatology occurred.

Neurotic symptoms were of course not the only reason that men were referred for treatment; long standing problems of personality and behaviour were also a factor in many referrals. But although the men's symptomatology decreased significantly during the research period, for the sample as a whole there was little evidence of changes in attitude or increased insight. When they were asked after three months and then after nine months whether they felt that they had learned anything substantial about themselves in the course of the treatment, the great majority of the men answered in the negative. Nor was there any evidence for the sample as a whole of changes in motivation as regards crime and treatment, or of changes in attitude towards the authority figures listed in the semantic differential. The only hint of change here came from the group treated men. They had initially expressed exceptionally low opinions of police and magistrates, but later rated these figures in the same way as the rest of the sample. The group-treated men also showed some increase in positive motivation towards treatment.

Given the nature and extent of treatment offered by the visiting psychiatrists, the negative findings of the research are hardly surprising. The men spent all their time in the ordinary atmosphere of the prison sub-culture, and periodic trips to the consulting room could not be expected to produce changes in attitude. That so few of them even felt that they had gained in self knowledge as a result of psychotherapy reflects the nature of the treatment given: in the main, the doctors focussed upon symptom relief and supportive psychotherapy. Neither could be expected to increase the patient's insight. But they did afford him support, and 75% of the sample said that they found their treatment helpful, the help consisting not of new insights gained, but of the relief of being able to talk to someone about current problems and frustrations. In the prevailing conditions, the main service of the therapist was to provide his patients with a sympathetic and listening ear.

Of this, the therapists themselves were well aware. They recognised that the work they were doing was mainly palliative, and that to a large extent it was concerned with treating problems which imprisonment itself had created. Hence all expressed concern about the fundamental need to change conditions in Wormwood Scrubs, first so that they should cease to be pathogenic, and then so that they could become therapeutic. Several of the doctors saw future hopes for prison psychiatric treatment as lying in the therapeutic community concept, and since the research was carried out one small step in this direction has been taken in Wormwood Scrubs, by the creation of a psychiatric unit within the prison hospital. It caters for some 20 men, i.e. for only a minority of those receiving psychiatric treatment. The men concerned go out to work in the ordinary prison workshops, but are otherwise based in the unit, the regime of which aims at being "clearly non-custodial and therapeutic with emphasis on the development of initiative and responsibility among the patients" (Glatt, 1974). The unit is staffed by officers who have volunteered for the work, and who have had some special training: they take part in the regular group therapy sessions on which treatment is based.

The new unit seeks to overcome at least two of the problems which the present research suggests are inherent in psychotherapy as practised in a conventional prison like Wormwood Scrubs. First, there is the need to change prison conditions, so that they become helpful rather than oppressive, therapeutic rather than pathogenic. In the absence of such changes, prison psychiatrists inevitably (and humanely) find themselves treating problems which the prison, rather than the patient, has generated. Secondly, there is a need to change a system in which a prisoner can be regarded as being "treated" because he sees a psychiatrist briefly two or three times a month. No therapist expects treatment to be effective under such conditions, and certainly the Wormwood Scrubs doctors had no illusions on this score. It is ironic, therefore, that judges should regard the availability of this "treatment" as justification for imposing lengthy sentences of imprisonment.

CHAPTER 8

Wormwood Scrubs and Grendon Compared

There were some important differences between the men in the two treatment samples, most of which were referred to in detail in Chapter 6. They related to two main areas: criminal and psychiatric. Grendon catered for the recidivist prisoner, Wormwood Scrubs mainly for the "star". The types of convictions incurred by the men in the two samples were similar, although drug and sex offenders were more common among the Wormwood Scrubs men.

Although the Wormwood Scrubs men were more disturbed, the two samples were broadly comparable as regards psychiatric status. They were of normal intelligence, and not psychotic. Neurotic disorders, though currently more severe in the Wormwood Scrubs sample, characterised both groups, with anxiety, tension and depression being common symptoms. There were more drug abusers in Wormwood Scrubs (43% were so diagnosed, compared with 13% in Grendon) but in other respects the samples contained similar proportions of men with pre-prison psychiatric problems.

Similar as they were in many respects, the two samples were subjected, as we have seen, to completely different regimes. Life in Wormwood Scrubs was not geared to a therapeutic purpose; its doctors did not control prison conditions. On the contrary, they spent much of their time treating disorders created by those conditions. Their role was to attend casualties, not to prevent them. Their patients were held in conventional over-crowded prison conditions: most of them were locked into their cells for a considerable part of the day, and the sex offenders forced to seek protection under Rule 43, spent the greater part of their time in what amounted to solitary confinement. Treatment for the Wormwood Scrubs sample consisted of trips to the psychotherapist made two to four times a month. The therapists who gave individual treatment were concerned primarily with helping distressed newly imprisoned men to adjust themselves to their predicament, and treatment was chiefly aimed at the relief of symptoms.

In Grendon, on the other hand, the men had considerable freedom and were confined to their cells only at night. They took part in group or wing meetings almost daily, and the whole organisation of prison life, and the way in which they were treated, was directed to the therapeutic purpose of helping the men to gain a better understanding of themselves, and a better ability to relate to other people.

It does not require research to establish the different effects which these regimes have upon their respective populations: one visit to each institution is enough to demonstrate the completely different prevailing atmosphere. But the research was able to point to some more detailed differences. One of these related to the amount of fighting in the two prisons. The men in both the samples were rated for previous violent behaviour, whether or not it had led to convictions; the assessment method used is described in Appendix 3, and the results are shown in Table 43.

From the above ratings, as well as from the conviction count, it will be clear that violence had in the past been an equally large problem for the two populations: over 60% of each had histories of violent behaviour, and a third of each had been involved in violence that had seriously endangered another's life or health. Half of each sample had convictions for violence. Both samples were asked at the three months interview whether they had been involved in any fighting since the last interview: of the 98 Grendon men, 5 answered in the affirmative (5%): of 35 Wormwood Scrubs men, 9 had been involved in fighting (26%), (chi^2 9·82 p < 0·001). The differing responses illustrate a point made in an earlier paper (Gunn, 1973) that violence is to a considerable extent situation specific. Here we see that men with similarly violent histories engage in significantly different levels of violent behaviour in prison, depending upon the regime in which they are held. Violence is against the rules in both prisons, but in Grendon many other factors tend to minimise its use: chief among them, the lack of tension, the emphasis on communication, and the fact that all inmates are part of a therapeutic community. In Wormwood Scrubs these conditions do not

Table 43   Violence Ratings for Grendon and Wormwood Scrubs Samples

	Wormwood Scrubs (42)		Grendon (107)	
	No.	%	No.	%
0 No convictions for violence, and never gets into fights	12	29	21	20
1 No convictions, but evidence of minimal violence — e.g. occasional fights or damage to property	3	7	20	19
2 Repeated acts of violence to persons or property, but no convictions; or, 1-2 convictions for violence. No acts causing serious personal injury (4)	10	24	23	21
3 Three or more convictions for violence, none seriously endangering life or health	4	10	8	8
4 One or more severely violent episodes, in which someone's life or health has been seriously endangered	13	31	35	33

exist: whether they are having psychotherapy or not, all the men mix together in a prison where the ordinary values of inmate sub-culture prevail. Tension can rise to a high level, aggravated by overcrowding and cellular confinement, and in these conditions fighting evidently remains a common occurrence.

The tendency of prisoners in Wormwood Scrubs to turn to violence bears on another important difference between the two prisons. In Wormwood Scrubs, unpopular men could only escape physical harm by asking to be isolated under Rule 43 from all contacts with their fellow prisoners. In Grendon there was no segregation block, and no one resorted to Rule 43 for his own protection. Every prisoner, however much his offence was disapproved of, took part in all the community's activities. In Grendon, men who in conventional prisons had taken the lead in attacks upon sex offenders, learned through contact with them (e.g. in groups) that such people are also human. For the sex offender himself, re-admittance to the community in Grendon, even though it is a prison community, is a considerable contribution to his rehabilitation.

At each re-interview, the men were asked whether they thought they had learned anything about themselves in the course of treatment. After three months, two-thirds of the Grendon men and 28% of the Wormwood Scrubs men answered in the affirmative; after nine months, 85% of the Grendon sample, but only 39% of the Wormwood Scrubs group believed they had learned much about themselves. The differences are highly significant, as Table 44 shows.

Table 44   Have You Learned Anything about Yourself
in the Course of Treatment?

	Grendon		Wormwood Scrubs		
	No.	%	No.	%	
After 3 months					
Yes†	65	66	7	21	chi² 18·51
No*	33	34	26	79	p < 0·001
	98	100	33	100	
After 9 months					
Yes†	64	85	9	39	chi² 17·41
No*	11	15	14	61	p < 0·001
	75	100	23	100	

† = Quite a bit, or a great deal.
* = Nothing, or a little.

Since most of the Wormwood Scrubs men and none of those in Grendon were receiving individual psychotherapy, the results shown in the table appear surprising at first sight. But there is no cause for surprise when the precise nature of treatment in the two regimes is remembered. In Grendon the whole regime and the whole day was aimed at giving the men better insight into themselves, whilst in Wormwood Scrubs the treatment was aimed mainly at symptom relief and support. The differences shown in the table are a natural consequence of the different treatment methods used in the two regimes. But the failure of psychotherapy to provide most of the Wormwood Scrubs men with any increase in insight, suggests that the treatment was unlikely to have much impact on the offender's personality and behaviour.

It was unfortunate that it proved impossible to retest the Wormwood Scrubs population on the MMPI, for the extraversion scales would have shown how the men's social functioning was affected by their experience of imprisonment. The Grendon men, by the time they were discharged, were reporting a markedly improved level of social adjustment and functioning, and a lessening of feelings of social hostility and withdrawal. The only aspect of the social attitudes of the Wormwood Scrubs men that could be retested was their rating of the various figures listed in the semantic differential, and their attitude to crime. The latter (as recorded by the attitude to crime questionnaire) showed no difference between the various testing occasions, and in this respect the Wormwood Scrubs men did not differ from their Grendon counterparts. However, the responses over time of the two groups on the semantic differential did display a very different pattern. Table 45 shows how the various elements were rated initially and three months later.

The Wormwood Scrubs men reported no significant change in their rating of prison officers and doctors, whilst the Grendon men showed a large increase in their approval of these figures. The difference again mirrors the difference between the institutions. In Grendon both the role of prison officers and doctors and their relationship with the men were quite different from those in an ordinary prison. Prisoners got to know staff closely, and the process was reflected in the attitude changes recorded on the semantic differential. The findings show how Grendon dissolved some of the accumulated bitterness and hostility that prison life fosters.

Table 45 also shows what are, from the psychotherapeutic point of view the most significant findings — the various ratings given to the "myself" element. Although this element stood apart from the others in our semantic differential in that the adjectives chosen were not designed to be specifically relevant to its rating, the rating scale nevertheless proved to be sufficiently sensitive to record changes in self-evaluation. At their initial testing, the two samples differed in their rating of "myself", with the Grendon men reporting significantly lower self-esteem ($p < 0.01$). This difference was found (Ch. 6, p. 139) to be statistically related to the longer periods they had spent in prison, and it may have been caused thereby. Yet after three months in Grendon, the men increased in self-esteem markedly, and reached the same level as that reported by the Wormwood Scrubs men at their initial testing. This change (which was subsequently maintained) is clinically important in its own right, but its importance is enhanced if self-esteem is in fact inversely related to previous prison experience: it shows that Grendon undoes some of the damage done by previous institutionalisation.

Table 45   Changes in Attitude after 3 months towards Elements in the Semantic Differential

| | Grendon (76 men) | | | | Wormwood Scrubs (27 men) | | | | |
| | Initial Rating | | 3 Month Rating | | Initial Rating | | 3 Month Rating | | F |
	Mean	s.d.	Mean	s.d.	Mean	s.d.	Mean	s.d.	
Social workers	55·1	10·7	55·5	10·8	57·1	9·9	54·5	9·1	2·00
Psychiatrists	60·2	7·8	60·9	7·0	58·9	9·6	58·6	8·7	0·39
Police	39·1	14·4	41·8	14·3	38·1	16·7	39·9	14·9	0·27
Magistrates	40·7	13·4	43·4	14·0	37·0	13·4	39·4	15·2	0·01
Prison officers	37·5	15·2	47·7	15·8	39·9	11·9	42·3	13·5	4·72*
Prison doctors	40·1	15·6	49·8	14·9	42·7	15·7	44·1	14·4	5·04**
Governors	43·2	14·9	46·8	13·8	46·1	11·5	49·4	11·1	0·00
Myself	52·4	9·2	56·4	7·2	56·3	6·0	55·3	8·4	6·19**

* p < 0.02
**p < 0.01

Among the Wormwood Scrubs sample, there was no change in the mean level of self-esteem, but further analysis showed that the overall lack of change was due to two opposing tendencies within the sample: whilst the minority of men who were treated on a group basis slightly increased their rating of the "myself" element, the individually treated prisoners reduced theirs. Both the Grendon and the Wormwood Scrubs results thus point to the value of group therapy as an antidote to the damaging effect that imprisonment has on self-esteem.

On all the items discussed above — the extent to which the men felt they had learned something about themselves, the extent to which they engaged in fighting, changes in the level of their self-esteem, and in their attitudes towards prison staff — the performance of the Grendon men during the treatment period was significantly different from that of the Wormwood Scrubs men. What of their mental state, and their symptomatology? Were there any differences between the groups in the degree to which they changed in these respects?

The psychiatric re-examination showed that both samples improved in mental state during the treatment period, but there was no statistically significant difference as regards the amount of change evidenced by each. The reduction in neurotic symptomatology and in manifest abnormality was substantial and similar in both groups.

The General Health Questionnaire was the only other measure of symptomatology which was repeated for both groups. Both reduced their scores substantially when their initial responses were compared with those made three months later, and as Table 46 shows, there was no difference in the amount of change which occurred in each group.

The above results have to be considered in relation to other relevant factors. More spontaneous improvement could be expected to take place among the Wormwood Scrubs men than among the Grendon sample, for two reasons. First, they were more disordered in terms of neurotic disturbance, so the degree of natural improvement which

Table 46   Changes over 3 months in Mean Scores
on the General Health Questionnaire

Grendon (76 men)				Wormwood Scrubs (27 men)				
Initial score		Score 3 months later		Initial score		Score 3 months later		
Mean	s.d.	Mean	s.d.	Mean	s.d.	Mean	s.d.	F
16·4	13·7	11·1	11·2	19·5	14·3	13·1	15·6	0·39 n.s.

could be expected to occur among them would be greater. Secondly, the Wormwood Scrubs men were mainly at the start of their sentences, and reduction in symptomatology would occur of its own accord as they gradually adjusted to their conditions of imprisonment. This tendency occurs among all newly imprisoned men, and it was seen at p. 148, Table 40, that the improvement on the General Health Questionnaire reported by the Wormwood Scrubs sample over nine months was in fact no larger than that reported by a random group of prisoners in the early stages of their sentences.

If these non-treatment factors were sufficient to account for much of the change in the condition of the Wormwood Scrubs sample, could the same be said of the improvement reported by the Grendon men? Here the situation was rather different. First, as the amount of initial severe neurotic disorder was lower, less spontaneous improvement could be expected to occur. Secondly, when the Grendon men were first assessed, they were well habituated to prison life, having on average already served more than a year of their present sentences. There seemed no reason to expect reductions in symptomatology to occur as a result of further habituation to prison life.

That the change in reported symptomatology which occurred in Grendon was in fact greater than would have occurred spontaneously without treatment, can be seen by comparing the General Health Questionnaire scores of the Grendon men with those of the random sample of prisoners who took part in the census. This was done in Tables 26 and 27 of Chapter 5; Table 26 showed that over nine months the Grendon men reported significantly more reduction in symptomatology than did the census sample, even though the latter contained many more recently sentenced men, who would be expected to improve their scores simply as a result of becoming used to prison life. When these recently imprisoned men were excluded from both samples, Table 27 showed that the census men reported no reduction in the mean General Health Questionnaire score between the two occasions of testing, whilst among the Grendon men there was a large and highly significant reduction. The census data thus point to an important difference which underlies the finding that both the Grendon and Wormwood Scrubs samples improved substantially and equally in neurotic symptomatology. The improvement among the Wormwood Scrubs men was similar to that which occurred among a random non-treatment sample of prisoners who were at a comparable stage of their sentences. But the improvement of the Grendon men could not be attributed to natural causes, and stood in marked contrast to the lack of improvement reported by a random sample of prisoners at similar stages of their sentences.

These findings show that Grendon differed from Wormwood Scrubs in that its treatment, although not specifically aimed at symptom relief, nevertheless produced in this area substantial benefits which could be attributed to the regime. The achievement is the more interesting in that it was obtained without the use of psychotropic drugs, whereas such drugs were being prescribed and taken by many of the men in the Wormwood Scrubs sample. The reduction in symptoms which the Grendon men experienced evidently stemmed from the environment in which they lived, an environment structured so as to enable problems and stresses to be openly looked at and shared.

Summary

Grendon and Wormwood Scrubs psychiatric services catered for somewhat dis-similar populations. Grendon dealt with recidivists and Wormwood Scrubs with "star" (i.e. first-time) prisoners. The Wormwood Scrubs prisoners were at the start of their sentences and were more disturbed. Treatment in the two situations was entirely different. The Wormwood Scrubs men lived in an ordinary prison and visited their psychiatrist only two to four times a month.

Whilst violence had been an equally large problem for both populations in the past, fighting was much commoner in Wormwood Scrubs than in Grendon.

At re-interview after three months, two-thirds of the Grendon men believed they had learned something about themselves in the course of treatment, whereas only one-fifth of the Wormwood Scrubs men thought this. There were no differences in the two populations in terms of their lack of change of their attitudes towards crime, but Grendon men shifted their attitudes towards authority figures whilst Wormwood Scrubs men reported no significant change. At initial evaluation the Grendon men showed significantly lower self-esteem, yet after three months in Grendon self-esteem improved markedly and reached the same level as that reported by the Wormwood Scrubs men at their initial testing. Among the Wormwood Scrubs men there were opposing trends; the group-treated men tended to improve in self-esteem whilst the individually treated men tended to deteriorate.

In terms of neurotic symptoms, both samples improved equally in the first three months; this finding tends to imply more therapeutic efficacy at Grendon for they were dealing with men later in their sentences when natural ameliorating processes had already taken place to a large extent.

Overall the results tend to emphasise the special benefits of group treatment, especially treatment carried out in a therapeutic community.

CHAPTER 9

After Release (1):
The Controlled Re-conviction Study

How should Grendon be evaluated? In our view, the appropriate method is to look at the interaction between the individual and the institution, and the results of this evaluation have been described in Chapter 5: Grendon makes people feel better, less hostile to authority and more able to handle their relationships with others.

But it may be asked, does Grendon help its inmates to cope better with life after discharge? Particularly, does it reduce their propensity to break the law? It is standard practice to pose this last question about the effects of custodial sentences, but the practice begs a more fundamental question: namely, is imprisonment, however it is served, an experience that can be expected to influence measurably the future criminal conduct of adult recidivists? The assumption that custodial sentences will have such an effect has a long history. At one time it was believed that solitary confinement, by giving the prisoner the opportunity to repent and turn away from sin, would have a decisive effect on his future propensity to commit crimes. When it became apparent that religious influences did not generally work in this way, nineteenth century penal ideology turned to deterrence: the argument was that if imprisonment was made sufficiently harsh — a "terror to evil doers" (Director of Convict Prisons, 1874) — the prisoner would eschew crime on release, so as to ensure that he would not return to prison. However, despite the harshest conditions, recidivism among prisoners continued, and the Gladstone Committee then concluded that what was necessary was to try to *reform* the prisoners, so that when they left prison they would be better people who would voluntarily avoid crime in the future.

All these ideas have the same underlying assumption: that because crime is something which the individual commits, if only the individual's propensity for it could be suppressed or removed — by conversion, terror, or reformation — he would cease to offend. Stated like this, the idea is obviously true: but it does not constitute the whole truth. An individual's decision to do one thing rather than another is one factor in how he behaves, but there are also many others. Crime occurs in the community, and criminal sociology has demonstrated how far it is socially created (Mannheim, 1965). An individual's criminal behaviour is powerfully influenced by environmental and situational factors: it has recently been shown, for example, in a study of residents in probation hostels, that their current offending behaviour is much more a function of the hostel environment than of their past histories or personalities (Sinclair, 1971). The importance of environmental criminogenic factors is grossly underestimated by those who believe that recidivists can be turned into future non-offenders, by removing them temporarily from the environment and subjecting them to a spell of imprisonment, whether of the psychiatric, rehabilitative or deterrent variety. In fact, innumerable factors influence the individual in his offending behaviour; some of them are environmental, some of them are personal and some are a mixture of the two. Among the factors that could be listed are: the norms of his community, i.e. of family, school, locality, friends, etc: the pattern of past behaviour, and of habit; attitudes to offending — e.g. to stealing; the force of immediate circumstances; current mental state — e.g. depression, or anger; alcohol or drug dependence; and the effect of any particular previous penal experience — for example in prison, or in an approved school. If re-offending is viewed in terms of this model, and if it is remembered that most prisoners return to their previous social environment on discharge, then whether a man has spent a part of a sentence in a particular prison (e.g. Grendon) could only be held to have very marginal significance in determining his future offending behaviour. Of course, for some individuals a particular experience in prison (as elsewhere) may prove to be of outstanding significance: but for recidivist populations as a whole, the contribution which a particular prison sentence makes to their future offending behaviour is unlikely — in relation to the total variance affecting re-offending — to be large enough to be measured. Hence it is not surprising that most studies of prison treatments show that there is no difference, in terms of re-conviction, between the treated men and untreated control groups (Martinson, 1972).

The belief that custodial treatment can have a decisive effect on future behaviour is nowadays often expressed in terms of a medical analogy. According to this "medical myth" (Clarke and Sinclair, 1974), crime is a symptom of pathology in the individual, the disorder being thought of as a disturbance of personality, attitudes or social functioning. The myth assumes that these disorders can be dealt with by subjecting the patient to a penal "treatment", which is conceived as acting on the illness like an antibiotic, and is therefore expected to cure the offender of his criminal propensities. This medical myth, like the earlier myths of religious regeneration, and deterrence, depends on a view of crime which largely ignores the criminogenic aspects of the social environment.

What of that small corner of crime where the offenders show evidence of mental abnormality or illness? Even here, there is little justification for regarding crime as a disease to be treated, or for assessing the efficiency of a psychiatric prison by its re-conviction rate. The men sent to Grendon had, as we have seen, many psychiatric problems, but their offending behaviour was not necessarily caused by these problems. For example, most of them reported abnormal levels of past and present psychiatric disturbance, but when the psychiatric findings were correlated with the data concerning criminal history there was little relationship and therefore little reason to expect that treatment for the psychiatric disturbance would, of itself, lead to an end of the offending behaviour. Of course, for some individuals there may have been a relationship between psychiatric disturbance and criminal behaviour: for example, in committing their offences they may have been directly influenced by the amount of anxiety and depression being felt. But even for this group, the positive contribution which a prison could make to their future patterns of offending behaviour was small: the Grendon regime certainly ensured that symptomatology reduced whilst the men were in prison, but could not influence its future incidence. A man could leave Grendon feeling well and with greater self-awareness, he might return to an unfavourable social environment, gradually become anxious and depressed again, and so resume the related offending behaviour.

Re-conviction studies depend upon the belief that certain spells of imprisonment can have measurable effects upon the future criminal conduct of offenders. In the course of our research we have come to reject this belief, at least in so far as it applied to the subject of our work — the adult recidivist. Re-offending is related to so many different variables that the influence of any part of a previous prison sentence can only be small. Our study of what actually happens in prisons also persuaded us that it was unrealistic to expect a particular prison programme to exercise a permanent — let alone dominant — influence over its discharged inmates' criminal behaviour. The regimes and treatments contained no ingredient that was sufficiently powerful. A particular prison sentence would represent only so small a proportion of the total variance affecting re-conviction, that it could not be expected to produce statistically measurable re-conviction effects. Yet it is upon such an expectation that the idea of evaluating prisons by their re-conviction rates depends.

If the future re-conviction rate of recidivist prisoners is unlikely to be affected measurably by the conditions under which they served their last prison sentence, is there any other way in which the effect of that sentence can be evaluated in terms of post-release experience? In theory, the men's social behaviour, attitudes and mental health could be looked at, and compared with what they were before. The difficulties of collecting reliable "before" and "after" data about a sufficiently large sample would however be immense — especially as the "before" data would really need to have been collected before the man was sentenced. It is unlikely that it would be practicable to conduct such a study. Probably the only practicable approach to evaluation would be to keep in continuous touch with the sample after their release and to ask them for their views and experience. Our research resources did not permit us to follow such a procedure, but we decided to try to keep in touch by letter with the men from our samples after they were released. Unfortunately, we were only able to obtain information from 40% of the men in this way. The results of the postal enquiry were nevertheless of some interest, and are discussed below.

Control Study

At the outset of our research we had planned to compare the re-conviction records of the Grendon men with those of a matched group of prisoners not receiving psychiatric treatment. We had originally believed that this would enable us to isolate any possible Grendon effect on re-conviction; it was not until later, after we had the opportunity to look both at the regimes and the men in Grendon and

Wormwood Scrubs, that we came to appreciate the fallacy of expecting that a spell of imprisonment in a particular prison could have a statistically measurable effect on the prisoners' future criminal records. However, the control group comparison had been set up before our views had developed in this direction, and since certain aspects of it raise questions of general interest, it will therefore be outlined here. Before doing so, however, a word should be said about our plan to use re-conviction data, since these are known to be an inaccurate reflection of the actual amount of offending behaviour that occurs (Walker, 1970; Hood and Sparks, 1970). To use absence of re-conviction as a criterion of success exaggerates the effectiveness of penal measures: for example, since less than half of all reported thefts are cleared up (and probably less than half of all thefts are reported) the number of thefts that result in convictions are obviously a poor guide to the number which occur. But re-conviction figures are usually the only hard data about re-offending which are available and they may be less imperfect for recidivists — with whom our study has been concerned — than for other groups, since an offender's chances of detection increase with the number of offences he commits (Walker, 1970).

The object of the control study was to compare our Grendon sample with a group of similar prisoners not receiving psychiatric treatment: the hope was that by comparing the re-conviction records of the two groups, any "Grendon effect" on re-conviction would be isolated.

In order to ensure that the men would have had at least one year at liberty before the re-conviction data were collected, only those members of our Grendon sample who were released from Grendon by May 1973 were included in the re-conviction study. Only 46 of our original 107 men qualified for this criterion (27 men had been transferred from Grendon to other prisons for one reason or another, and the remaining 34 had not been released by May 1973), so in order to increase the size of the group to be followed up, it was decided to include in it 15 other men who were leaving Grendon by May 1973. These men were given the same battery of tests and interviews as had been given to the original sample, but were seen once only, on average four weeks before their release.

The task of matching these 61 men with similar non-Grendon prisoners was a daunting one. It was accomplished only because of the generosity of the Home Office in allowing us to use data from the Parole Index. This Index contains very detailed information about all prisoners eligible for parole, i.e. prisoners with sentences of more than

18 months. By searching its cards it was possible for us to find for each of the Grendon men a prisoner with whom he was matched on seven, and usually eight, variables. The index also enabled us to select only those prisoners who would be released by May 1973. The variables selected for matching were: (1) age, (plus or minus three years if necessary); (2) number of previous prison sentences (plus or minus two, if necessary, except where there was no previous sentence); (3) total length of previous prison sentences (plus or minus up to two years if necessary, except where there was no previous sentence); (4) current offence — main charge; (5) marital status; (6) occupation in last job (census social class categories); (7) predicted possibility of re-conviction. This last item was calculated by the Parole Index authorities in the form of a score between 0 and 100, based largely on past criminal history. Calculations with the same formula were made for the Grendon men, and matching was carried out within a margin of plus or minus ten points.

The eighth variable was the nature of the living arrangements to which the prisoner would be going on his release (e.g. wife, parent, hostel, etc.). In the majority of cases matching on all eight variables was possible, but if it was not, this eighth item was dropped as a matching criterion.

By this process controls for our 61 men were selected from the parole index. Arrangements were then made for one of us to see them in their respective prisons and give them the same series of interviews, tests and questionnaires which had been used for the Grendon sample. Only in this way could we discover whether the controls were in fact comparable on matters which the Parole Index did not cover, but which were clearly important for our study — e.g. motivation, mental state and personality.

The Parole Index often provided more than one possible control for a given Grendon prisoner, and the man whose prison was nearest to London was then selected. Despite this procedure, extensive travelling throughout the country was necessary in pursuit of the control sample and 28 prisons had to be visited. Occasionally, when a control was seen, he was found to be receiving psychiatric treatment; in that case, another match was selected.

After the controls had been interviewed and assessed, they were compared with the 61 Grendon men on all the variables which had been collected in the Grendon study — i.e. on criminal, social, psychiatric and psychological characteristics, on motivation and on attitudes. Where variables had been assessed repeatedly for the Grendon men (attitudes, mental state, etc.), it was the data from the initial assessment that was compared with the controls.

The comparisons showed that the initial matching on the eight parole index variables had worked well; e.g. the average age of the Grendon men was 26·02 (s.d. 4·63) and that of the controls 26·64 (s.d. 5·31) t = 0·69. The initial matching had also produced secondary matching in many other important areas: for example, no differences emerged on history of maternal or paternal loss, on current social responsibilities (will anyone be financially dependent on you when you leave prison?), or on most of the criminal variables. Indeed, so far as social and criminal history was concerned, there were differences in only four areas.

One of these related to the occupational status of the men's fathers. Although the two groups had been matched for their occupational status, when they were asked about their fathers' main (or longest) employment during their own childhood, more Grendon men than controls said that their fathers had been engaged in professional or intermediate occupations—i.e. Social Classes I and II. Information on this was available for 51 Grendon men and 53 controls: ten of the former (20%) and only two of the latter (4%) placed their fathers into the two highest social classes (X^2 = 5·09 p < 0·025), while significantly more of the controls said that their fathers had been employed in unskilled work (31%) (16) as compared with 12% (6) X^2 = 4·09 p < 0·05).

The second area of difference was probably related to the difference in paternal occupational status: there was a slight trend for the Grendon men to have acquired more in the way of formal educational attainments (O levels, technical or commercial certificates), and they scored significantly higher on the Heim AH4 Intelligence Test. Because of lack of time, the controls were given only Part II of the test to complete—i.e. that part which is least educationally loaded: the mean score of the controls on this part of the test (N51) was 35·47 s.d. 11·52, and that of the Grendon men (N51) was 42·45 s.d. 12·91, t = 2·78 p < 0·01. That the Grendon men as a group were more intelligent and more often had fathers of higher occupational status, is almost certainly a reflection of Grendon's selection policy: it is articulate men, ready and able to talk about their problems who—other things being equal—are most likely to be regarded as suitable for the regime.

Finally, there were a few differences between the groups as regards their criminal history. On the vast majority of the criminal variables on which they were compared, they were however very similar: e.g.

there were no differences as regards age of first offence, approved school experience, total number of convictions, time served on previous sentences, and the number of convictions for larceny, fraud, violence, robbery, sex, arson, drunkenness and motoring. The differences which arose were in respect of three types of criminal variables: the controls were found to have been less heavily involved in illegal drug-taking; they had made more money from crime, and they were currently serving longer sentences. Table 47 shows these differences.

Table 47   Criminal Variables on which Controls and Grendon Men Differed

	Grendon 61		Controls 61		t matched	p<
	Mean	s.d.	Mean	s.d.		
Length of present sentence in months	31·93	12·19	43·19	12·09	5·03	0·001
Number of drug convictions incurred	0·52	1·46	0·07	0·31	2·37	0·05
Drugs rating (criminal profile)*	1·21	1·56	0·44	0·97	3·21	0·01
Theft rating (criminal profile)*	2·67	1·04	3·02	0·85	2·74	0·01
Financial gain (criminal profile)*	1·43	0·96	1·84	1·02	2·24	0·05

*See Appendix 3.

The largest difference relates to the length of the current sentence; it was caused by the fact that we selected the controls from the parole index, which meant that the shorter term men were more likely to have been discharged by the time of selection. The difference on sentence length may also be connected with the differences on the theft and financial gain scales; the controls had in the past made more money from crime, and it is possible that their current offences were financially more ambitious — and therefore more heavily punished — than those of the Grendon men. The higher mean score of the controls on the theft scale reflected mainly the higher proportion among them who were rated as having ever made substantial gains (£1000 or more) from stealing: 23% of the controls fell into this group, compared with only 10% of the Grendon men. Similarly, on the financial gain scale, 23% of the controls, compared with only 7% of the Grendon men, were rated as having largely been dependent upon crime financially. The other difference between Grendon men and their controls was in drug-taking.

The drugs rating scale showed that 57% of the Grendon men, but only 23% of the controls, had engaged in illegal drug taking on more than one occasion, and the difference in the number of drug offences incurred by each group was a further reflection of this.

Thus taking the social and criminal information collected for both groups, four main differences were found, apart from the current length of sentence: the Grendon men were more intelligent, they said their fathers were of higher occupational status, they had been much more heavily involved in drugs, and considerably less dependent on crime for their financial support.

How did the two groups compare on the psychological variables? Only 46 of the controls completed the MMPI, so comparisons could be made only between them and the Grendon men with whom they were matched. No significant differences emerged between the two groups on the seven scales of the MMPI selected for use: like the Grendon men, their controls had scores which for most of the scales were highly abnormal when compared with the American norms. In one respect however, the Grendon men were different from their controls: they had a higher mean score on the "F" scale, suggesting a greater tendency to call attention to themselves and to their problems. (The Grendon mean was 74·24, s.d. 17·4 and the controls' mean was 68·04, s.d. 15·08, matched t (N46) = 3·32, p < 0·01). The likeliest explanation is that the Grendon men were more inclined than the controls to see themselves as psychiatric cases and to require that others should see them as such.

The psychiatric interview, like the MMPI, showed the two groups to be remarkably similar: the level of manifest abnormality was the same, and there was no significant difference in their mean total symptom scores. Just over half of each group was found to be disturbed to a clinically significant extent. This even matching as regards current disturbance was confirmed, as far as neurotic symptoms were concerned, by the similar performance of the two groups on the General Health Questionnaire. However, although the present mental state of the groups did not differ, the Grendon men reported a higher incidence of pre-prison psychiatric problems, as can be seen in Table 48.

It is clear from this table that although their symptomatology in prison is not different, the Grendon men had a rather different

Table 48   Previous Psychiatric History

| | Grendon (60) | | Controls (60) | | | |
	No.	%	No.	%	X²	p<
Attempted suicide	22	37	13	22	2·58	n.s.
Alcoholism*	19	32	8	13	4·78	0·05
History of O.P. treatment	19	32	4	7	10·54	0·01

*Defined as use of alcohol causing significant social or personal damage to the individual or his family.

psychiatric history from the controls. Their greater previous involvement in drug taking has already been mentioned; they also had more previous history of alcoholism, and they had made much more use of psychiatric treatment in the health service.

An explanation for this last finding emerged when the groups were compared on their attitudes to treatment and to psychiatry; here important differences became apparent. The questionnaire about attitudes to psychiatry showed 54% of the controls compared with 12% of the Grendon men expressing little or no desire for treatment. Every item on the attitude to psychiatry questionnaire discriminated between the two groups at a statistically significant level, and there was a large difference between their mean scores. (Grendon (N59) mean 19·95, s.d. 3·8, Controls (N59) mean 15·08, s.d. 3·9, matched t = 6·85 p < 0·001.)

The same picture emerged from the interviewers ratings. Over half (59%) of the controls were assessed as having no desire for treatment, compared with 5% of the Grendon men. At the other end of the scale, 18% of the controls compared with 51% of the Grendon men were assessed as having a strong desire for treatment. However, the size of the difference should not obscure the fact that as many as 18 per cent of the controls were expressing a strong desire for treatment which they were not receiving.

The attitude to the crime questionnaire also showed significant differences between the two groups, with the Grendon men reporting a rather stronger desire to abandon crime: their mean score (N59) on the scale was 13·56, s.d. 3·8, whilst that of the controls (N59) was 12·05, s.d. 3·6, matched t = 2·23 p < 0·05).

The distribution is different principally at the extreme ends of the scale, with a comparatively high proportion of the controls showing little desire to abandon crime, and a comparatively high proportion of the Grendon men expressing a strong wish to do so.

The last set of comparisons to be made were on the semantic differential, which was completed by 41 of the controls. Their responses were compared with the 41 Grendon men with whom they were matched. With one exception, the figures in the semantic differential — prison officers, magistrates, police, psychiatrists, "myself", etc. — were rated almost exactly the same way by the two groups. The only difference concerned social workers, of whom the Grendon men had a rather better opinion than the controls ($p < 0.05$).

Discussion

The parole index gave us what was probably an unparalleled opportunity to collect a matched control group; no prison research worker could have had or hoped for a better one. By enabling us to select controls from a pool of some 4000 men about whom detailed social and criminal information was recorded, the index made it possible for us to match each Grendon man with his control on seven or eight criminal and social variables. This initial matching produced secondary matching in many other areas, so that on the vast majority of data on which the two groups were compared — social, criminal, psychological, psychiatric and in their attitudes to themselves and to authority figures — no differences emerged.

Nevertheless, although with the facilities made available to us we were able to ensure matching to this unusual degree, a few differences between the groups did exist, and were in our view serious enough to destroy the possibility of regarding them as satisfactorily matched. The Grendon men were more likely to have come from a higher social class background and they were more intelligent. They had been much more heavily involved with drugs than the controls, and they reported more alcoholism. Although they had as many convictions for offences of dishonesty, the Grendon men had made less money from stealing, and had been less financially dependent on crime. Finally, there were differences in attitudes to psychiatry and crime. The Grendon men tended to see themselves as psychiatric cases, they were more motivated to have treatment, and they had made more use of treatment in the past. They also had significantly more negative attitudes to crime.

All this suggests perhaps that in the criminal behaviour of the Grendon men there was more irrational, and less financial, motivation than among their controls. It certainly raises fundamental difficulties about comparing the two groups in terms of their post-prison offending behaviour for they were not similar in respect of important pre-prison variables.

The difficulty is enhanced because the ways in which the Grendon men differed from their controls did not have a single direction that could be regarded as making them more, or less, likely to return to crime. Some of the differences can be regarded as making the Grendon men more likely to recidivate: e.g. their alcoholism and their greater involvement in drugs. Other differences go in the opposite direction — the controls have in the past been more heavily dependent on crime for their support, and they express, while in prison, less intention of abandoning crime. Yet other differences have an unknown relationship to the likelihood of re-offending and re-conviction: e.g. does the fact that the Grendon men see themselves as psychiatric cases, and are much more likely to seek psychiatric help, have any bearing on their propensity to offend or to be convicted? (It will later be seen that the largest differences between Grendon men who were and were not convicted, lay in their attitudes to psychiatry.) What, in re-conviction terms, is the relevance of the finding that the fathers of the Grendon men were of higher occupational status than the fathers of the control group? Is the superior intelligence of the Grendon men likely to have any bearing on their future criminal behaviour, or on the likelihood that they will be discovered in it? These questions, together with the differences between the groups that can more clearly be related to the likelihood of re-offending, demonstrate that our control group was in fact no such thing. Nor, unfortunately, can it be assumed — which it would be both tempting and convenient to do — that the differences between the groups will cancel each other out.

The object of our matching exercise had been to find a group of untreated prisoners who would be like the Grendon men on relevant pre-prison variables, so that when the two groups were compared in terms of re-conviction, any Grendon treatment effect on the re-conviction rate would be isolated. At the end of the exercise we found that the two groups were not sufficiently alike. Neatly though they were matched for nearly all the items which criminologists traditionally take into account when they set up re-conviction studies, important differences existed in other areas which it is less customary to measure — attitudes to psychiatry, and to crime, and previous financial dependence on stealing. It would have been all too easy to omit some of these measures and to conclude that the two groups were evenly matched, but they were not.

Our attempt to find a true control group of men similar to the

Grendon prisoners, but untreated, thus proved to be unsuccessful. The failure sprang from the fact that the men who get to Grendon and who stay the course are specially selected; they are people who see themselves as psychiatric cases and are motivated to have treatment; and they are unlikely to have been criminal in a very professional sense. The only way of ensuring that a control group would be matched on these, as well as other pre-sentence variables, would be to set up a system under which a pool of men selected as suitable for Grendon would be randomly allocated between Grendon and non-treatment prisons. From an ethical standpoint, such a procedure is unlikely to be acceptable; but even if adopted, it would be unlikely from a research point of view, to yield results. The inherent weaknesses and difficulties of using random allocation procedures to study institutional penal regimes have recently been demonstrated (Clarke and Cornish, 1972).

In reporting our failure to find a properly matched control group for the Grendon men, we find consolation in two considerations. One is a finding that may prove to be of general interest, mainly the importance of looking at and controlling for, areas such as attitudes, and past reliance on crime for a living. Re-conviction studies do not usually take these into account, perhaps because they are frequently based upon data obtainable from the official records; but in the present research they were not only the factors which differentiated our experimental group from their controls, they were also the factors which were found most strongly to be related to re-offending and re-conviction.

Our second consolation is that the failure to establish a proper control group did not detract from our study. When we began our research we accepted the usual idea that prison regimes could be expected to have measurable effects on their inmates' re-conviction rates. Hence the control study was set up to measure the contribution which Grendon would make to this rate. But as we proceeded with the research, became familiar with the men in our samples and the regimes to which they were exposed, we began to realise the fallacy of expecting that in their future re-conviction careers the influence of one particular part of one prison sentence would prove to be statistically measurable. The experimental variable in our research design—i.e. the Grendon treatment—represented so small a proportion of the total variance affecting re-conviction, that it could not be expected to produce measurable effects. Hence the re-conviction data from a perfectly matched control group would not have added to our knowledge of the Grendon treatment effect. Had it been possible to construct such a group for the Grendon sample, we would — by the end of our study — have hypothesised that its re-conviction rate would be the same as Grendon's. In terms of pre-release variables, the groups would have had equal chances of re-conviction, and we did not expect that the experimental variable — the prison in which they finished their last sentence — would affect these chances. In the event, our controls were not satisfactorily matched, and the fact that we found no significant differences between the Grendon group and the control group in terms of re-conviction rates (X^2 0·58) cannot be properly interpreted. For the record 43 of the Grendon men (70%) and 38 of the controls (62%) were re-convicted during the follow-up period (usually about 2 years).

CHAPTER 10

After Release (2): Group Differences and Some Case Histories

Postal Enquiry

Originally our plan of research had envisaged a post-release comparison not only of the Grendon men with their controls, but also of the Wormwood Scrubs sample with a matched control group of similar but untreated prisoners. However, only 18 of the 42 men in the Wormwood Scrubs sample were released by May 1973, so it was only for these 18 men that matches could be selected.

The plan of the post-release study was not only to collect re-conviction data for the various groups, but to try to keep in touch with them by letter, and find out how they were getting on. All men from Grendon and Wormwood Scrubs who were to be discharged by May 1973, and their controls, were asked whether they would agree to take part in a postal follow-up survey. Most of them were agreeable and supplied us with an address. Arrangements were then made to write to each man at six-monthly intervals after his release. A General Health Questionnaire was enclosed with the letter, and also a form (a copy is given in Appendix 11) asking about the man's experience in four main areas. These were (1) employment (number of jobs, length of the longest, unemployment, etc.); (2) living arrangements (whether living alone, with wife, girl friend, etc., and whether happy with their present living arrangements); (3) psychiatric problems (suicide attempts, amount of drinking, drug taking, and whether general practitioners or psychiatrists had been consulted about any problems);

(4) criminal activities (offences committed and whether or not prosecuted for them).

These forms were sent out to each man for whom an address was available, six months, twelve months and eighteen months after release. On each of these occasions, completed forms were received back from about 40 per cent of the total sample. Table 49 shows the proportion of men from each group of the sample who sent in forms twelve months after release.

Table 49 Men Participating in the Postal Enquiry 12 Months after Release

Sample	Total	No. participating	Proportion participating %
Grendon	61	25	41
Grendon controls	61	18	29
Wormwood Scrubs	17	6	33
Wormwood Scrubs controls	18	8	44
	158	57	39

The proportion of men from each sample who responded at six months and eighteen months was very similar to the proportion who responded at twelve months, although they were not always the same men: e.g. just over half of the 62 men who replied at six months, also replied at twelve months.

It is apparent from Table 49 that the number of respondents was too small to enable comparisons to be made between either of the two treatment groups and their controls—even had matching been good enough to make such comparisons worthwhile. However, since a considerable amount of data was available from the men who replied, it seemed worth examining it; although it could not be used for the purpose originally intended, it would at least provide for some 40 per cent of all the men in the sample, a glimpse of how they fared after release. The data was therefore examined as a whole, regardless of which sample group the respondents had been in.

The first step was to see whether the men who sent in forms differed significantly from those who did not. Comparisons were therefore made on all the 170 variables which had been collected in prison at the initial assessment. Very few statistically significant differences emerged, as can be seen in Table 50, which compares the men who sent in forms at twelve months with those who did not. There were even fewer differences when the men who responded at six months were compared with those who did not.

The men who participated in the postal enquiry tended to have been somewhat less involved in theft and fraud, even though there was no difference between the groups in the number of convictions incurred for these two offences. It was also clear that the respondents were those who, in prison, had evidenced more neurotic symptomatology, and less well integrated personalities; and they had shown a greater tendency to regard their criminal behaviour as connected with their psychological problems. These factors were no doubt the reason that these men were more interested than others in keeping in touch with members of the Institute of Psychiatry. That they had, when in prison, expressed more unfavourable opinions of magistrates seems difficult to explain: there was a trend ($p < 0.10$) for them also to have made more hostile ratings of police and prison officers.

In addition to comparing the two groups in terms of the data collected in prison, they were also compared on the re-conviction data received from the CRO (Criminal Records Office), in order to see whether there was any tendency for the responding group to be the men who had been re-convicted less. There was however no such tendency: they had been re-convicted as often as the men who did not write to us ($X^2 = 0.52$).

The comparisons between those who did and those who did not take part in the postal enquiry thus showed that the two groups were sufficiently alike to make the analysis of the postal questionnaires worth while. Two sets of analyses were carried out: one on the questionnaires of the men who responded at six months, and one on those who responded at twelve months. The results were very similar, and in the following account it is the information from the twelve-month enquiry which is presented.

The first point of interest which emerged from the questionnaires, was how much fuller a picture of re-offending behaviour they gave than did the CRO. At the twelve-month enquiry, information was available from 60 men on this point: 42 of them said that they had committed further offences, but the CRO information showed that only 32 had been convicted. Only one of the 18 men who said they had not offended during the year had in fact been convicted.

Table 50   Postal Enquiry 12 Months after Release: Differences between Men who Participated and Those who Did Not, in Terms of Data Collected in Prison

Variables at initial prison assessment	Participants*			Others					
	Mean	s.d.	N	Mean	s.d.	N	t	p<
Neurotic symptom score	11·47	6·63	(58)	9·39	5·99	(97)	1·99	0·05
MMPI ego strength scale	39·08	8·38	(53)	41·62	6·79	(97)	2·01	0·05
Response to AP scale item "My criminal behaviour has nothing to do with psychological illness"	2·25	1·23	(56)	1·78	1·29	(97)	2·27	0·05
Attitude to magistrates	34·72	11·58	(46)	40·97	14·03	(91)	2·60	0·05
Theft rating (criminal profile)	2·63	1·13	(60)	2·93	0·87	(97)	1·82	0·10
Fraud rating (criminal profile)	0·60	1·12	(60)	0·99	1·34	(97)	1·88	0·10

*Included among the respondents, both here and in the subsequent discussion, are three men who did not send in questionnaires, but for whom post-release information was available from other (e.g. probation) sources.

The men who said they had re-offended were compared with those who said they had not, on all the variables that had been collected at the initial prison assessment. Table 51 lists the items on which the two groups differed.

The largest difference between the men who re-offended and those who did not, lay in the extent to which the former had previously engaged in stealing behaviour, but the number of stealing convictions did not distinguish the groups. The second largest difference was in respect of family and personal relationships: the re-offenders had been assessed in prison as evidencing markedly more pathology in these two areas. (For the method of assessment used, see Gunn and Robertson, 1976a, b and Appendix 12.) Other differences between the groups showed that the re-offenders had more previous custodial experience, and had tended to start offending at an earlier age; they had more history of drug and alcohol abuse and they had in prison expressed less guilt about past offences, and a more hostile attitude to prison officers. It is worth noting that offenders and non-offenders did not differ on any of the measures used to assess their mental state while they were in prison (i.e. psychiatric and MMPI findings) or on the extent to which they had pre-prison experience of psychiatric treatment.

This picture—taken in prison—of the men who had become re-offenders twelve months after release, was generally similar to the one which emerged from the postal enquiry carried out six months after release. Information after six months was available for 63 men: 27 of these said they had offended, and 36 had not. When these two groups were compared, the non-offenders tended to be the men who in prison had expressed more anti-crime attitudes, who had low scores on the theft and violence rating scales, and who held more favourable views of authority figures such as police, prison officers, etc. There was some evidence that as time at liberty increases, chronic problems, such as a difficulty in forming or maintaining relationships, alcoholism, and drug taking, seem to become more important in their relationship to re-offending: none of these factors distinguished the offenders from the non-offenders at six months, but all were significant, or nearly so, twelve months after release.

Did any differences in their post-release experiences distinguish the offenders from the non-offenders? Table 52 shows those items of the follow-up questionnaires on which, twelve months after release, the groups differed significantly.

It is evident from the table that in terms of their post-release experiences, the offenders were more unsettled and unhappy than the

Table 51 Postal Enquiry 12 Months after Release. Differences between Offenders and Non-Offenders in Respect of Data Collected in Prison

Variables at initial prison assessment	Non-Offenders			Offenders			t	p<
	Mean	s.d.	N	Mean	s.d.	N		
Theft rating (criminal profile)	1·89	1·45	(18)	2·95	0·79	(42)	3·66	0·001
Rating of pathology in family relationships	0·81	0·98	(16)	1·70	1·02	(40)	2·98	0·01
Rating of pathology in personal relationships	1·19	0·65	(16)	1·95	1·01	(42)	2·80	0·01
Alcohol problem	0·13	0·34	(16)	0·95	1·23	(42)	2·64	0·05
Attitude to prison officers	43·62	12·76	(13)	32·55	14·13	(33)	2·46	0·05
Months served before present sentence	15·50	21·52	(18)	28·17	20·17	(42)	2·18	0·05
Response to AC item "I feel guilty when I think of my offences"	2·75	1·12	(16)	2·00	1·28	(40)	2·05	0·05
Attitude to prison doctors	45·46	13·55	(13)	35·12	17·00	(33)	1·96	0·10
Financial dependence on crime rating (criminal profile)	1·22	1·11	(18)	1·79	1·02	(42)	1·90	0·10
Drugs rating (criminal profile)	0·56	1·34	(18)	1·40	2·04	(42)	1·88	0·10
Response to AC item "I would like to make a lot of money from crime"	3·06	0·99	(16)	2·30	1·50	(40)	1·86	0·10
Age at first offence	17·50	6·18	(18)	15·19	3·90	(42)	1·75	0·10
Attitude to police	40·85	14·26	(13)	35·52	14·79	(33)	1·74	0·10

Table 52   Postal Enquiry: Differences between Offenders and Non-Offenders 12 Months after Release

Variables 12 months after release (from questionnaires)	Non-Offenders			Offenders*			t	p<
	Mean	s.d.	N	Mean	s.d.	N		
Weeks out of work	6·06	8·67	(18)	16·72	18·52	(25)	2·27	0·05
GHQ score	3·50	6·07	(14)	22·78	19·68	(32)	·57	0·01
Drinking rate‡	1·39	0·84	(18)	2·08	1·18	(37)	2·21	0·05
	Yes	No	N	Yes	No	N	X²	p<
Happy with living arrangements	15 (83%)	3	(18)	13 (43%)	17	(30)	5·84	0·02
Still living with wife†	7 (78%)	2	(9)	3 (23%)	10	(13)	Fisher	0·05
Seeing a doctor for nerves, etc.	1 (6%)	17	(18)	17 (51%)	16	(33)	8·85	0·01

*Where the men completed their forms in prison (i.e. on fresh sentences) information was only used insofar as it related to their pre-sentence circumstances. Imprisoned men were all excluded from the "weeks out of work" item, and also from the GHQ item.

† This item was applicable only to men who had been married when initially assessed in prison.

‡ The questionnaire asked whether drinking had been very heavy, heavy, moderate, very little or nil, and the replies were coded on a five-point scale, ranging from 0 (nil) to 4 (very heavy).

other men. They reported that they had been drinking more heavily, were much more depressed and anxious—their mean score on the GHQ was very high—and had far more often visited a general practitioner (though not a psychiatrist) for nerves, depression or headaches. Their marriages had broken down more frequently, and they were generally unhappy with their present living arrangements. Finally, they had experienced considerably more unemployment than the men who did not re-offend.

In the unhappy group self-portrait painted by the offenders twelve months after release, it is impossible to disentangle cause and effect among the different components: the relationships between the offences, the high symptomatology, and the unemployment etc., could not be established from the questionnaires. Obviously many relationships are possible—e.g. a man may become depressed through continued unemployment, and then commit an offence; or he may lose his job because of an offence, and then become depressed. Whatever may be true for an individual man, the general picture obtained from the questionnaires emphasises that re-offending does not occur in a vacuum: employment, current mental state, marriage stability, living arrangements, and drinking patterns are all related to it.

For the present study, one of the main questions of interest was the relationship of offending to psychiatric abnormality. The men who re-offended tended to report high levels of symptomatology and to visit doctors (but not psychiatrists—the correlation between re-offending and seeing a psychiatrist was only 0.07, N = 50) much more frequently than the non-offenders. However, as noted, the relationship between these variables and the others connected with re-offending could not be established from the questionnaires. Since the re-offenders were the men whose marriages had broken down, who were unhappy with their living arrangements, and who were often facing imminent court appearances, it is not surprising that their neurotic symptomatology was high. However, this is not evidence that neurotic predisposition caused the men to offend, for in terms of the psychiatric and psychological (MMPI) assessments made in prison the re-offenders did not differ from the other men. Except for their greater history of involvement with drink and drugs, the re-offenders did not differ on any of the psychiatric or psychological variables which had been assessed in prison; they had shown no greater tendency to abnormality in terms of the findings of the MMPI or the psychiatric interview, and their pre-prison psychiatric history—mental hospital admissions, suicide attempts, etc.—was no different from that of the other men.

Re-conviction data

Since the postal enquiry produced information for less than half of our potential follow-up group, official re-conviction records were the only data available for the whole population. The weakness of these records as an evaluative measure was discussed in the previous chapter, but in the absence of better data it seemed worthwhile examining them.

Our first step was to see what differences would emerge if, irrespective of the prison they had been in, we compared re-convicted men with those who were not re-convicted: 158 men were available for the comparison—i.e. they had been released by May 1973. As Table 49 showed, 61 of these men were from Grendon, 61 were Grendon controls, 18 were from the Wormwood Scrubs treatment sample and 18 were matched controls for that sample. By the time the re-conviction data was collected the 158 men had been released, on average, for just under two years; 112 (71%) were found to have been re-convicted and 46 were not. Of these 46, however, 26 had replied to our postal enquiry and 9 of them (35%) said that they had re-offended; thus it seems likely that at least a third of the non-re-convicted group had in fact committed further offences.

Before comparisons between the re-convicted and non-re-convicted men could be made, it was necessary to ensure that the two groups were comparable in terms of length of time since release. No difference emerged in this respect; when the re-conviction data were collected the re-convicted men had on average been released for $22 \cdot 12$ months (s.d. $4 \cdot 95$), and the non-re-convicted men for $21 \cdot 76$ months (s.d. $5 \cdot 37$) t = $0 \cdot 41$ n.s.

A comparison was then made between the two groups over all the 170 variables which had been measured at their initial assessment in prison—i.e. social and criminal history, psychiatric data, MMPI, attitudes to crime and to psychiatry, motivation for treatment, and attitudes to authority figures and to self. Table 53 shows the only significant differences which emerged from these comparisons.

The differences are all of the expected and well known kind: that re-conviction is positively related to the amount of previous offending. None of the psychological, psychiatric or attitudinal variables distinguished the men who were re-convicted from those who were not.

A similar comparison was then carried out among the Grendon men to see what differences would emerge if the re-convicted men were compared with those who had not been re-convicted. When the

Table 53 Differences between Re-convicted Men and Those who were not
Re-convicted

Variable as assessed initially in prison	Re-convicted (112)		Not re-convicted (46)			
	Mean	s.d.	Mean	s.d.	t	p<
Total No. of larceny convictions	11·02	7·6	7·16	5·9	3·38	0·01
Months served before present sentence	29·82	30·1	16·51	19·1	2·97	0·01
Age at first conviction	15·04	3·9	16·71	6·4	2·02	0·05
Theft rating (criminal profile)	2·91	1·1	2·58	0·3	2·01	0·05

official re-conviction data were received the 61 Grendon men had been at liberty on average for two years: 44 of them had been re-convicted (73%) and 17 had not.* It has of course to be remembered that re-conviction is not synonymous with re-offending: of the 17 men who were not re-convicted, 5 had in the course of the postal enquiry admitted to further offending, and it is unlikely that the remaining 12 were all genuine non-offenders. Of the 44 men who had been re-convicted, 19 had received prison sentences, one had been made the subject of a hospital order, and the rest had been dealt with by non-custodial measures. The main types of offence were larceny (23 men) drugs (7 men) motoring (6 men) and violence (5 men).

Before the re-convicted men could be compared with those who were not, it was necessary to ensure that they had been at liberty and at risk for the same length of time. No statistically significant differences emerged: for the 44 re-convicted men, the mean number of months since release was 24·84 (s.d. 4·53) whilst for the 17 unconvicted men, it was 23·00 months (s.d. 5·80) t = 1·28, n.s.

What differences did the re-conviction data show between the Grendon men who were re-convicted and those who were not? From the point of view of the Grendon study, one of the chief interests was to see whether changes which occurred in Grendon on the items measured in our research—attitudes, personality (MMPI), psychiatric state etc. — were in any way related to the men's performance after release.

---

*On p. 179 the number of re-convicted men was given as 43: this is because in that section, each Grendon man was matched with his control for the length of time he had been at liberty, and any convictions which fell outside this period were not counted.

In the event, however, the number of men available for this analysis proved to be small. As previously explained, only 46 men in the follow-up group had been part of our original Grendon sample, and it was only for these men that re-assessment data throughout the sentence was available. For each of them calculations were made of the extent to which he changed between the initial and final assessment on the variables that were retested—i.e. the semantic differential, the MMPI, attitudes to crime and psychiatry, interviewers' assessment of motivation for treatment, and psychiatric mental state. When this had been done, the re-convicted men were compared with the others to see whether they differed in the amount they had changed. The groups, unfortunately, were very small—there were 33 re-convicted men and 13 who had not been convicted, and the figures were reduced further because of missing data on some of the variables: e.g. only 24 of the convicted and 9 of the un-convicted men had completed the MMPI on two occasions. Because of the small numbers, the analysis of change, which showed no differences between re-convicted and non-re-convicted men, has to be treated with some reserve.

Another analysis which had originally been planned, was to see whether there were differences in the re-conviction rates of the three wings. With only 17 un-convicted men in the sample, the figures were too small for any meaningful analysis to be made.

The 17 un-convicted men were compared with the 44 who had been re-convicted on all the variables which had been collected about them at their initial assessment. Table 54 shows the items on which the groups differed significantly. There was no difference between them as regards the amount of time they had served in Grendon.

Since the 17 men who were not re-convicted include five who were self confessed offenders, another analysis was made in which these five men were removed from the un-convicted group and counted among the convicted. The resultant picture did not differ from that shown in Table 54. The table shows three areas in which there were significant differences between men who were re-convicted and those who were not, and once again it is interesting that none of the variables relating to psychiatric abnormality distinguished the groups. The first area of difference related to previous offending: the re-convicted men had been more heavily involved in thefts and frauds, and less often convicted of sexual offences; they had started to offend at a younger age, and had more previous custodial experience. The second difference was in attitudes to the police: the men who were not re-convicted had, in the semantic differential, expressed significantly

Table 54 Grendon Re-convicted Men compared with Grendon Non-re-convicted Men

Variables as assessed in Grendon	Re-convicted			Not re-convicted			t	p<
	Mean	s.d.	(N)	Mean	s.d.	(N)		
Total score on AP scale*	19·00	3·56	(44)	22·41	3·25	(17)	3·41	0·01
Number larceny offences	12·16	8·77	(44)	5·88	5·30	(17)	2·74	0·01
Fraud rating	1·18	1·42	(44)	0·24	0·96	(17)	2·60	0·05
Months served before present sentence	37·02	33·98	(44)	15·06	20·06	(17)	2·48	0·05
Theft rating	2·86	0·76	(44)	2·18	1·42	(17)	2·29	0·05
Attitude towards police	34·95	14·53	(37)	44·94	15·29	(16)	2·26	0·05
Assessment of motivation at interview	3·07	1·02	(44)	3·65	0·58	(17)	2·19	0·05
Number of sex offences	0·48	1·35	(44)	2·29	5·31	(17)	2·07	0·05
Age at first conviction	15·09	3·36	(44)	17·65	6·11	(17)	2·05	0·05

*Items 2, 3, 5 and 6 of the AP scale (see Appendix 5) discriminated between the groups at greater than the 1% level.

more favourable views of the police. (Could these views have been reciprocal, and thereby relevant to the prosecution rate?) The third area of difference, and the one which was most powerful in discriminating between the groups, lay in attitudes to psychiatry: the AP questionnaires showed that the men who were not re-convicted had in prison expressed more favourable views of psychiatry, and in particular (as was indicated by the large differences on items 2, 5 and 6 of the questionnaires) had been more inclined to regard their criminal behaviour as a manifestation of psychological illness. The interviewers had also given the men who were not re-convicted higher ratings on the scale which measured motivation for treatment.

A comparison of Table 53 with Table 54 shows that both for the total sample, and for the Grendon sample, variables relating to previous criminal history distinguish the re-convicted men from those who were not re-convicted. However, among Grendon men but not among the whole sample, an even more powerful discriminator — in fact the most powerful one — between the re-convicted and non-re-convicted men is their attitude to psychiatry. In view of the difference between the samples in this respect, it was decided to analyse the data separately for Grendon and non-Grendon men and the 158 men were divided into four groups on the basis of whether or not they had been to Grendon, and whether or not they had been re-convicted. The data on criminal and attitudinal variables were then examined for these four groups, and the items which showed significantly different distribution between the groups are shown in Table 55.

It will be seen from the table that whilst criminal factors (number of convictions, and months previously served) distinguish the re-convicted from the non-re-convicted both in the Grendon and in the non-Grendon groups, motivation for psychiatric treatment was related to re-conviction in the Grendon group alone. It may be that the Grendon men who had high motivation for treatment, and a tendency to view their criminal behaviour as a psychiatric problem derived particular value from the treatment they received in Grendon: this explanation would give support to the hypothesis put by Dr. Gray that Grendon is of most benefit to highly motivated men. However, it may simply be, among men going to Grendon, that very high motivation is part of a general "less criminal" factor (fewer previous offences, and less custodial experience) which is associated with lack of early re-conviction. The number of men in the analysis (only 17 were not re-convicted) and the data available were insufficient to determine the question.

Table 55 Re-conviction Differences between Grendon and Non-Grendon samples

Variables as assessed initially in prison	Grendon				Not Grendon				F	p<
	Not re-convicted (17)		Re-convicted (44)		Not re-convicted (38)		Re-convicted (59)			
	Mean	s.d.	Mean	s.d.	Mean	s.d.	Mean	s.d.		
AP Score	22·4	3·4	19·0	3·6	15·9	4·3	16·0	4·2	15·4	0·001
Rating of Motivation	3·6	0·6	3·1	0·9	2·3	1·1	2·7	1·2	7·5	0·001
Total number of convictions	16·3	9·3	21·8	10·8	13·7	8·4	18·0	9·5	5·0	0·002
Months served before present sentence	15·1	20·7	37·0	33·4	17·2	18·5	24·4	25·8	4·93	0·002

Some Case Histories

The crudeness of re-conviction as a measure, and its uncertainty—so many offences never result in convictions—make it a very unsatisfactory way of considering prisoners' post-release careers. Our postal survey attempted to seek fuller information: offences, as well as convictions, were enquired about, and so were other facets of post-release experience, such as work, living arrangements, symptomatology, etc. However, the number of areas which could be covered by the post-release questionnaire was strictly limited, and apart from the fact that questionnaires were received from less than half of the population, they could at best give only a very incomplete account of the shape and nature of a man's career after release.

The best way of assessing how the men had fared after release would undoubtedly have been to keep in touch with them personally. Our resources precluded us from doing this, but we were able to interview a few of the ex-Grendon men, to hear about their life since release, and to get their views about Grendon in retrospect. Six men were seen—four of them were once more in prison, and two were free. They were not specially selected, other than that the two had kept in touch with us through the postal survey, and all six were in the proximity of London.

The experiences of each of these six men are summarised below. In a research report like the present one, which describes and discusses its subject in terms of mean scores and standard deviations, the reader may sometimes feel that the individual has been lost sight of. These case histories may perhaps serve as a reminder that the population which we rather ruthlessly reduced to a mass of statistics, did of course consist of individuals who differed from each other in their histories, problems, and attitudes; in the use they made of Grendon; and in their experiences after release—particularly in the crucial matter of their good (or bad) luck as regards re-conviction.

Case 1

A man of 26, sent to Grendon towards the end of an 18-month sentence for motoring offences: he was there for 6 months. He had by then incurred some twenty convictions for a variety of offences—burglary, larceny, violence, drunkenness—and had spent 3 years in prisons or borstals before the 18-month sentence.

His offending career had started at the age of eleven; his home background was disturbed, he did not know who his father was, and he had spent three years of his early life in approved schools. He had never settled, became heavily involved in drug taking, and relied on stealing for a living.

At the initial psychiatric interview in Grendon he was found to be seriously disturbed, with marked neurotic symptomatology; he said he tended to commit offences when lonely and depressed. When he left Grendon, his symptomatology was improved, and he said he had learned a great deal.

After his release he went to his pre-arranged job, which he lost within six months because of heavy (illegal) drug taking. He was unable to find another job. He began breaking into meters for cash; and stole letters in the hope of finding money in them. Every job application he made was unsuccessful, and he was unemployed for more than three months. Afterwards he emphasized how it was this situation that had driven him back to crime: in his view "It depends not on you, but on other people".

Then his luck changed. He was accepted for a job, and he did not lose it when, months later, his employer found out about his record. He had been in the job for almost two years when he was seen. He said that apart from his initial drug taking, and stealing while he was unemployed (for none of which he had been caught), he had engaged in no criminal activity. Fear of losing his job was an important restraint, which, he said, had now made him law abiding in even the smallest matters. He felt he had too large a stake in life to want to endanger it.

He lived together with a girl friend, and they enjoyed a full social life.

Asked about the value of Grendon's treatment, he said that Grendon had helped and perhaps hastened changes in himself that would have occurred in any case. The best thing about Grendon was how it helped people to understand others. In group therapy "You find you all have the same fears. You get to understand people". He also emphasized the value of the "Any Questions" sessions: "You're supplied with ideas and information about outside people. If you live in a criminal society, you can't overcome that barrier, you can only *imagine* what's on the other side. In Grendon you can question the people outside and find out what they're like . . . you become more balanced." He had found Grendon's treatment very helpful for himself, adding "I don't think the effects are immediate. You don't get the benefit till a year later. Grendon is the first stage of a transition process. You are bombarded with ideas which will cause you to change your attitude".

When this man came to the Institute of Psychiatry for this interview, he had been out of Grendon for almost three years, and was well established in his home life, his social life and at work: he was, and felt himself to be, an undoubted success. However, an indispensable element in his success was of course his luck: he had committed a series of drug and larceny offences during his first year of freedom, but had not been caught. Was he a success or a failure?

Case 2

Aged 24, with 17 convictions for property, motoring and drug offences. He had been to borstal, and went to Grendon while serving his first prison sentence — 3 years — for further burglary and motoring offences. He spent 11 months in Grendon.

He had been involved in drug taking since he was twelve, and had never engaged in any settled way of life; most of his offences had been committed against a background of drug addiction, which in turn was related to his tendency to run away from difficulties into the unreal world created by drugs.

When seen in Grendon, his mental state was normal; he was diagnosed as a severe drug addict.

In his first months at Grendon, the staff found him isolated and aloof, but gradually he became more positive and confident, and his relationships with his parents, as well as with people in the prison, improved markedly.

He was released to his parents, settled well and worked steadily. He acquired a steady girl friend, and lost interest in and contact with his old delinquent and drug-taking associates.

After nine months, he had an accident at work, and had to stay away for a while. He became rather unhappy and morose, and went off to visit (in another town) his old drug-taking friends one weekend. For the first time since his release (he said), he had a "smoke" (cannabis), and was arrested for possession. He was bailed for three months, returned home and resumed work. When his case was heard he was sentenced to 12 months imprisonment.

This man's experience was the exact reverse of the man in the previous case. The latter had a short spell of offending immediately after release, for which he was not caught: he then settled well. The present man settled well, and was a law abiding citizen for nine months, when his isolated recourse to cannabis resulted in a further spell of imprisonment. He was seen in prison.

Asked about his experience at Grendon, he said it had helped "a tremendous amount". In the first place, "it taught me to talk", something he had previously found almost impossible. This enabled him to take part in the give and take of group therapy. "I started to talk to people with similar problems to my own, and gave more thought to what other people said. I faced reality, and learned to accept myself as I am."

As a result of this process, many changes took place in himself, he said. He admitted to himself in Grendon that his offences had been committed "to impress people"; and as his relationships with others improved, he no longer felt that he had to impress them in this way.

In helping him to get a better understanding of himself, Grendon had helped him with his relationships with others: "I'm not putting on an act all the time now: I can get closer to people and form friendships." After his release he found he could talk to his parents, "the first time ever", and he developed a close and satisfactory relationship with a girl. Whereas previously he had spent his evenings in the West End, or in local pubs, his interest was now centred on his girl friend, and he had even become positively motivated towards work — since work was a means of building up resources for his future: "I've really enjoyed drawing wages; opening my first bank account and watching it grow."

An outsider would find it hard to assess how far Grendon had specifically contributed to this man's changed life style: after all, most young men settle down eventually. But he believed he could never have gone "straight" for nine months had it not been for Grendon, and he attributed the changes in himself to his experience there, in particular to the way Grendon had given him insight: "It was a breakthrough, I started to understand myself."

Although this man's post-release experience had so many positive features, in terms of re-conviction and re-imprisonment he has, of course to be categorised as a "failure": unlike Case No. 1, luck was not on his side.

Case 3

Aged 28, with 12 convictions for thefts and breaking. He had served 2 years on a series of short previous sentences, and was sent to Grendon towards the end of an 18-month sentence for a minor robbery: he spent only 4 months in Grendon.

All his offences had been connected with drinking, and frequently he was so drunk that he had no memory of them afterwards. His history showed that he resorted to drink in order to alleviate feelings of depression. He had made many suicide attempts. Hospital treatment for alcoholism (aversion therapy) had not proved helpful to him.

At the psychiatric interview in Grendon he evidenced a considerable degree of neurotic symptomatology, and was diagnosed as a neurotic alcoholic.

Two months before he left Grendon, his wife said that she did not want him back. He persuaded himself that he would be able to change her mind.

Fresh discharge arrangements were hastily made, and on his release he went to a hostel, and found himself a job at the local employment exchange, having told them about his record. He was delighted to have got the job, and confidently approached his wife for a reconciliation: but she was adamant. He walked around a park, trying to think it out, then went into a pub: "To hell with it: and that was it." He came out "paralytic", and threatened a man unknown to him with violence, in a successful attempt to get more money for drink. He repeated this procedure several times during the next two weeks. He could not later remember exactly what he did, and says he was shocked and frightened to hear the details of his attacks at his trial: he had not known that he was capable of such violence.

Whilst he was free, he went to see his probation officer to ask for help; he explained that he was in serious trouble, and a psychiatric appointment was arranged for him. But neither the probation officer nor the psychiatrist was able to offer him any practical help.

He was caught less than two months after his release from Grendon: he said he could remember thinking "Thank God I've been arrested". He was given a 6-year sentence (for robbery, assaults, etc.). His offences were much more serious than any he had committed before.

He was seen in prison about five months after his re-conviction. When he was asked about treatment at Grendon he said he had never really participated in it: "I didn't allow them to get through to me: I was blocking them. I'd get angry when people tried to tell me things. I didn't learn a great deal. I was still the same person as before."

As he frankly confessed that he had wasted his time in Grendon, he said he could not assess the value of its treatment. He regretted the lack of a Grendon after-care scheme: he felt there was a need for a phasing out system, perhaps in the last six months, so that men could try out life "with a thread to hold". Then if difficulties occurred, help and support could be given. "At the moment, you're thrown out there, and if it goes wrong, then ten to one it's another prison sentence."

This man's account emphasised the importance of motivation in any psychotherapeutic treatment programme. No such programme can be expected to help a person who is blocking its attempt to do so.

The account also demonstrates how a prison of itself is powerless to assist a man to cope with his subsequent social circumstances. This man's pattern of offending had always been rather clear-cut: he easily became depressed, he drank to alleviate his distress, and he committed offences whilst drunk, in order to get more money for drink. Grendon could among other things, try to help him with his depressive problem whilst he was in the prison, but obviously the prison could not exercise a continuing influence over his mental state, or his reaction to adverse circumstances when he was released. This man was alone in the world. He had put all his hopes into a reconciliation with his wife, and when that failed, his immediate and impulsive reaction was to paralyse the pain by means of drinking. Subsequently he turned for help to some of the official agencies — probation officer and psychiatrist: but they were unable to offer him the assistance he needed. Possibly they did not appreciate the gravity of the situation, but more important than any lack of understanding, is the lack of provision for emergencies of this sort (see also Gunn, 1974); the necessary facilities for social first aid within the community scarcely exist.

Case 4

A married man of 27, who had been in trouble with the law since he was thirteen. His early home background was very poor; his parents had separated when he was young, and he then lived with his father, a thief, and a highly unsatisfactory stepmother.

He became a professional thief — all his friends were "villains" — and he had engaged in all sorts of offending behaviour, from petty theft and pimping, to robbery with violence. He had 30 convictions, mainly for larceny, wounding and motoring. He came to Grendon for the last year of a 4-year sentence for robbery: prior to this sentence he had already spent more than 5 years in prisons and borstals.

At the initial psychiatric interview, he complained of many symptoms, especially anxiety and depression. He had sought psychiatric treatment in the past, and previous reports mentioned a history of depression and a strong self-destructive element in his character.

He was released to his wife's home, but found it empty when he got there. He met up with new criminal associates, engaged in a couple of break-ins with them, but was not caught. In the midst of these activities, he said, he suddenly lost his taste for them — lost the spirit, the defiance, the interest and the motivation. Crime, which used to be a thrilling activity, and in which he greatly enjoyed the mutual support of his mates, ceased to be an attractive pastime.

"I've simmered down" was how he put it, when he was seen 17 months after release. The simmering down had affected his whole life style. Once a reckless and dangerous motorist (with more than a dozen convictions), always impelled to prove he was the fastest and most daring driver of them all "I now drive like an old clergyman". And his leisure time, once devoted to crime and drink, was now spent pottering about in a friend's garage, or in making things for his home. "I've become a bore."

About a month after he left Grendon, he got a job and had held it for 16 months when he was seen. The job, which involved travelling, suited him in that he did not have to work closely with anyone else: "I've always been interested in work: what used to mess me up at work was my relationships with people."

He had set up home with a new girl friend — "It's not perfect, but it's a working relationship". He had often been asked to help with "jobs" — banks, post offices, wages, etc. — but had consistently refused. He had totally lost interest in crime for its own sake.

He did not attribute his "simmering down" to Grendon — he thought it would have happened anyway — but he felt he had gained a considerable amount by going there. The best thing about Grendon was "being able to get things off your mind — to talk to people and not feel embarrassed. You always find someone else has had the same experience". Grendon had changed his attitudes towards people. Although he was still very liable to lose his temper with those close to him (e.g. his girl friend) he had, in general, become more tolerant and more able to understand other people's points of view. He said he had gained a good deal from the Grendon "Any Questions" sessions: they made him realise that people like magistrates and police, really believed in what they were doing — "You see them as human beings". As a result, he felt his attitudes to authority had become more balanced.

Apart from the initial breaking offences, he had also broken the law by continuing to drive, although he was disqualified: his disqualification still had 18 months to run, after his discharge from Grendon. His job required him to drive, and he felt he had no alternative but to take the risk. He was not caught. He had committed no other offences and said he had no wish to: "I'm happy as I am . . . I have now been out of prison for over a year for the first time in my life . . . ."

Case 5

Aged 21, with 36 convictions, 26 of them for stealing, and the rest for motoring. He was serving 17 months for burglary and associated motoring offences and spent the last 5 months of his sentence at Grendon. Before his sentence he had already spent nearly 3 years in borstal and prison.

All his thefts had been committed in order to get money for drugs. He was heavily involved in the soft drug scene. His life had been unsettled for many years, he lacked ambition and was frequently described as "inadequate".

At our psychiatric interview on admission to Grendon he was diagnosed as a drug abuser with a residual paranoid state.

When he left Grendon he made no secret of his intention of returning to the drug culture, and indeed in Grendon he had mainly associated with other drug offenders.

On release, he returned to his wife, and took a job as a decorator. He continued to mix with "the same sort of people I'd always mixed with"—i.e. the people who admired his reputation as a "speed fiend"—and took amphetamines, barbiturates and cannabis heavily at weekends: "It makes my weekends more successful." But during the week he did not take drugs, and for six months he worked. His flat was then searched, and he was charged with possession of drugs. He was granted bail, and before the hearing took place, another search led to further charges being made. He was sentenced to 18 months imprisonment for possession of drugs. By this time, his marriage had broken down.

When he was asked about Grendon treatment, he replied that it must have helped: not only was he out longer than ever before (8 months) but during this time he had worked and refrained from stealing—something quite unprecedented for him. Previously he had always got his money for drugs by stealing. "I got a few values and priorities sorted out in Grendon, like working for my money and not stealing." But his attitude to drugs had not changed, and his return to a well known circle of drug-taking friends made his re-arrest a virtual certainty.

Case 6

A man of 22, with a 3-year sentence for wounding, of which he spent the last year in Grendon. He came from a broken home, had an approved school background, and by the time he received the 3-year sentence he already had 11 convictions, for larceny and violence, and had spent over 2 years in prison.

When seen at our first psychiatric interview, he was suffering from non-severe neurotic symptoms of various kinds, but at the final interview he appeared to be more seriously depressed. He said that he became violent when tense, and had a history of alcoholism.

On release, he went to live with a girl friend, and got a job. But he started suffering from bad headaches, stayed away from work, and got depressed. He embarked on a very unsettled life, wandering about and taking drugs. Later he became involved with a group of people with whom — often for money — he engaged in sadistic activities. On several occasions, by his own account, he almost killed one of his (willing) victims, and after one such event went to a doctor to ask for help. He was given a psychiatric appointment for three months ahead but was back in prison before the date arrived. Despite attempts to restrain himself he returned to his sadistic activities. He was eventually arrested for some stealing offences, committed for kicks rather than for need. He said he "felt relief at being taken out of circulation". He had become frightened by his violent behaviour and the pleasure it gave him, but was unable to extricate himself from his way of life. "I was glad to get to court. I didn't know where it would end." He had been free for ten months. He got a 2-year sentence for larceny. His other activities apparently never came to police notice.

He was interviewed in prison two months after starting his new sentence. Asked his views about Grendon treatment, he said it had proved helpful to him in several ways. "You are more aware of yourself and more responsible for yourself." But he felt that the basic difficulty about Grendon was that it was a prison, and therefore could not really help him with learning to cope with ordinary life. He said "Most of us have been locked up since we were thirteen. People just don't realise what it's like. I want to fit in with what's normal, but I feel I'm getting worse and worse. The every day things out there are beyond me". He suggested that Grendon should be in a town, and that its walls should be demolished. "Then run it on the same lines, with the inmates mixing with civilians. They (i.e. the inmates) should be forced into the life stream."

He said he had learned a considerable amount in Grendon. He said his attitudes to people in authority had changed: "I don't hate them so much, I've begun to sympathise with them: they are just as much controlled as we are." He had also, as a result of his Grendon experience, lost his lifelong fear of doctors, and after his release had consulted doctors and sought psychiatric help. Grendon had also been helpful in other ways, e.g. he said it had changed his attitude to drink: he no longer drank to excess. "Before I went to Grendon, I blamed the drinking. Now I know that it's my troubles that make me drink. I know the drinking is entirely up to me." He also said Grendon "made me feel more responsible for myself . . . more honest . . . and it helped me with my relationships . . . I learned to tolerate people I detested . . . now I can manage people *up to a point*". He emphasised this qualification: his relationships with women and with people close to him remained a major difficulty.

It was clear from this man's account that he had enormous problems. He said he had found his Grendon experience valuable, and useful in a specific number of ways. But Grendon was a prison, and he had spent his childhood in approved schools and most of his adult life in prison: what he wanted, he said, was help of the Grendon type to be made available to him in the community, so that he could improve his ability to cope with the real world. It is interesting that he did in fact turn for help to the medical profession, when he felt that his behaviour was becoming out of control; but all that he was offered were tablets, and the promise of a psychiatric appointment a quarter of a year later.

Consideration of these six cases illustrates how, obviously, the factor of "having been to Grendon" was by itself incapable of helping men to cope with the pressures and problems of their post-release circumstances. Several of them said that they wished that Grendon after-care, or Grendon type facilities, had been available to them in the community, to help them through periods of crisis. They included the two men who turned to doctors for help when they felt themselves to be losing self control, and it reflects the lack of suitable community facilities that neither of them got the support they were looking for.

Past prison experience clearly cannot permanently insulate people against the pressures and circumstances which lead to re-offending. But this is not the same as saying that Grendon had no influence. On the contrary, with one exception — the man who said that he had never genuinely participated in the treatment programme — all the men felt that they had learned a good deal at Grendon, and had benefited from going there. Attitudes had changed, relationships with others had improved, greater self-understanding had been achieved. But these changes were not reflected in the figures for re-offending, much less in the figures for re-conviction. The young man (Case 2) who was re-imprisoned for smoking cannabis, had worked for 9 months after his release, had refrained from the habitual stealing with which he had previously been involved, and had established greatly improved relationships with his family. His whole life style had changed, but his re-conviction and re-imprisonment reflected none of this improvement. On the other hand, the men in Cases 1 and 4, who had committed what most people would regard as more serious offences — stealing, breaking, and driving whilst disqualified — but who were not caught, have to be counted as successes from the re-conviction point of view. Re-conviction records probably tell us more about law enforcement procedures than they do about offenders. They certainly do not tell us the essentials about the offenders, which in the case of all these three cases, was that despite some re-offending, they had radically changed their way of life and become settled, working members of the community.

We do not wish to suggest that these changes were wholly due to the treatment in Grendon. Some of the men said they felt Grendon had simply hastened a process that would have happened anyway, although others attributed their improved life style mainly to Grendon's effect. The important point is that the men felt that they had benefited in various specific ways from their stay in Grendon. They might of course have benefited equally, or more, had similar treatment been available to them in the community, but Grendon had no option in this matter: it is a prison, and has to keep its men in custody. This unalterable fact Grendon puts to constructive use. We have already seen in Chapter 5 that whilst men were in the prison, their symptomatology improved, their relationships with others became easier, their attitudes to authority figures became less bitter and their self-esteem rose. The accounts of the few released prisoners whom we saw, suggested that what happened at Grendon was not purely ephemeral. Certainly, the prison was unable to prevent the men offending again: given the recidivist histories of the sample, and the fact that most of them returned to their former environment, this was not surprising. But the interviews showed that the men felt that they had gained at Grendon something that had been of lasting value to them in the free world. There was one exception: the man in Case 3, who confessed that he had never participated in Grendon treatment: "I was blocking them; I didn't allow them to get through to me." His account demonstrates what Dr. Hamblin-Smith (1922) emphasised half-a-century ago, that psychiatry in prison, like psychiatry elsewhere, can only help non-psychotic patients who want to be helped. In fact, as we have seen, men sent to Grendon varied considerably in their motivation for treatment and in their wish to abandon crime, and there were those, like the present example, who came and left with little wish to look at themselves, or to change their patterns of behaviour. It cannot be expected that Grendon could substantially benefit them, and this emphasises both the fallacy of trying to evaluate institutions by overall measures such as re-conviction rates, and the need to look more closely at the interaction between the individual and the institution.

Summary

This chapter and the previous one described several aspects of our efforts to look at the post-release experiences of our various samples. The first was an attempt to compare the Grendon men with a group of matched prisoners who were not receiving psychiatric treatment. The idea was to compare the re-conviction rates of the two groups, with a view to seeing whether it reflected any Grendon treatment effect. The project foundered on two obstacles. One was the problem of finding a suitably matched control group. No research workers could have hoped for a better opportunity to assemble such a group than was given to us by the Parole Index, but although the group which we assembled was like the Grendon men on the great majority of the social, criminal, psychological and psychiatric variables measured, they nevertheless differed in a few important respects, most of them connected with the Grendon selection process. The Grendon men had in the past been less financially dependent on crime, they were more anxious to turn away from criminal behaviour, and they were much more likely to view their criminal behaviour as part of a psychological problem. They had also more often had histories of drug taking and of alcoholism. These differences made it impossible to regard the two groups as alike in their chances of re-conviction, the more so as nearly all these variables were, in fact, found to be related to re-offending. Our conclusion was that it would in practice be virtually impossible to find an effective control group for the Grendon men, the obvious alternative method — random allocation — being ruled out not only for ethical but for practical reasons. Clarke and Cornish (1972) have demonstrated that, theoretically attractive as this method is, it is not in practice a satisfactory way of studying the effects of different types of institutional treatment.

The second problem about the control study was even more fundamental, and related to the use of re-conviction as the evaluative measure. Re-conviction data provides a very incomplete measure of re-offending, but is nevertheless used because in most studies, including the present one, no other hard post-release data is available for the whole population. But by the time we had done our research, and become familiar both with the men in our samples in Grendon and Wormwood Scrubs, and with the treatment they received, we had become persuaded that it was pointless to use re-conviction rates as an evaluative measure. This was partly because of their inaccuracy but mainly because it became apparent that most of the factors, such as social and environmental influences, which affect a recidivist's prospects of re-conviction are not of a kind which can be affected by prison treatment of the sort under study. The experimental variables in our research design — i.e. the treatment given during the man's last sentence — represented so small a proportion of the total variance affecting re-conviction that it could not have been expected to produce measurable effects. Had we been able to form a properly matched control group for the Grendon men, we would therefore have hypothesised that its re-conviction rate would not differ from Grendon's. (In fact, the re-conviction rate of our inadequately matched group did not differ from Grendon's.) This hypothesis does not mean that we regard Grendon's treatment as valueless: it means only that we regard re-conviction rates as a valueless measure of Grendon's treatment, for they measure things which prisons cannot realistically be expected to influence.

The best way of looking at the long-term effects of Grendon's treatment would have been to keep in touch with both the discharged Grendon and control men. This was beyond the resources of our research, so an attempt was made to keep in touch with them by post. The Grendon men and their controls, and the Wormwood Scrubs men and their controls, were all asked to take part in a postal survey after their release. Questionnaires were sent out to them every six months, enquiring how they were getting on, and asking for specific information about employment, living arrangements, psychiatric problems and criminal activities. Our hope was that in this way we would get a fuller picture of the men's lives than was provided by the re-conviction data. Unfortunately, however, the response was incomplete, and uneven as between the four groups: it was therefore impossible to examine the groups separately, or to compare them with each other. However, since 40% of the sample as a whole provided us with information, we did get a glimpse of how a substantial minority of the men fared after release. This minority did not seem to be un-representative: when compared, in respect of the variables collected in prison, with the men who did not write to us, very few differences emerged, nor was there any trend for those who participated in the enquiry to have been re-convicted less often than those who did not.

Of the 60 men who wrote to us twelve months after release, 42 said they had re-offended (re-conviction data, however, showed that only 32 men had incurred further convictions). The 42 self-reported re-offenders were compared with the 18 men who said they had not committed further offences. In terms of the data which had been collected in prison, it was found that the men who did not re-offend were those who had previously been less heavily involved in thefts, who had less previous prison experience, who had less pathological personal and family relationships, less alcoholism, and more guilt feelings about their previous offences. Their replies to the postal survey showed that since leaving prison they had, when compared with the re-offenders, experienced less unemployment, less marital breakdown, less neurotic symptomatology, and had been drinking less heavily; they were also more likely to have been satisfied with their living arrange-ments. The picture is of the men with the worst prognosis in criminal and social terms, re-offending again within twelve months, and our respondents' written accounts showed that this re-offending did not occur in a vacuum: on all sides — employment, accommodation, marital relationships, and symptomatology — the re-offenders reported more difficulties. Again this emphasised how limited is the positive contribution which a prison can make to its inmates' future chances of offending: the problems the men faced were concerned with living in the community, and these are not problems which prisons can alleviate.

One final point of interest from the postal survey should be mentioned. When the self-reported offenders were compared with the men who said they had not re-offended, the groups did not differ on any of the psychiatric or psychological assessments which we had made in prison. There was no tendency for the more abnormal or more disturbed men to have re-offended more than others.

This finding was repeated when the re-conviction data were analysed for all men in our study (whether from the Grendon or Wormwood Scrubs samples or from the control groups): on average the men had then been at liberty for twenty months. A comparison of the 112 re-convicted men with the 46 not re-convicted showed that they differed only on variables relating to criminal history (age at first conviction, previous custodial experience and previous involvement in theft). None of the psychiatric, psychological or attitudinal variables distinguished the two groups. Nor, when the re-conviction records of the Grendon sample were looked at separately, was there any tendency for the re-convicted Grendon men to have been more disturbed or abnormal than those who were not re-convicted. When Grendon men who were re-convicted were compared with those who were not there were differences in only two areas. One was the usual criminal one, with the re-convicted men having more custodial experience, more larceny offences to their name, and an earlier age of first conviction. The other and larger difference was the attitude to psychiatry, which was markedly more favourable among the non-convicted. This was an interesting difference because it did not occur among the non-Grendon men and therefore suggested the possibility of an interaction between initial high motivation and treatment at Grendon. There was, however, no evidence that re-conviction was related to changes in attitude, psychological functioning or psychiatric state which occurred in Grendon, but the figures available for this part of the analysis were very small.

CHAPTER 11

How Many Psychiatric Cases are there in the Prison Population?

So far we have examined the psychiatric facilities provided at two prisons. These examinations cannot, of course, tell us anything about the demand for these services. Our control study illustrated that there is probably a large residual pool of prisoners who have psychiatric symptoms and would like to be considered for psychiatric treatment. However, this was not a random sample of the prison population. To gain some idea of the prevalence of psychiatric disorder within the sentenced population of H.M. prisons and to determine the overall level of demand which such a population might exert, a census survey is required.

We were fortunate for in February 1972, the Home Office Research Unit carried out a census of the prison population in the South East Region. This was a 10 per cent random survey of all adult sentenced males, other than fine defaulters, who were in prison on 2nd February of that year. We undertook to add a psychiatric component to that census, our aim being to provide an estimate of the number of men in prison who could be regarded as psychiatric cases, and to make an estimate of the demand for services by measuring the extent of motivation as we had done in our other studies.

The definition of a case was the first problem that exercised our minds. Traditionally psychiatric studies try to place patients in diagnostic categories such as schizophrenia, depression, personality disorder and the like. For 1 per cent of the prison sample we were able to do something of this sort but we have not made this our prime objective. Diagnoses cannot be made by questionnaire: an interview with a psychiatrist is required. We could not interview all 10 per cent of the prisoners, only 1 per cent. However, even if we had had facilities to interview every prisoner we do not believe that a simple labelling exercise would have served our purpose. Certainly by such a process we could have selected a small group of severely ill (usually psychotic) prisoners who by any standards would be regarded as psychiatric cases. Certainly we could have selected a group of men with very few psychiatric problems whom we would have been happy to label normal and who would be happy to be labelled as normal. However, this would have left us with a large group in the middle, perhaps the majority, who were neither clearly normal nor clearly mad. In ordinary clinical practice such patients largely determine their own labelling and treatment arrangements by the initiative they take and the motivation they exhibit. Only in the severest cases, where there is no dispute about the presence of intense disturbance or madness, are the patients own wishes over-ridden and compulsory treatment powers applied. Few patients who are convinced that they have a psychiatric problem and persuasively ask for help are rejected entirely. For the majority what determines whether a person gets psychiatric treatment or not, is an interaction, between the services available, the level of symptomatology exhibited, and the degree of motivation. In an abstract epidemiological survey of this kind the interaction effect between supply of services and demand is artificially removed. There is no way round this problem, except an elaborate action research programme which would also be slightly artificial, but it has to be borne in mind in what follows. We had a further difficulty though, we were working in prisons. The man in prison is already compulsorily detained because of his behaviour. It may be tempting for society to capitalise on this by trying to add compulsory treatment (i.e. a method of changing behaviour) to the compulsory detention. It may be tempting for the prisoner to use psychiatry as a means of escaping punishment even though in other settings he would have no medical motivation at all. The method we have chosen tried to get round this difficulty, but in any case we were not convinced it is as great a problem as is often thought. Prison doctors are particularly aware of the need to avoid compulsory treatment in prison and normally try to get a man into a NHS hospital if compulsory treatment is required. Many prisoners are aware that treatment in prison does not ameliorate the prison sentence. Indeed, since treatment may mean time away from the workshops, cannot usually be given in an open prison, and does not improve social status as a prisoner, it may make the sentence more irksome.

Our method of case identification, as will be seen, has attempted to take into account symptomatology, motivation, and previous history. Furthermore, we have tried to validate this method against the views of practising psychiatrists.

The Questionnaires

We sent a series of questionnaires to the 811 men who had been randomly selected by the Home Office, and 629 satisfactory replies were received, i.e. we obtained completed forms from 78% of the original population. Of the 182 men from whom no reply was received, 40 (5%) had not been given their forms because of administrative errors; 78 (10%) were known to be refusers and 64 (8%) failed to return the forms for unknown reasons. Given that much of the information we were asking for was of a personal and confidential nature, we felt that a successful response rate of 82 per cent (not including those lost through errors of administration) was satisfactory.

All those men who did not reply to our forms initially, were given a second chance to do so and, at the same time, were asked to state their reasons for not replying if they still did not wish to give us the information for which we asked. Of those men who gave a reason for not replying, a little over half stated that they simply "couldn't be bothered" or made other remarks which indicated that they did not like filling in forms. Nineteen men stated quite bluntly that they did not believe the project was what it claimed to be or that they resented being used as "guinea-pigs". The suspicions of this group are surely understandable in the prison context. As one man put it—"I want nothing to do with these London psychiatrists".

A covering explanatory letter was sent to each man from one of us. This contained the reason why our forms had been sent to that particular man and attempted to allay any fears he might have about the confidential nature of the information he was giving us.

Five forms had to be completed. The first of these which we labelled "Medical History" consisted mainly of a series of psychiatric questions which required a "yes/no" type of answer. Questions were asked about epilepsy, previous in-patient or out-patient treatment in a mental hospital, previous psychiatric treatment in prison and a desire for such treatment. Men were asked whether they would like to go to

Grendon and also about their drinking, gambling and drug-taking behaviours. The question of previous suicide attempts was also raised and a space was provided for comments. The form is reproduced in Appendix 13.

In addition we sent our two attitude scales (see Chapter 2) on attitudes to psychiatry (AP) and to crime and criminal behaviour (AC). In both, a high score is held to reflect "good" opinion so that the man scoring highly on the AP is saying that he thinks psychiatry is useful and that psychiatric treatment is relevant for his needs. In order to obtain a high score on the AC, a man would have to say that he feels guilty about his criminal activities and would like to stop offending.

The General Health Questionnaire (see p. 49) was also sent to each man, but in view of its difficulty with chronic problems we added a further questionnaire, the Self Rated Symptom Scale (SRSS). This has 35 questions and is slightly more likely than the General Health Questionnaire to pick up chronic symptoms, because it asks whether individual symptoms have, in the previous week, been affecting the respondent "not at all", a "little", "quite a bit" or "extremely". Details of the scale, and the questionnaire itself, are given in Appendix 14. Unfortunately we made the error of printing it on two sides of a single sheet, many men did not turn over and so, as will be seen from the tables, more data than usual has been lost on this variable.

Altogether, 123 questions were asked but we calculated that only 15-20 minutes were needed to complete our forms. By asking about desire for treatment, neurotic pathology and previous psychiatric history, we hoped we would obtain a comprehensive psychiatric profile.

Before we were able to say anything about our results, we had to establish that our material was reliable and that gross errors had not been introduced into the sampling procedure through the 22% of the sample for whom no response was obtained.

The short term stability of the AP, AC, GHQ and SRSS had already been established and so we felt that it would be economical to incorporate our measurement of this aspect of reliability for our psychiatric history into the psychiatric interviews which were to be carried out on just over 10 per cent of our sample. All the items listed in our questionnaire were asked again by the team of psychiatrists approximately two weeks after all the men had returned their forms. The correlations which were obtained between our interview and questionnaire responses are presented in Table 56. This table demonstrates how data, even data which is considered historical and objective, is affected by the collecting medium. "Barbiturate taking" for example was badly collected by the questionnaire because of an error in the question; it was dropped from further analysis.

Table 56   Correlations between Questionnaire and Interview Responses N = 90

Item	r
Suicide attempts	0·87
LSD taking	0·85
Previous inpatient treatment	0·79
Amphetamine taking	0·77
Desire for treatment	0·74
Previous prison psychiatric treatment	0·73
Cannabis taking	0·71
Other drug use	0·71
Previous Grendon treatment	0·66
Heavy drinking	0·57
Previous head injury	0·56
Heavy gambling	0·56
Previous outpatient treatment	0·55
Alcohol problem	0·49
Opiate taking	0·47
Barbiturate taking	0·28
Epilepsy	No epileptic men interviewed

All items with interview/questionnaire correlations of less than 0·60 (under the line) were also dropped except "alcohol problem". This was retained because of the overwhelming importance of an alcohol item in a psychiatric examination of a prison population and it was chosen in preference to "heavy drinking" because a more detailed analysis of part of this data by Bowden (1975b) revealed that the majority of the unreliability in relation to the drinking questions comes from the group of prisoners who answer their questionnaires "Yes I drink heavily, but no I do not have a drink problem". Bowden personally examined the men at five of the twenty-one prisons in the census, these prisons represented as comprehensive and unselected a population as possible, none being institutions which specialised in alcoholism. Eighty-one men were studied one month after completion of the questionnaire. He also found that men who had admitted problem drinking on their questionnaire denied this in 33 per cent of cases at interview. This finding is not entirely new, Hochstim (1962) compared three ways of collecting sociomedical data, and found that they elicited more drinkers by mail and telephone enquiry than by personal interview. It is also part of a wider phenomenon. The more emotionally loaded a question is for an individual the more likely he is to fake good (Heron, 1956). Ellis (1947) studied love affairs in a group of 69 female undergraduates, first on interview and a year later with an anonymous questionnaire, and showed that the more ego-involving was the enquiry the less interview responses matched those from the questionnaire. So, in the present study, the majority answered the interview more favourably, and presumably less revealingly, than they answered the questionnaire.

This is an important idea which broadens the whole problem of reliability. At a common sense level it does not seem particularly surprising. Most people are aware how much easier it is to write difficult painful letters than to say the same thing face to face. Most psychiatrists are aware how long it can take some patients to pluck up courage to talk about some really key problem in their life (such as drinking, sexual deviation, criminal behaviour). On the other hand, clinicians continue to assert that the interview is all important as a fact finder and rarely is it advocated that interviews can be supplemented by questionnaire.

Sample Bias

As our project was additional to a Home Office Research Unit survey in which the prison files of 811 men were being examined, we had an opportunity to compare the men who completed the questionnaires (responders) with those who did not (non-responders) on data external to our own to see how far the responding sample could be taken as representative of the whole. We were well aware of the danger of placing too much reliance on data gleaned by a team of coders from files not specially prepared for research purposes. Nevertheless, as the comparative opportunity presented itself we thought it better to take it, in spite of the limitations, than to ignore it. The data supplied by the Home Office Research Unit was in the form of several hundred items of social, criminal, and medical information. We chose 154 items limiting ourselves to only one or two items from each major area and trying to select items we thought more reliable. The variables on which the responders and non-responders differ are presented in Table 57. The data refers to 626 responders and 181 non-responders because we had difficulty in interpreting the material in respect of 4 cases. They

Table 57 Responders Compared with Non-Responders

	Responders (N = 626)				Non-Responders (N = 181)				X^2	$p <$
	Yes	%	No and NK	%	Yes	%	No and NK	%		
Substitute parent before 15	122	(19)	504	(81)	16	(9)	165	(91)	10·59	0·01
Illiterate	14	(2)	612	(98)	11	(6)	170	(94)	5·68	0·05
Mostly out of work last 5 years†	78	(14)	462	(86)	37	(24)	117	(76)	7·27	0·01
Behaviour problems as a child	163	(26)	463	(74)	31	(17)	150	(83)	5·63	0·05
Possible psychotic episodes	19	(3)	607	(97)	15	(8)	166	(92)	8·34	0·01
In open prison	69	(11)	557	(89)	32	(18)	149	(82)	5·50	0·05
Been refused parole*	130	(32)	281	(68)	48	(50)	48	(50)	10·73	0·01
Vagrancy offence on record	61	(10)	565	(90)	35	(19)	145	(88)	11·75	0·01

†Unrateable cases, usually because of institutionalisation, omitted (N = 450).

*Short-termers are not considered by the parole board (N = 411).

also differed in terms of age, the responders having a mean age of 31·4 years (s.d. 8·7) and the non-responders a mean age of 34·6 years (s.d. 11·5 t = 4·03 p < 0·001). Both mean ages are rather high because of the selection criteria used by the Home Office in choosing their sample. They excluded fine defaulters and prisoners under 21.

The list of differences between responders and non-responders may seem at first sight to be a large one, but it must be remembered that the two groups were compared on 154 variables and differed significantly on only 9 (i.e. less than 6%). Our main concern was to identify those differences which might have contributed either to an over-estimate or an under-estimate of psychiatric cases in our sampling.

In terms of the components which made up our questionnaire we supposed that an important one, desire for treatment, would have been very different between the responding and non-responding groups but we had no way of testing the size of any such difference.

The nature of some of the differences found, indicates that those men who did not respond to our forms were, as a group, somewhat more disturbed than those who had replied. For example, they had a poorer work record as measured over the previous five years — a larger proportion had had some history of psychotic disturbance and had been charged with a vagrancy offence. However, this pattern is perhaps offset to some extent by the fact that more of the responders had been regarded as behaviour problems when they were children, had tended more often to come from broken homes and were less often to be found in open prisons. The last of these factors is particularly important in that most men in open prisons would have been unlikely to be very disturbed or to be thought of as psychiatric cases.

The fact that a disproportionate number of non-responding men had their parole claims turned down would suggest that anger at authority in general had played a part in determining whether or not our forms were completed. However, we have no reason to suppose that this factor was itself related to pathology. In any case, the real numbers involved in the last variable are very small. Illiteracy was found to be a factor in determining response to our questionnaire and since illiteracy is often associated with subnormal intelligence, it is possible that a higher proportion of those men who did not respond and who were also illiterate had had some previous psychiatric experience. However, here again, the real numbers involved were very small and would be unlikely to have had any marked effect on our final case estimate.

It is very difficult to draw conclusions from these data but we tentatively suggest that the non-responders were a slightly more anomic group with an increased likelihood to suffer psychiatric and social pathology. Put the other way we found no evidence that the responders were particularly likely to suffer from excess pathology and so give a distorted over-estimate of the numbers of psychiatric problems in the prison population.

Questionnaire Results

The basic characteristics of the population, as ascertained by the questionnaire, are set out in Tables 58 and 59.

Table 58

	N	Mean	s.d.
Length of current sentence (months)*	596	34·6	28·7
No. of months served	626	12·1	15·5
Age (years)	629	31·4	8·6
SRSS	513	6·4	6·4
GHQ	611	15·9	14·8
AP	613	16·4	5·2
AC	607	13·3	4·3

*Excluding lifers.

Table 59   Medical History

	Yes	%	No	NK
Epilepsy	9	(1·4)	620	0
NHS IP psychiatric treatment	76	(12)	551	2
Been to Grendon	26	(4)	601	2
Other prison psychiatric treatment	56	(9)	572	1
Desire for prison treatment	238	(38)	383	8
Desire for Grendon	172	(28)	446	11
Drink problem	94	(15)	534	1
Gambling problem	55	(9)	567	7
Cannabis taking	179	(29)	440	10
Hallucinogen taking	83	(13)	536	10
Amphetamine taking	134	(22)	485	10
Other drug abuse	45	(7)	574	10
Any illicit drug	199	(32)	420	10
Suicide attempts	99	(16)	511	19

From Table 58 it will be seen that there is a strong bias towards longer-term prisoners who are older than the average first offender. This is largely related to the inevitable sampling bias produced by looking at a resident population.

Validation by Interview

A proportion of the census sample were randomly selected on a roughly 1 in 10 basis for interview. In the event 1·3% of the total sample were interviewed by eleven Maudsley trained psychiatrists. Interviews were carried out in all the twenty-one census prisons. The fact that all eleven had received their psychiatric training at the same hospital was an advantage, as it ensured a degree of agreement between interviewers. We used the structured psychiatric interview schedule devised by the General Practice Unit at the Institute of Psychiatry and our psychiatrists were given special training in its use.

All interviewing took place within one week. The Monday of that week was devoted to training and briefing our psychiatrists who, in addition to the mental state examination already mentioned, were required to make an assessment of desire for treatment and to ask all the items listed in our "Medical History" questionnaire. Desire for treatment was assessed using the five-point rating scale which had been developed in our study of Grendon prison.

We hoped that by the end of their interviews our psychiatrists would have enough information to allow them to rate each man as to whether or not he could be regarded as a psychiatric case. We supposed that their judgments would have been based on a number of factors and, in particular, the three which we had attempted to measure using our questionnaires; motivation (desire for treatment), current pathology, past psychiatric history. We asked them to assess, in the light of these factors, whether they would have regarded the man as suitable for psychiatric treatment under ordinary health service arrangements. By correlating case status with the responses obtained at interview, we reasoned that we would have sufficiently strong criteria to extrapolate from the relatively small interview sample to the total census population. The model used in this exercise is best described by the diagram on page 219 opposite.

Although 106 men were interviewed, only 90 of these had completed and returned questionnaire forms and it was on the responses of these 90 men that our various calculations and extrapolations have been

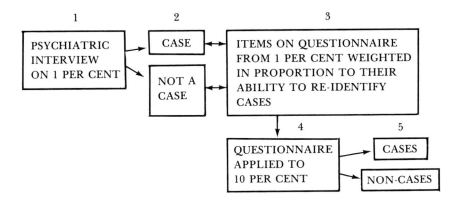

based. Thirty-one of the 90 men (34%) were regarded by a psychiatrist as being cases.

The small group of 16 questionnaire refusers were examined separately. Four of the men were called cases by the interviewing psychiatrists:

003 A 22-year old drug abuser, strongly motivated for treatment, who gave no reason for not filling in the forms.

116 A 34-year-old alcoholic. Depressed, lethargic and too apathetic to fill in forms.

379 A 50-year-old rapist under constant prison hospital care for a severe depressive illness. Just too ill to fill in forms.

497 A 34-year-old robber recently involved in a prison disturbance. An angry paranoid man who complained of rage attacks. He refused to fill in forms because he hated prison authorities.

The non-case non-responders had a variety of other reasons for not filling in their forms including illiteracy, suspiciousness, a refusal to be "catalogued" and "aversion" to form filling and so on. Out of our 106 interviews we found 35 cases.

For the sake of completeness we also asked the interviewing psychiatrists to categorize the cases into one or more of the diagnoses given in the International Classification of Diseases. The list is given in Table 60.

One obvious omission from Table 60 is mental retardation (310-315) in its various forms. This is simply because we did not have psychological facilities available to us and were therefore not in a position to comment about intellectual abilities.

Our next task (stage 3 of the diagram), was to correlate case status with all the responses which the 90 men made both at interview and on their questionnaire forms (Table 61).

Table 60   Diagnostic Labels and their Frequency
Amongst the Interviewed Cases

ICD Category and No.	Times used	
	Total	Primary
295 Schizophrenia	1	1
296 Affective psychosis	1	1
300 Neurosis	9	9
301 Personality disorder	22	16
302 Sexual deviation	3	1
303 Alcoholism	13	5
304 Drug dependence	3	0
		33*

*Diagnoses missing for 2 cases.

Table 61   Correlations between Case Status and:
(a) Interview data (b) Questionnaire data

(a) *Interview data*

(only those correlations which were significant to greater than the 0·1% level are listed)

Item	'r'
Total score on Mental State Interview*	0·59
Desire for treatment	0·59
Drinking rated as a problem	0·45
Previous psychiatric treatment in prison	0·35
Suicide attempts	0·32

*A number of the items which go to make up the total score on the mental state interview were highly related to case status. However, as the total score had the highest correlation, a list of individual item correlations was considered unnecessary.

(b) *Questionnaire data*

Item	'r'
Desire for treatment	0·53
Score on the AP scale	0·51
Score on the SRSS	0·40
Desire to go to Grendon	0·40
Score on the GHQ	0·39
Previous in-patient treatment	0·37

A number of important factors emerged from this analysis. In the first place, with regard to the psychiatric interview, it was clear that case status was highly and equally related to present mental state and motivation. The third element in our battery, psychiatric history, was also related to case identification but to a much lesser extent—the correlation between being a case and previous in-patient treatment being 0·28 (p < 0·01).

As regards the relationship between questionnaire items and case status, it was found that mental state as measured by our tests was less highly related to case status than the mental status assessment made by the psychiatrists themselves. Furthermore, previous psychiatric history became more important in case determination. Both these trends are important as they indicate areas of possible error. The success of our model was highly dependent upon our ability to associate our questionnaire data as closely as possible with the material collected at interview and the relative lack of power in our measurement of pathology clearly set us at a disadvantage.

Stages 4 and 5 of our model were completed in the following manner. A computer programme was written which was designed to do three jobs. In the first place, it examined questionnaire items and combinations of items for accuracy of case status as defined by our psychiatrists. Secondly, it made an estimate of the prevalence level of cases according to the item or item combination being used and, finally, it listed the case numbers of all prisoners identified as cases by any given formula.

The accuracy of individual scales and questions for identifying cases was tested and the four items which provided the highest level of correct identification are listed in Table 62.

We believed that we would probably achieve a greater degree of accuracy by using a combination of items. A discriminant function analysis was carried out between cases and non-cases and the eight items which discriminated most highly between the two groups were

Table 62   The Accuracy of Individual Items in Predicting Case Status

Item	Non-Cases*	Cases*	Accuracy level
Attitude to psychiatry scale	20 (or less)	21 (or more)	80%
Desire for treatment	No	Yes	79%
SRSS	7 (or less)	8 (or more)	77%
GHQ	15 (or less)	16 (or more)	72%

*Scores

given weightings. These weightings were calculated using a pro-
portional system described by Billewicz *et al.* (1969) and are
represented, along with their respective weightings in Table 63.

Table 63   Weighted Scores of Discriminatory Items

Item		Weighted Scores
Attitude to Psychiatry — score of 21 or over	Yes	+ 11
	No	− 3
Desire for treatment	Yes	+ 7
	No	− 4
Had psychiatric treatment in prison	Yes	+ 8
	No	− 1
Any in-patient psychiatric treatment	Yes	+ 8
	No	− 1
Drink problem	Yes	+ 7
	No	− 1
Desire to go to Grendon	Yes	+ 6
	No	− 2
SRSS Scale — score of 8 or over	Yes	+ 4
	No	− 3
Previous suicide attempts	Yes	+ 5
	No	− 2

As is clear from Table 63, the system used for weighting items
allowed negative scores to be given for negative responses and positive
scores to be given if a symptom or sign was present. The total weighted
score was then calculated for each man and the computer programme
already referred to was used to assess the power of the various
combinations of items. Not surprisingly perhaps, we found that the
highest rate of correct identification was produced using all items and
was found to be 85% accurate. This means that only 15% of cases
were identified as false negatives or false positives. A false negative is a
man rated as not a case by the weighting system but called a case by the
interviewing psychiatrist; a false positive is a man called a case by the
weighting system but rated as not a case by the interviewing psychiatrist.

It should be noted that in this case-identification process the
computer programme was searching for the most accurate or most

specific combination of weighted items, i.e. the combination which gave the fewest false positives and the fewest false negatives when the weighted questionnaire data was evaluated against the actual doctor's decision. This is undoubtedly the right choice of cut-off point for an epidemiological exercise such as this, and it turned out to be men with total weighted scores of 3 or less who were regarded as non-cases and those with 4 and above were classified as cases. Different cut-off points would have given different numbers of false positives and false negatives. If we had wished to make the instrument less specific but more sensitive, i.e. to concern ourselves less with accuracy but more with eliminating false negatives, then we could simply have pitched the cut-off point at a lower level. Such a procedure would perhaps be suitable for clinical screening when it would not matter if over-identification took place, but when care would be needed to avoid case material slipping through the screening net.

Using the most accurate cut-off point our overall estimate of the number of cases in the census sample was found to be 31%. Taken at its face value, this means that about 1 in 3 of all men in prison could, in our terms, be regarded as patients within the framework of psychiatry in the community. The figure does not mean that a third of the prison population is "mad" in lay terms, or that an equivalent proportion of men would actually seek psychiatric help once they were out of prison. Indeed, we know from asking them that only about 20% of the total group had in fact had psychiatric treatment.

Because of our inability to obtain a strong measure of manifest abnormality, we have been forced to rely upon expressed desire for treatment. Not that this is, in our opinion, a bad thing in itself. If we restrict ourselves to talking solely about case status, then the place of motivation in our theoretical estimate of cases is very important. However, the relationship between motivation and case status is rather complex and this is neatly illustrated by some of the false positives and false negatives that were thrown up in our case identification procedures.

The following four men were not called cases by our psychiatrists at interview but were classified as such using our weighted score technique:

The first man was a thief who was serving a 15-month sentence. The psychiatrist regarded him as a pathological liar and as an exaggerator and he also noted his strong desire for treatment but regarded his symptoms as secondary to imprisonment. A prison medical officer (in our estimation) may well have taken him on for short term amelioration had he been noticed (which he was not). His weighted score was 15.

The second man was serving a long sentence for manslaughter. Our interviewing psychiatrist rated him as not a case because his severe depressive feelings had abated with anti-depressant medication. However, the strong desire for treatment was noted and the prison doctor treating him clearly disagreed with our survey psychiatrist, for we later discovered that the prisoner had been referred to Grendon. His weighted score was 19.

Our third case was another long sentence man whose offence was rape. The psychiatrist correctly detected his motivation for treatment and his symptomatology and we believe that he simply made a rating error. The man's weighted score was 22.

Our fourth and final example is a man who was serving two years for a larceny offence. He was a clear-cut alcoholic who desired treatment (although not at Grendon nor in a prison setting because of his anti-authority views). Previous trials of treatment had been unsuccessful and so our survey doctor rated him as not a case. His weighted score was 21.

The following three men were called cases by our doctors but had relatively low weighted scores:

The first of these was a burglar who was serving 18 months. He was an alcoholic (who denied his drink problem on his questionnaire) and who told the survey doctor that he did not want treatment. He was nevertheless rated as a case on account of the severity of his problem. His weighted score was −18.

Our second example is a man who was serving a medium-term sentence for an offence of robbery. Although he was asymptomatic in prison, he was an alcoholic with violent outbursts when drunk who expressed at interview a strong desire for treatment. His weighted score was −11.

Our final example is another robber who was serving a medium-term sentence. He also had a drink problem but had no other pathology and had no desire for medical help. His weighted score was −20.

Comparisons with other Studies

Unfortunately it is almost impossible to compare this exercise with other work, not only because very few psychiatric prevalence studies have been carried out in British prisons, but also because we are not using the usual epidemiological methods. Bluglass (1966) for example, examined every fourth convicted prisoner received into Perth prison. He studied 300 in all and estimated that some 46% of these men were psychiatrically abnormal (1·9% suffering from psychosis, 11·2% from alcoholism and drug addiction, 14·2% from subnormality). He was, like most workers, using a purely pathological approach. In other words, if at examination he deemed a man to have psychiatric abnormalities then he was given a diagnosis and counted as a case. We have chosen a different method in an attempt to get nearer to what happens in practice and to try and avoid some of the circular reasoning which the pathological approach leads to in psychiatry. Even in physical medicine, where objective criteria are available there is an interaction between services supplied and numbers of cases for treatment. Perhaps the best-known example of this in recent years was the diabetic survey of an English town which produced so many new individuals diagnosed as diabetic and requiring treatment, that the research team had to set up a clinical service. In real psychiatric practice doctors do not go into a population, interview individuals not attending the services and say "I think you have neurotic problems you ought to come for treatment". Theoretically it would be possible to do this for severe psychiatric disturbance, but for the most part whether we, or our neighbours take our neurotic problems to a psychiatrist depends not only on severity, not only on our own perception of our problems as neurotic, but also on our attitude towards those problems and towards the psychiatric services. Motivation, or desire for treatment is crucial in ordinary voluntary psychiatric practice. It is only when pathology is so severe that a relative and two doctors agree that judgment is impaired that the patient's wishes can be discounted.

In our view these problems are especially troublesome in prison surveys. Firstly, motivation for treatment is undoubtedly more complex. Some prisoners even with severe symptoms, will resist all help because of their fear of psychiatry and so they are untreatable unless manifestly ill. Other prisoners may see treatment, especially if it means a change of location, as a soft option and will plump for it even if they have few or no symptoms. More important than all this though is the temptation for the researcher to fall into the circularity of noting that many individuals have numerous social and personal problems, consequently labelling the people concerned as personality disordered, and thence ascribing their social and personal problems to the personality disorder.

To reiterate, it is in an attempt to circumvent these problems that we have defined cases in terms of three factors, motivation, pathology, previous history. Our criteria allow pathology to overwhelm motivation and motivation to overwhelm pathology in extreme cases, but for the most part a man needs a mixture of pathology and motivation, with perhaps a positive previous history before he is labelled a case.

The Demand for Psychiatric Help

We cannot say that we are entirely satisfied with our own efforts at case identification, and we feel that a more useful method of presenting our data would be to look at it in terms of the individual parameters which were used to identify case status. By doing this, we avoid the numerous theoretical pitfalls involved in simply discussing cases and we can also get some idea of the demand for services, the degree of psychological disturbance in prisons and the extent to which prisons and psychiatric hospitals are dealing with the same population of men.

As we see from Table 59 (page 217) over one-third of the men in our sample responded in the affirmative when they were asked whether or not they wanted psychiatric treatment in prison. It can be objected that some men responded in this way to fulfil our expectations. However, this must be set against the fact that psychiatric status still carries a certain stigma with it, in or out of prison but especially amongst prisoners. Whilst it is probably true that public attitudes towards psychiatry have altered radically in the past twenty years or so, most people continue to associate psychiatry with the more florid and exotic types of madness and do not readily accept such a status for themselves.

In our opinion, a far more important qualification in regard to our response rate is to be found in the possibility that a large number of men have misconceptions about both the practice and "powerfulness" of psychiatric treatment. For large numbers of the public a psychiatrist is someone who reads people's minds, interprets their dreams, is very interested in their sexual fantasies and, most important, somehow makes them better by being able to do all this: someone who dispenses magic, in fact.

We think that a large number of men who told us that they would like psychiatric treatment have false expectations about what that treatment may amount to. One piece of information exists which tends to confirm our view. As part of their survey, the Home Office Research

Unit noted whether or not psychiatric help had been provided during the period of a man's present sentence. The figures they produced indicated that some 27% (169) of the men who answered our questionnaires, had had some sort of psychiatric treatment from a psychiatrist or doctor, and that a further 5% (31) had taken part in group counselling or discussions. However, in response to our question "Have you ever had psychiatric help in prison?" (i.e. on any sentence), only 9% (56) responded in the affirmative. Even if the 5% who had had group counselling were regarded as not having had treatment, the difference between the proportion of men who said that they had had treatment and the proportion who had had treatment in terms of the criteria used by the Home Office, is very large and is highly statistically significant ($X^2 = 37\cdot4$). We would suggest that a large part of this difference is due to disparity between expectations about treatment and the reality of treatment. The other likely cause of the disparity is the fact that we asked about psychiatric treatment in our questionnaire thus implying treatment by a psychiatrist, whereas the Home Office Research Unit have considered any psychological treatment (for example, the administration of psychotropic drugs) as representing psychiatric practice. This latter type of treatment corresponds to general practice in the National Health Service and it is rather unfair to regard it as being equivalent to psychiatry in the terms which we used. Nevertheless, if a man is being treated with psychotropic drugs he is receiving help for his psychological problems. As this type of treatment accounts for a large proportion of everyday psychiatric practice, we feel that our original point regarding expectations and reality, remains valid. In terms of raw numbers the demand for psychiatric help is very large indeed. By our estimate, approximately ten thousand men would say yes if asked whether or not they would like such treatment in prisons. A simple sum indicates that the 60 part-time psychiatrists at present employed by the Home Office, in the Prison Department, could not cope with a case load of ten thousand men, especially if those men were expecting any form of psychotherapy.

The Prevalence of Psychiatric Disorder

The distribution of scores, provided by our sample, on the General Health Questionnaire indicates a high degree of disturbance and psychological discomfort in the population. Our subjects produced a mean score of 15·95 (s.d. 14·8) compared with the pathology threshold of 11/12 of the test (Goldberg, 1972). Feelings of anxiety and depression are common in prison.

To what extent can this relatively high rate of neurotic complaining be attributed to the effects of imprisonment alone? We cannot give a complete answer to this question but, to some extent, we have been able to measure the contribution made by imprisonment. We re-tested men who were still in prison nine months after completion of our initial assessment procedure. Our main reason for doing this was our interest in determining the long term stability of some of the tests which we had used in the Grendon and Wormwood Scrubs parts of our studies. However, it was noted in the course of this exercise that those men who had been serving the early part of their sentences when the census was carried out tended to produce the largest reductions in score on the GHQ at re-testing. In order to test this we divided the re-tested group into two sections, one comprising those men who had completed six months or less of their sentences at initial assessment and the second group made up of all other men. A two-way analysis of variance was carried out to examine the possibility of an interactions effect between change in score on the GHQ and belonging to one or other of these groups. The results of this analysis are presented in Table 64 and it is clear that, as a group, the early-sentence men show a marked reduction in symptom scoring when compared with those men who were not in the early part of the sentence. It is also clear from the table that early-sentence men tend to have higher scores on the GHQ initial assessment ($t = 1.96$ $p < 0.10$). The GHQ asks about symptoms in terms of how a person feels "normally" or usually and it seems reasonable to suppose that men report feeling more anxious and depressed than "usual" during the first few months of sentence. At nine months reassessment such symptoms will either no longer be unusual or will have dissipated with adjustment to prison. Prisons are not very pleasant places and it is hardly surprising that we have found a large number of men who complain of feeling anxious and depressed.

Table 64   Occasions Times Groups Interaction Effect for '6 months or less' men compared with '7 + months' men'

	0-6 months (50)				7 + Months (85)				F	
	Initial		9 Months		Initial		9 Months		2 way	
	Mean	s.d.	Mean	s.d.	Mean	s.d.	Mean	s.d.	A of V	p<
GHQ score	21·4	15·5	15·5	15·2	15·9	16·2	16·3	16·7	6·46	0·01

We feel that in regard to the planning of psychiatric facilities to meet this degree of disturbance, it would be better to broaden the scope of our vision beyond the specifically psychiatric sphere, to the area of prison management. In our view it would be pointless to suggest some form of linear increase in the number of part-time psychiatrists employed by the Prison Department to match the degree of disturbance evident in any particular prison. We do not wish to suggest that prisons alone are responsible for all or even the major part of the high level of disorder found within their walls. Prisons have to cope with many men who are extremely disturbed, and very disturbing, but this simply serves to bring us back to our point regarding management. We would suggest that, as they are organised at present, many prisons exacerbate the problems already inherent in the population of men with whom they have to cope. Seen in these terms, our findings have considerable relevance for the general question of prison management.

Previous Psychiatric History

Something in the region of 20% of our sample reported that they had had either out-patient or in-patient treatment outside prison. Only 6% (37) reported that they had received both types of treatment. A further 6% said that they had only in-patient care and 6% claimed that they had been treated only as out-patients.

This is the best indication we have of the size of the population which is shared by both prisons and psychiatric hospitals. A number of these men, we do not know how many, will alternate between prisons and hospitals on a regular basis. Perhaps their numbers justify a rationalisation of the system which presently exists whereby all aspects of the Prison Medical Service operate independently of the National Health Service.

Some Illustrative Cases

All these points about cases, demand for services, prevalence of disorder and so on appear a bit academic when put in terms of figures alone, so by way of illustration we will end with three vignettes of cases taken from our control or normal sample (see Chapter 9) who presented psychiatric problems.

Case A

A 35-year-old man serving 10 years for rape. As with several rapists we have seen in this study and elsewhere he proved very difficult to interview. At first he refused to be interviewed at all saying that people only wanted to accuse him of things he hadn't done. His prison record indicated that he was frequently in trouble for aggressive verbal outbursts. Eventually he calmed down and agreed to chat at which point he poured out a torrent of anxieties and guilt. He scored very highly on the GHQ (40) expressing suicidal ideas. He talked of his fetishism and his previous convictions for stealing women's underwear from clothes lines. He also described marked obsessive symptoms including checking and indecisiveness and described himself as a perfectionist. He was very reluctant to talk about his offence but related it to difficulties with his wife which he then took out on a strange woman. At the beginning of his sentence he had been offered psychiatric treatment but he turned it down; however, it was clear at interview that if his initial hostility could be overcome and his ambivalent feelings brought into the open he would have been a suitable candidate for individual psychotherapy. Predictably he failed to keep in touch with us during our follow-up.

Case B

A 30-year-old man serving 5 years for armed robbery. He was coming to the end of his sentence but he had lost a great deal of remission because of his continually violent behaviour. Boastfully he told of how many people he had attacked, severely hurting some of them. He described how a small slight would send him into a rage which he could not then control. He only scored 10 on his GHQ with only a few neurotic symptoms appearing. However, at interview it was clear that he had a multitude of neurotic symptoms and some very defensive ideas amounting at times to paranoid feelings. The interview was not easy at first because he was convinced he was being set up for certification and transport to Broadmoor (hence his low GHQ score). In spite of all his difficulties and his recognition of them, he refused to consider the idea of psychiatry. It has never actually been offered to him, presumably because of his lack of motivation. He did agree that a prison like Grendon might suit him, however, and it is possible that his motivation would improve if he were sent there. When pressed about the nature of his problems he said "I've traced my ancestry back to the sixteenth century and my family has a disease of the blood, still, I suppose blood circulates through the brain".

Case C

Another man who had a low score (12) on his GHQ. He was serving 18 months for burglary and illustrates the difficulties of seeing a prison sentence in isolation. He was a man of 23 who had spent most of his life since school in institutions of one sort or another. A year or more had been spent in various mental hospitals which he usually begged and pleaded to accommodate him, only to discharge himself soon after arrival. At interview he talked endlessly of his suicide attempts, his hypochondriacal pains, his phobia of dying (and hence sleeping), his constant taking of his own pulse. His motivation for prison psychiatric treatment was very high, indeed he had written to his M.P. about it. However, he has been rejected on every sentence on grounds of untreatability. It would be hard to argue that a short course of psychiatric treatment, or even Grendon would change him very much. What came across so clearly at interview was the chronic and crippling nature of this man's neurotic disorder and therefore his need for consistent help on both sides of the prison wall.

Summary and Conclusions

We added a psychiatric component to a prison census carried out by the Home Office Research Unit in February 1972. Rather than carry out a straightforward diagnostic survey, we decided to try and identify the proportion of men who could be regarded as psychiatric cases in practical terms. A series of questionnaires was sent out to 811 men. They contained three major components which we regarded as crucial in determining case status; current mental state, desire for treatment and previous psychiatric history. Thirteen per cent of our 10% sample, 106 men in all, were interviewed by a team of psychiatrists. At the end of each interview the psychiatrist made a decision about case-worthiness. Using these interviews, we established questionnaire criteria which allowed us correctly to identify 85% of cases in our interviewed population. These criterion items were then used to identify cases in the total census group and we found that about one-third of the population could be regarded as cases using this method of identification.

Because of the conceptual problems involved in case identification we also examined our data in terms of desire for treatment, manifest pathology, and psychiatric history, independently. We found that about one in three men were willing to have psychiatric help in prison. There was some evidence, however, to suggest that there was a discrepancy between their expectations of treatment and the real nature of psychiatric practice. Nevertheless, the salient point of this finding, in our view, is that a large amount of goodwill exists towards psychiatry and we feel that this could be made use of. We concluded that a large amount of psychological disturbance exists in the prison population. Although we could not distinguish between the abnormality inherent in the population and the specific contribution made to manifest pathology by imprisonment itself, we believe that the latter factor certainly contributed to the anxiety and depression which existed. We think that our findings have relevance for the wider aspects of prison management. We found that about one in five men in our sample had had previous psychiatric treatment in the National Health Service.

CHAPTER 12

Psychiatric Data from the Census Questionnaire

Whilst the main purpose of the census was to establish the extent of the demand and need for psychiatric services in prisons, the information which was collected also enabled us to examine specific problem areas. This chapter is divided broadly into three sub-sections. The first deals with the relationships between sentence length and the material collected in the census. The second section comprises the work done on addictions and compulsions (drugs, alcohol and gambling) and the final part of the chapter is a report on the relationship between type of offence (and offender) and neurotic symptomatology.

1. Sentence Length and Psychiatric Characteristics

For administrative purposes, the Prison Department divides the prison population into three separate sentence groups (i) short-term men, i.e. those men serving under 19 months; (ii) medium term prisoners, i.e. men with sentences between 19 and 48 months, and (iii) long termers, defined as being those men serving sentences of over four years. The census questionnaires were therefore analysed with a view to seeing whether these three groups differed in psychiatric characteristics.

In the first place, it was noted that medium-term men produced a higher response rate to our forms than did the men in the other two groups, 85% compared with 72% for short-term men and 75% for long-sentence men. An administrative explanation exists to explain the relatively poor performance of the short-term group in that they were statistically less likely to have received our forms because of their release date. Indeed, of the 23 men who were due for release within a few days of the date of our census, 19 were serving sentences of less than 19 months. However, no reason can be found to account for the difference in response rate between medium- and long-term prisoners.

As might have been expected, both age and the length of time in prison on present sentence were factors on which the groups differed (Table 65).

When the men were asked whether they had ever (on this or previous sentences) had psychiatric treatment in prison there was no significant difference between their responses; 7% of the short-term, 8% of the medium-term men and 13% of the long termers reported that they had had such treatment. But the three groups did differ in the extent to which they currently wanted treatment: desire for treatment increased with sentence length (Table 66). Whilst only one-third of the short-term group stated that they wanted treatment almost half (48%) of the long-term group made a positive response to this question. A similar but more pronounced trend was also found in regard to the question of whether or not a man would like to have gone to Grendon, but this may have been connected with the fact that Grendon was known not to take men with short sentences.

The three groups also differed in their attitudes to psychiatry and to crime. As a group the short term men were less inclined than the other two groups to express desire for psychiatric treatment as reflected by the AP scale. There was also a tendency for sentence length to relate to more socially desirable responses in terms of the AC scale (Table 67).

Perhaps the most interesting feature of our results was the relative lack of distinctiveness between the various administrative groups in terms of the variables which reflect psychological disturbance. For example, the groups presented very similar distributions in terms of their GHQ and SRSS responses and reported no differences in relation to their drug taking, gambling behaviour and attempted suicides. There was a tendency for men serving long sentences to report less problem drinking than medium-sentence men, a figure of 8% compared with 14%. Both these groups reported less problem drinking than the short term group, where 21% of the sample said that they had such a problem. The difference between the three groups was significant ($X^2 = 11·20$ p < 0·001). To some extent this marked difference may be due to the effect of a longer time in prison serving to blur the memory of drinking as being a problem for the individual.

Table 65

	Short Term		Medium Term		Long Term		F	p<
	Mean	s.d.	Mean	s.d.	Mean	s.d.		
Months served so far*	3·7	2·8 (217)	9·9	6·5 (273)	29·8	24·0 (136)	7·3	0·001
Age	30·1	8·5 (217)	31·2	8·3 (274)	33·7	9·2 (138)	7·3	0·001

*Data missing for 3 men.

Table 66   Desire for Treatment and Desire for Grendon

| | Desire for treatment* | | | | Desire for Grendon** | | | |
	Yes	No	X^2	$p<$	Yes	No	X^2	$p<$
Short term	71 (33%)	146			45 (21%)	172		
Medium term	102 (38%)	167	8·02	0·01	72 (27%)	194	11·20	0·01
Long term	67 (49%)	70			55 (41%)	80		

*Data missing for 6 men.
**Data missing for 11 men.

Table 67   Attitude to Psychiatry and Attitude to Crime

| | Attitude to Psychiatry* | | | | Attitude to Crime** | | | |
	Mean	s.d.	(N)	F	Mean	s.d.	(N)	F
Short term	15·5	5·4	(212)		12·6	4·3	(208)	
Medium term	16·9	4·9	(266)	4·7	13·3	4·1	(265)	5·4
Long term	16·6	5·3	(135)	$p<0.025$	14·1	4·2	(134)	$p<0.01$

*Data missing for 16 men.
**Data missing for 22 men.

Whatever the explanation, it was interesting that the proportion of problem drinkers in the three groups bore an inverse relationship to the proportion of men in each group who expressed a wish to have treatment.

2. Illegal Drug Taking

Questions were included in the Medical History questionnaire (Appendix 13) concerning the prisoners' drug-taking activities. They were asked:

Have you ever taken drugs other than those prescribed by the doctor? Yes/No
If "yes" — please tick which ones:
Hashish or cannabis (pot)
LSD (acid)

Amphetamines (blues, etc.) or methedrine
Pethidine
Cocaine
Others (please state which)

In the reliability check that was carried out on the 90 men who had completed questionnaires and also been seen by a psychiatrist the correlations in Table 68 were obtained.

Table 68   Type of Drugs Reported
Questionnaire and Interview Correlations (N = 90)

LSD	0·85
Amphetamines	0·77
Cannabis	0·71
Other drugs	0·71
Opiates	0·47

On the whole the agreement seems quite good. However, since the doctors were able to go into greater detail in their interviews and discuss the varieties of drugs as well as the frequency with which they had been taken, it was not surprising to find some discrepancies in the men's replies. There were nine individuals who admitted verbally that they had been involved with drugs at some time, while failing to report this on their forms. Conversely, there were three men who denied any such experience to the doctor, but admitted it in writing. It seems likely, therefore, that a small proportion of the group which we have labelled "non-drug-takers" correctly belong to the drug-taking sample. This is another illustration of the point that using both questionnaire and interview rather than one or the other will reveal more positive information. However, since this should have served to minimise any differences found, it is unlikely that the results discussed below would have been materially affected.

Altogether according to the information received from the 629 forms which were returned suitable for coding, 199 men (32%) had taken drugs illegally at some time, 420 (67%) specifically denied doing so, and 10 (2%) were not prepared to answer the questions. Experimentation with some sort of cannabis was clearly the most common activity reported: no less than 179 prisoners (90% of the drug-takers) ticked this, and an additional man told the doctor he had smoked hashish although not admitting it on his questionnaire. Of this group, 47 individuals had apparently confined themselves to cannabis, i.e. 23% of those we have considered as drug takers.

We also analysed the data of the prisoners taking drugs illegally to discover how, if at all, those who admitted breaking the law in this respect differed from the rest in terms of the other information they gave on their questionnaires. The factors which were found to distinguish significantly between the two groups are listed below in Table 69.

The drug abusers were, on the whole, young men: nearly three-quarters of them were less than 30 years old on the day of the census. They more often reported a history of out-patient psychiatric treatment and/or hospitalisation, and heavy drinking. Their scores on the neuroticism scales were significantly higher than those of the non-drug-takers, and they expressed stronger motivation for psychiatric treatment, and less towards giving up their criminal behaviour. These men had obtained psychological help while in prison more frequently than the other offenders in the survey, and a higher proportion of them currently wished for such treatment either in Grendon or elsewhere.

Individuals who reported some involvement with illegal drugs thus seemed to constitute a more neurotic and currently unhappy set of men than those who denied such experimentation. Since on all but one* of the eight variables used to distinguish "cases", the drug takers differed significantly from the non-drug-takers; we found that 44% of the former compared with only 25% of the latter ($X^2 = 21·35$, p $= <0·001$) were identified as "cases" by our case identification procedure.

It was thought that men who said they had restricted themselves to some variety of cannabis might be less likely to emerge as cases than the rest of the drug-takers. Accordingly the 45 individuals in the "cannabis only" group were isolated from the 152 who had tried amphetamines or combinations of drugs. Table 70 shows the proportion of "cases" in the three resultant groups.

These figures confirm that in our survey those whose drug activities were limited to cannabis were less likely to have been picked out as cases than the 152 men taking other drugs illegally. However, they still displayed a higher level of apparent psychiatric disturbance than did the prisoners who denied all illegal drug-taking.

---

*Suicide attempt: 39 (20%) drug-takers reported a suicide attempt compared with 56 (14%) non-drug-takers $X^2 = 3·70$ p $<0·10$.

Table 69 Differences between Drug-takers and Non-Drug-takers (data missing in 10 cases)

	Drug-takers (199)			Non Drug-takers (420)			X^2	p<
	Yes	%	NK	Yes	%	NK		
Aged under 30 years	142	(71)		183	(44)		40·69	0·001
History of OP Psychiatric treatment	37	(19)		38	(9)	2	10·53	0·01
History of IP Psychiatric treatment	32	(16)		41	(10)	1	4·55	0·05
Heavy drinker	66	(33)	1	85	(20)	2	11·58	0·001
Prison psychiatric treatment ever	33	(17)		23	(6)		18·95	0·001
Psychiatric treatment desired now	110	(55)		123	(29)	7	35·92	0·001
Wish for Grendon prison (including those currently there)	81*	(41)	2	83*	(20)	8	20·73	0·001
	*6 currently in Grendon			*9 currently in Grendon				

	No.	Mean	s.d.	No.	Mean	s.d.	t	p<
SRSS	161	7·9	6·8	347	5·7	5·9	3·73	0·01
GHQ	197	19·1	15·7	405	14·4	14·2	3·70	0·01
AP	197	17·1	5·5	408	16·0	5·0	2·63	0·01
AC	196	12·1	4·3	404	13·8	4·1	4·75	0·01

Table 70 Number of Cases Identified

	Amphetamines only or more than one drug (152)		Cannabis only (45*)		Non-drug-takers (408*)		X^2 due to linear regression	$p <$
	No.	%	No.	%	No.	%		
Cases	70	(46)	16	(36)	101	(25)	24·01	0·001

*2 men could not be classified.
*12 men could not be classified.

3. Drinking Behaviour

The medical history questionnaire also contained two items which were intended to give a crude outline of the drinking behaviour of the 10% sample of men serving custodial sentences. None of the individuals who came into the survey was imprisoned for non-payment of fines, and none who completed the questionnaire had been sentenced to less than two months. It follows, therefore, that many men whose drinking resulted in a short period of imprisonment will have been excluded.

The prisoners were asked to answer "yes" or "no" to the following:

"Are you a heavy drinker (of alcohol)?"

"Do you have a drink problem?"

Of the 811 men who were circularised with the initial questionnaire, 628 replied to at least one of the items on drinking. Of these, 467 (74%) denied both heavy and problem drinking, 67 (11%) reported that although they drank heavily it did not constitute a problem for them and 94 (15%) rated themselves as problem drinkers. These figures indicate that just over a quarter of the census sample were reporting heavy and/or problem drinking. There were 155 prisoners who acknowledged heavy drinking and 88 (57%) of these considered they had an alcohol problem. Possibly because the questions could have been interpreted as referring to the present situation, a small number of men (six in all) denied high consumption of alcohol while saying "yes" to a drinking problem.

As a result of the study by Dr. Paul Bowden (see p. 213) it was decided to follow the same divisions in discussing the main sample. The prisoners have therefore been divided into problem, heavy, and not heavy categories, according to their replies on the written questionnaires. We are probably safe in assuming that the individuals who fall into the problem group could also be termed heavy drinkers, although as indicated above they did not invariably acknowledge this to be the case.

There was a tendency for the problem drinkers to be serving lesser sentences than the other two groups and also to have been in prison for a shorter time by the date of the census. Many of the individuals whose drinking is seriously affecting their behaviour may become involved in relatively petty crimes, rather than committing the more sophisticated type of offence. It is also very likely that the longer a man has been shut away from society, the less he remembers any problems he may have had when alcohol was available to him. The figures are given in Table 71.

Tabel 71   Length of Current Sentence and Time Spent in Prison on This Sentence

	Problem Drinkers			Heavy Drinkers			Not Heavy Drinkers			F	p<
	N	Mean	s.d.	N	Mean	s.d.	N	Mean	s.d.		
Sentence in months	92	27·8	25·1	63	36·8	28·8	440*	35·7	29·5	3·10	0·05
Months served	94	8·4	10·8	65	11·6	10·2	465	12·9	16·8	3·35	0·04

*Lifers excluded.

When we compared all abnormal drinkers with the rest we found a uniformly higher level of problems and aberrant behaviour amongst the heavy as opposed to normal drinkers. However, the breakdown into three instead of two groups produced less clear cut results. Tables 72 and 73 below list all the variables on which significant differences were apparent. The first part of Table 72 gives those which showed a linear trend with the problem drinkers being at one end of the scale and the normal drinkers at the other, and the second half those for which the chi-square value distinguished between the groups, but no linear trend was found. Table 73 gives the result of the two tests administered to assess the level of neurotic symptoms amongst the prisoners, and the two attitudinal tests. The receipt of both in-patient and out-patient treatment in a mental hospital, and the admission of heavy gambling, show a distinct trend between the three groups, with the problem drinkers having the highest positive response on each of these questions, and the not heavy the lowest. There was also an association between drinking excessively and taking cannabis. Reported suicidal behaviour did not show a meaningful relationship to alcohol, although it might be that the heavy (no-problem) group also tend to deny suicidal attempts. The neuroticism questionnaires show the expected graded relationship with excessive drinking and the reported attitudes to psychiatry fit in with this. Attitudes to criminality on the other hand are "worse" among the heavy (no problem) drinkers than either of the other two groups. There is then a small suggestion that as Bowden has postulated the heavy (no problem) group are different from problem drinkers. Whether this is in terms of under-reporting problems, or in terms of being more criminal and less psychiatric cannot be settled from these data. It is worth recalling that only 43 per cent of the heavy (no problem) drinkers were consistent between interview and questionnaire.

The three groups were similar in terms of whether they had ever been given psychiatric treatment while in custody, either at Grendon Underwood or at some other prison. This was true also when we compared all abnormal drinkers with the rest. However, as we can see from Table 74 below, both in respect of a general desire for some sort of psychological help in prison, and the more specific wish to be treated in Grendon, there is a distinct linear trend, with the problem drinkers expressing the most interest in psychotherapy, and the normal drinkers the least.

Table 72 Differences found between Prisoners According to their Reporting of Drinking Behaviour

	Problem Drinkers N = 94			Heavy Drinkers N = 67			Not Heavy Drinkers N = 467			X^2 due to linear regression	P <
	Yes	%	NK	Yes	%	NK	Yes	%	NK		
OP Psychiatric treatment	19	(20)		11	(16)		46	(10)	2	9.0	0.01
IP Psychiatric treatment	21	(22)	1	8	(12)		48	(10)	1	9.6	0.01
Heavy gambling	24	(26)		10	(15)	1	43	(9)	4	19.7	0.001
										X^2d.f.2	p <
Gambling problem	20	(21)		3	(5)		32	(7)	5	19.5	0.001
Cannabis ever	34	(36)	3	28	(42)		116	(25)	6	10.6	0.01
Hallucinogens	12	(13)	3	16	(24)		54	(12)	6	6.5	0.05
Attempted suicide	29	(31)	3	6	(9)	3	65	(14)	15	18.2	0.001

Table 73 Neuroticism and Attitudinal Tests

| | Problem Drinkers | | | Heavy Drinkers | | | Not Heavy Drinkers | | | | |
	N	Mean	s.d.	N	Mean	s.d.	N	Mean	s.d.	F	p<
SRSS	74*	10·4	7·9	60*	7·3	5·7	378*	5·6	5·9	19·41	0·001
GHQ	92	22·0	16·8	67	18·0	14·3	451	14·5	14·2	10·72	0·001
AP	91	18·8	4·8	67	16·1	5·4	454	15·9	5·1	12·11	0·001
AC	92	13·2	4·2	67	11·4	4·7	447	13·5	4·1	7·40	0·001

*SRSS had a poor response rate (see p. 212).

Table 74   Desire for Psychiatric Treatment in Prison

	Problem Drinkers 2 men in Grendon N = 94			Heavy Drinkers 2 men in Grendon N = 67			Not Heavy Drinkers 11 men in Grendon N = 467			X^2 due to linear regression	p<
	Yes	%	NK	Yes	%	NK	Yes	%	NK		
Treatment desired during current sentence	59	(63)	1	31	(46)		148	(32)	6	34·2	0·001
Wish for Grendon now (including those currently there)	39	(42)		22	(33)		107	(23)	10	14·1	0·001

4. Gambling

The men were asked on the questionnaire to say if they gambled heavily, and if this activity posed any problem for them. There were 622 prisoners who gave an answer to at least one of these questions, and of these 46 (7%) admitted both heavy and problem gambling, 9 men (1%) said that although they did not think they gambled heavily it was a problem nonetheless, and 31 (5%) reported heavy gambling only. On the strength of these figures it would not appear that heavy and/or problem gambling was particularly prevalent in our sample of prisoners: in all we found only 86 individuals (14%) who answered affirmatively to at least one of these questions.

5. Factor Analysis

The term "criminal" is often used without qualification, implying that "criminals" represent a class of people who are similar to one another and distinct from other people. Evidence for the distinctive nature of the criminal is usually produced by using populations of men or women who are imprisoned. It can be readily demonstrated, for example, that, as a group, prisoners produce different distributions from the non-prisoner population in terms of variables such as social class and age and it has also been shown more recently that they produce different distributions for personality dimensions such as extroversion and neuroticism (Eysenck, 1964).

However, such distinguishing features as have been found to exist hardly justify the assumptions of homogeneity and separateness which are implicit in the non-qualified use of the term "criminal". In the first place, the amount of overlap which occurs between the criminal and non-criminal groups is enormous, particularly in relation to the personality dimensions referred to and, in the second place, a large amount of variation exists within the criminal (prisoner) population. We felt therefore that it would be worthwhile taking a closer look at the relationship between neurotic symptomatology and types of offending.

All the information which had been collected in the course of the census was put together with the social and criminal information collected by the Home Office Research Unit. A principal components analysis was carried out using all these variables and, when the two principal components of the factor matrix were orthoganally rotated, the dimensions produced reflected (a) psychiatric disturbance and (b) recidivism.

The position and loading of a number of relevant variables on these dimensions is produced in Fig. 1. As will be seen there, the component represented by the vertical dimension is defined by variables such as "amount of previous custodial treatment" and "number of previous larceny offences". The horizontal dimension is used to represent the psychiatric component in the analysis and is defined by manifest neurotic pathology and motivation for treatment.

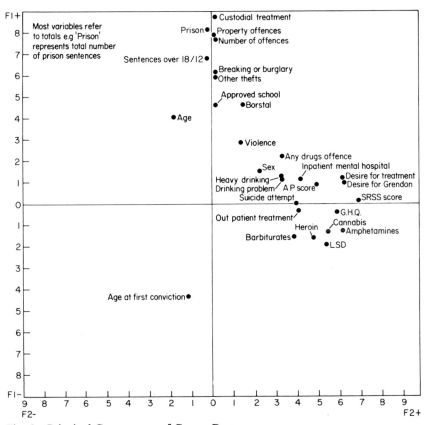

Fig. 1   Principal Components of Census Data.

The position of the various categories of offending in regard to these dimensions is of interest as there is a trend for property offences to load highly on the "recidivist" dimension and not at all on the psychiatric. Other types of offences such as violence, sex and especially drugs, all load more highly on the psychiatric dimension and are less closely linked with a history of recidivism. However, it has to be remembered that these variables refer to the number of offences committed and not to actual offenders. In order to clarify the position with regard to offenders, we divided those men who had replied to our census forms into four groups on the basis of their predominant offending pattern. These were property, drugs, sex, and violence. Three raters were used for this grouping procedure and a very high degree of inter-rater agreement was achieved by ensuring that each man was assessed independently by at least two raters. Any differences which did occur were discussed, and a consensus decision was reached. It was found that when property offenders were compared with the other three categories of offender, the distribution of the groups differed in terms of the self-rating symptom scale ($t = 2.06$ $p < 0.05$), the property offenders having lower scores on average.

The point which emerges from all this is a simple one which is often forgotten, namely that it is meaningless to talk of prisoners or criminals as if those terms represented homogeneous groups of people in regard to psychological abnormality. Our analysis demonstrated that within the prison population anxiety and depression are associated more closely with certain types of offence and offender than with others, but nevertheless enormous variations occurred within the various groups. At the level of the individual, general statements about the relationship between neuroticism and crime lose something of their value and their authority, and it is, of course, with the individual that sentencers and prison authorities have to deal.

Summary

1. There were few psychiatric differences between the short, medium and long-term offenders, although the long term men were older and more desirous of psychiatric treatment.

2. In the census 32% of the men admitted illegal drug-taking at some time, experimenting with cannabis being the commonest activity. The drug-takers were much more likely to be "cases" using the criteria previously devised (Chapter 11). This was still true when cannabis only takers were compared with non-drug-takers.

3. Seventy-four per cent of the census sample denied both heavy and problem drinking, 14% described themselves as problem drinkers. There was a tendency for these problem drinkers to be serving shorter

sentences, they showed much more psychiatric symptomatology, and were more likely to have tried taking cannabis.

4. Only 14% of the census sample reported either problem or heavy gambling.

5. A factor analysis of all the census data produced two independent components of psychiatric disturbance and recidivism. When the prisoners were divided into four groups, property offenders, drug offenders, sex offenders, and violent offenders, the property offenders were distinguished from the other groups by a lower neuroticism score.

CHAPTER 13

Final Remarks

Research Techniques

For the most part the reader will draw his own conclusions about the methods used in this series of studies. However, we believe that we should re-emphasise three important aspects of the research methodology at this point.

(a) Control Studies

It is difficult to conceive how a research team could have been better placed than we were to collect a control sample matched to our cohort. Indeed, by most standards, we achieved remarkably good matching. However, we were not able to match on several crucial variables, the most important being motivation for treatment. This of course invalidated a direct comparison between the two groups. What should be emphasised is that if we had not measured motivation we would not have known that the groups differed in this respect. On how many other crucial variables, which we did not measure, did the groups differ? How many other matched control studies suffer from this same deficiency?

In theory random allocation might have been a method of overcoming the difficulties we encountered in matching, but Clarke and Cornish (1972) have demonstrated the inherent defects of using random allocation as a means of evaluating penal treatments. They highlight five main difficulties. Firstly, the ethical problems raised by the practitioners doing the treatment and hence the difficulty of obtaining consent for such a trial. Next, the confusion caused by the variety of goals attributable to any institution; this makes the choice of one or two simple success criteria fallacious. In this study, for example, we have been examining improvements in health, changes in attitude, and re-conviction. We could have examined many others. Can all these be controlled for simultaneously? Thirdly, random allocation between the institution to be measured and another system presents large practical problems. In this study at what point would the random allocation have taken place? Before the man's motivation had been tested or after? What happens psychologically to motivated men selected for Grendon, who are rejected capriciously at the last moment? Would not resentment affect the result? What happens alternatively, if men are selected before their motivation is tested? How do we analyse the group who drop out because of lack of motivation? Fourthly, even if random allocation could be achieved the results would not be very much more value than those obtained by a simple descriptive study. Any institution is a complex unique system and the effective variables (if any) cannot be identified with precision. Some individual members of staff may be powerful therapeutic factors. Hence it is not possible to generalise to other situations in the same way as it is, for example, when a large sample of patients suffering from a readily identifiable discrete disease is shown to benefit from a particular chemical. Fifthly, institutions change with time, even as the experiment progresses. At the end of the experiment it will be impossible to test for the significance of these changes even if they have been measured. We would add a sixth reservation to this list. The process of random allocation, the experiment, the observation, changes the nature of the treatment programme and so the original concept is altered anyway. In the 1930s the now famous Hawthorn effect was noted. Simply by paying attention to a particular group of workers, by observing them, their productive levels were changed (Roethlinberger and Dickson, 1939). These observational effects are almost certainly present in institutional research and many other such intrusions would be introduced by a random allocation procedure. In the event our lack of a satisfactory control group was not a disadvantage. We were able to describe the systems used, and we were able to note some of the changes which took place in the men. It soon became evident that the type of regime applied in Grendon is largely concerned with the social adjustment of an individual to a prison environment. It would be an unwarranted assumption indeed to equate social adjustments in prison, attitude change and a reduction of symptoms with post-release variables such as a reduced crime rate, better work rate, and so on. These factors take place outside of prison and are at least as affected by the post release environment as by the pre-release environment.

(b) Re-conviction Data

It follows from the above that we do not regard re-conviction as a satisfactory test of the efficacy of Grendon. Undoubtedly many people assume that one of the aims of any prison, including Grendon, is to prevent a man committing further offences after release. Furthermore, many people expect Grendon to be better than other prisons in this regard. We believe that this is to over-simplify the issue and to misunderstand the potentials of institutions. Prisons have many functions: punishment, deterrence, and containment, must be high on the list. Fulfilment of a public sense of justice and a need for retribution is surely the main reason that we go on paying for a system of total institutions that have in studies throughout the world been shown to be harmful. Prisonisation (as Clemmer (1940) called it) seems to be an almost inevitable consequence of prolonged imprisonment; certainly many of the Grendon subjects could be said to be suffering from it at the time of their transfer to Grendon. Prisonisation is a negative factor detracting from a man's ability to cope with society. It is hardly something we would inflict on someone if our first concern was with "rehabilitation" or the prevention of further convictions. One interpretation of our results of the Grendon study is that the therapeutic community reduces or eliminates the prisonisation effect of previous imprisonment; a remarkable effect if that is correct.

Even if the prevention of anti-social behaviour were the main concern of the penal system, then re-conviction figures would still be a poor guide to efficacy. As we have seen, re-conviction does not tell us much about a man's behaviour; the best way to keep the re-conviction figures down is to have an inefficient police force! Secondly, if re-conviction is a good guide to "success" in the broadest sense we cannot necessarily attribute that success to the last spell of imprisonment.

If crime prevention is to be a realistic exercise, then attention must be paid to the environment in which a potential offender finds him or herself. Re-conviction figures, if they have any meaning at all, are a better guide to the effectiveness of after-care arrangements, than of the experiences of an institution left behind. If, say, an alcoholic were admitted to a hospital, did well in treatment, and was then discharged to a distant part of the country, would it be appropriate to test the efficacy of that hospital treatment by investigating the patient for relapse of drinking two or three years later? The answer must be "No": the hospital treatment is effective if it gets the man off the drink, gets him thinking about his situation, and prepares him for discharge to an environment where he will be sorely tempted. If that phase is successful, further success will depend on a number of issues including close follow-up, and good out-patient work. The relapse rate after two or three years is probably an indicator of the efficacy of the after-care arrangements if it is a legitimate measure of treatment at all. So it is with a prison psychiatric service: all that can be done in the institution is to cope with the present and prepare for discharge. After discharge the only therapeutic agent available is the follow-up service provided.

(c) Previous Evaluative Studies

Many previous attempts have been made to evaluate penal institutions in terms of re-conviction data. In view of the approach we have adopted and the uniqueness of Grendon we do not propose to review that literature. For reviews the reader is referred to Martinson (1972), Cornish and Clarke (1975), Brody (1976). Suffice it to say that the overwhelming conclusion is that a wide variety of institutional management systems do not influence re-conviction rates.

Only two previous studies have examined Grendon. Again both of these have been in terms of re-conviction data; neither has been published. In essence the first study finds no relationship between going to Grendon and a lowered re-conviction rate. It has been reviewed by one of us elsewhere (Robertson, 1974). The second study was carried out by a university student (see Gray, 1973b). He believed that he found the length of stay in Grendon to have a significant relationship with conviction. Unfortunately, however, his dissertation did not employ sufficiently rigorous statistical techniques to sub-stantiate this view. His unpublished paper has also been reviewed by one of us elsewhere (Robertson, 1974).

(d) Groups v. Individuals

The third research issue we wish to emphasise is obvious and yet so fundamental, and so frequently neglected that it deserves restatement. The statistical analyses have been applied to groups. Within those groups there are wide variations; it is always possible to find a number of individuals completely defying the group trend. Clinicians, and the processes of law, tend to be concerned with individuals not groups. The rules and results which apply to groups do not apply to individuals. It is one thing to say that a group of men with certain characteristics can be expected to change in a particular way by a specified form of treatment but any individual with those characteristics may defy all expectations. All dynamic particles and objects show some degree of randomness. Within a group the randomness of one individual is partially counteracted by the randomness of others, for the individual chance is of great significance. Furthermore, intelligent individuals can take decisions to go against group trends.

With modern data collecting and statistical techniques the reproductive behaviour of large groups of people can be predicted with remarkable accuracy. What we cannot do, nor will ever be able to do, is to predict when John Smith will fall in love, whom he will marry, and when his children will be conceived. He contributes to the group data but he is an individual making individual decisions.

In the past, criminology has paid a lot of attention to prediction using statistical techniques. Only gradually has it become quite clear that however sophisticated the statistical technique, it cannot predict the behaviour of an individual. In this project we want to emphasise that our group results are just that, they give us information about Grendon, about the population receiving psychotherapy at Wormwood Scrubs, about the prison population but they do not give us clinical information about individuals.

Psychiatry and Crime

One dangerous effect of a book such as this could be to advance the notion that criminal behaviour and psychiatric disorder are inextricably intertwined, or that the correct management for criminals is a course of psychiatric treatment. We hope that we have avoided these pitfalls and made it clear that we do not subscribe to either of these naive notions. Moreover, it cannot be emphasised too strongly that studies of prisoners do not tell us much about criminals. Prisoners are only a small selected sample of criminals. Most of us break the law from time to time, some of us get caught and are then designated criminals. Only a very few of us get sent to prison.

Nevertheless, we did demonstrate that prisoners show a lot of psychiatric symptoms. We found that approximately one-third of the sentenced population could be defined as "cases" using our criteria, over one-third of the prisoners wanted psychiatric treatment, 32% had taken drugs (especially cannabis) illegally, a quarter reported either heavy or problem drinking, and 7% reported either heavy or problem gambling. One important prevalence we were not able to comment on is the level of psychosis among the sentenced men, although the data from our census (Table 60) suggest that it is a small problem in the order of 1-2% of the sentenced population.

What do these high prevalence levels of psychological disorder in prisons tell us? Not a lot on their own because some important issues are unknown. Firstly, we do not know whether these levels are exceptionally high ones as we do not have compatible data from a similar group of adult males outside of prison. Secondly, we do not know what contribution imprisonment makes to the genesis or alleviation of psychological problems. Thirdly it may well be that courts differentially select the neurotic, the inadequate, the handicapped for imprisonment. An earlier study by one of us indicated that the prevalence of epilepsy in H.M. prisons is above that in the general population (Gunn, 1977).

Throughout we have emphasised that nothing in our data suggests a general association between mental disorder and crime, nor between mental disorder and recidivism. Indeed, our factor analysis of the census data produced two independent factors which we have called "psychiatric disturbance" and "recidivism". However, the epilepsy study mentioned above did find associations between anti-social behaviour and the disorder in particular individuals. In the present study, too, we observed associations between criminal activities (e.g. sexual crimes) and psychiatric disorder in particular individuals. Everybody knows that a psychotic illness (or an episode of madness) can lead to bizarre, sometimes dangerous, sometimes anti-social behaviour. There are also complex relationships between psychological disorder in other individuals; Case 6 on p. 202 illustrates the story of a man whose numerous neurotic problems included sadism which in turn led him to violence. Our conclusion is that it is correct to assess the psychological component which may or may not contribute to anti-social behaviour in individual cases, but incorrect to make broad generalisations about the relationships between psychiatric disorder and crime or even about personality structure and crime.

The high number of cases we identified in our census survey raises three questions. Are our prisons being used as a form of mental hospital or asylum? Evidence from other sources suggests quite strongly that they are (Bowden, 1975a, Gunn, 1974). Secondly, how much neurosis is generated by the process of imprisonment? Some data on this are presented in Chapter 11. Thirdly, how legitimate is it to expect the prisons to carry a heavy load of psychiatric pathology? Is it reasonable to expect the prisons to take on a quasi-medical role so that it is possible for courts to send patients to prison in order to receive medical treatment? Clearly there are too many cases for the National Health Service, as currently constituted, to cope with, and equally clearly it is right for medical practitioners to minister to the medical needs of prisoners. In these circumstances it may be tempting to see the prisons as an alternative to the Health Service for some patients. Nothing in our study leads us to believe that this view should be encouraged.

Insofar as Grendon is of therapeutic benefit to its inmates we are not convinced that its results could only be obtained at Grendon or in a prison. Given that Grendon treatment is an entirely voluntary arrangement, there seems no good reason to suppose that similar treatment could not be available within the National Health Service. The fact that it is not is another matter, but it would seem to be a mis-use of justice simply to send people to prison because of the psychiatric care they may get when they are in prison.

Psychiatric Treatment in Prison

In this study we have concentrated upon psychotherapy within the prisons. We believe that we have demonstrated that the therapeutic community approach adopted in Grendon reduces neurotic symptoms, improves attitudes, and generally relieves the effects of prisonisation. We also believe that the data suggests that the group techniques employed at Wormwood Scrubs are more useful than the individual techniques. However, we have not commented on physical methods of psychiatric treatment (such as drugs and ECT) which are also used within prisons nor have we discussed hormonal treatments or behaviour therapies which are used for the treatment of sexual disorders. Brain surgery (amygdalectomy in particular) is almost never used in British prisons (Prewer, 1974) and therefore needs no discussion here although it would raise very serious ethical problems if it were to be used.

We found no evidence whatever of non-psychotic individuals being coerced into treatment. Transfer to Grendon requires a man's consent for example, and a man could request his transfer away from Grendon any time he wished. The main complaint we heard from the prisoners was that there is too little psychiatry available: more want it than can obtain it.

Whilst it is clear that the Northfield experiment of the Second World War (p. 23) inspired the current Grendon programme, and in that sense it is in a modern psychiatric tradition, we do not see anything exclusively medical in the current regime. No doubt a psychiatrist should be involved in a good therapeutic community programme, especially one that many precipitate breakdowns, uses drugs, or screens out the mentally ill; however, the day-to-day activities at Grendon were largely run by non-psychiatrists. There seems to be no reason why the principles of Grendon could not be extended to other prisons. Such units would need to be small and to have an above average staff ratio but they need not be as expensive as Grendon.

One of the greatest problems facing psychiatric treatment in prison is precisely that it is in prison. Many of the advances of modern psychiatry are related to the de-institutionalising of psychiatric care. Modern psychiatry may not yet have grasped how large a part of its work is concerned with the care of the chronic sick, but, in Britain at least, it has fully grasped that community care embracing sheltered accommodation, sheltered work, day care and out-patient care are the essentials of good treatment. Prisons are set apart from society, they have few or no links with local communities. In such a setting it is extremely difficult, if not impossible, to practice good modern psychiatry, especially the psychiatry of chronic disorders such as most neurotic prisoners present. The practitioners at both Wormwood Scrubs and at Grendon expressed frustration that they are dealing with a predetermined interlude in a man's life. However hard they try, and at Grendon they have a number of ingenious ways of getting round the problem, the medical and hospital staff at the two facilities cannot offer a comprehensive follow-up service nor take on their patients for long-term care where it really matters — in the community.

If, as we believe, most of the keys to offending behaviour lie in the community, it follows that we also believe that the prevention of behavioural problems in psychiatric patients must also take place in the community. In the past the problems of forensic psychiatry have been associated with institutions. Now, as general psychiatry puts more and more emphasis on community work, forensic psychiatry, which is after all a branch of general psychiatry, should do likewise. If forensic psychiatry in the community were to become a reality, then regimes such as Grendon could be linked to it by a flexible use of the parole system.

The Butler Report

In recent years the problems associated with the mentally abnormal offender have been increasing and by 1972 the government decided to set up a special committee under the chairmanship of Lord Butler to examine these problems. The report of this Committee was published in August 1975 (Home Office, DHSS 1975). It is a detailed and complex document which will have a profound effect on the practice of psychiatry in Britain. The report was published after our research was completed, hence the small amount of attention given to it.

Grendon prison is mentioned in the Butler Report but in disappointed tones. Previous reports by Gray (1973) and Newton (1971) are quoted as indicating that the re-conviction rate for prisoners leaving Grendon is much the same as for prisoners leaving other gaols, although with the reservation that "reconviction rates are not the only or even necessarily the most valuable yardstick for evaluating the success of an institution such as Grendon". Our own thoughts on this issue are set out earlier in this chapter and the research methodology of the particular studies mentioned has been examined by Robertson (1974). Our research in this book is referred to, but one of the obvious conclusions that follows is not drawn. The methods used at Grendon may have significant lessons for prison management in general and may be transferable (now that the methodology is clearly worked out) without necessarily being so expensive; indeed, the new unit being developed at Wormwood Scrubs (p. 155) and the "C" Wing at Parkhurst (Prewer, 1974) are examples of this already happening. It would be a pity if the Butler Report were to be read as discouraging this trend.

Some attention is paid by the Butler Committee to after-care arrangements, although they are more concerned with the after-care of NHS patients than of prisoners. They recognise the importance of the probation service in this work and give some impetus to the further development of hostel and / day training arrangements in the community. They also endorse a policy put forward by one of us (Gunn, 1971) for the setting up of special crisis walk-in, 24-hour clinics in large urban areas to give a service to potential offenders and families in distress at the moment of greatest need. Clearly the findings of the current project tend to endorse these recommendations. We would go further and say if we, as a community, are really concerned to help the mentally abnormal offender, if we are really concerned to prevent him "getting into trouble" and appearing in the re-conviction statistics, then we will pay maximum attention and give maximum resources to community services which will assist him. Offences are committed in the community in response to community situations; that does not necessarily mean that the community is responsible for crimes committed in its midst. Offenders, even mentally abnormal ones, carry that burden themselves. However, it is a burden which could be and ought to be shared to some extent if we are going to make any impact on offending behaviour. Institutions cannot develop powerful control mechanisms which extend in a mysterious fashion into an offender's post-discharge future. Individual officers at Grendon already offer more than an institutional service. When the ex-inmate in distress rings up his old wing officer and says "help" he may find that officer giving up his spare time to fly to the rescue, but such an *ad hoc* system cannot provide an extensive service; certainly no after-care service in England can be entirely linked to one institution. In the future we shall undoubtedly continue to use the prison service for punishment, for containment of the persistently dangerous, for the first stages of treatment of some mentally abnormal offenders. It will be our decision as a community, whether we also concern ourselves with crime prevention in the community; institutions cannot take that responsibility away from us.

Appendix 1

SOCIAL AND CRIMINAL HISTORY INTERVIEW

Each man was asked about his background, and his social and criminal history. The interview was conducted in association with the official prison file. The manual of instructions for the interview schedule itself is presented in Robertson (1974 Appendix 1, p. 365). The following areas of behaviour were among those covered by the schedule:

1. Criminal History

(a) Age at first court appearance.

(b) A detailed account of the number and nature of previous convictions including the present offence. A conviction was defined as an offence for which a man had been found guilty. Several convictions incurred at one court appearance were counted separately. Offences were categorised into eleven types: fraud, stealing, violence other than robbery, robbery, homicide, rape and attempted rape, sex other than rape, arson, drugs, drink and motoring.

(c) Length of current sentence.

(d) The length of time served in prisons, borstals or detention centres before present sentence (this was calculated and recorded in months and represented the *actual time* that a man had spent in either borstal or prison).

(e) Length of present sentence so far served.

2. Social Background

(a) The men were asked about the nature of their home life until the age of 15. Parental loss (maternal and paternal) was noted, as was the age at which this loss first took place. In the data presented in this book, loss was defined as separation from the parent figure for a period of at least one year before the age of 15; absence did not have to be continuous.

(b) The social class of the man and his father was recorded. The criterion for rating this variable differed between man and parent. The father's usual, or longest, occupation during the prisoner's childhood was categorised, while for the man himself, occupation at the time of the offence was coded.

(c) Educational status was measured in terms of whether the man had any formal qualifications. Four categories were used: no formal qualifications; technical or commercial certificates; "O" levels; "A" levels.

(d) Marital status at the time of the offence was recorded: there were 5 categories in this section: single, widowed, divorced, separated, and married. Among the married were included any men who had lived together with the same woman for over two years.

(e) The extent of a man's social responsibility was assessed by asking him whether or not he expected to be financially responsible for the upkeep of anyone other than himself after he was released from prison. The categories available for this rating were: wife; children; "other".

(f) Information was sought about the process whereby the men came to be receiving treatment. They were asked which prison they had come from and from where the pressure for referral had emanated.

Categories for "pressure for referral" were: court request; prison medical officer's opinion; outside pressure (e.g. probation officer), and other pressures.

Reliability

Extensive pilot work on the interview was carried out in Grendon before the study commenced in June 1971, and the final schedule was, in fact, the third edition of the instrument which had been produced.

The combined test/retest and inter-rater reliability of the schedule was assessed. A cross over design was adopted and a two week interval period was allowed between interview occasions. The second edition of the schedule produced the following results when 60 Grendon men were interviewed by this procedure:

1. Age: no discrepancies.
2. Age at first conviction: 6 discrepancies.

These were caused by the fact that the raters were using a different criterion for this variable. A mutually agreeable definition was decided upon and this was written into the manual.

3. Nature and number of offences: a number of minor discrepancies were found to exist. As with the previous variable, the differences were due to lack of definition. The position as regards these variables was clarified and the agreed definitions put into the manual.

4. Length of present sentence: no discrepancies.
5. Length of time served on present sentence. Only one or two discrepancies arose with this variable, none of them amounting to differences of more than one month. Given the two week interval in between interviews it was decided to regard agreement between raters as satisfactory.

6. Variables relating to early home life and the existence and degree of parental loss were found to be highly reliable.

7. There was 90% agreement for the social class rating of man and father.

8. There was also 90% agreement with regard to marital status and there was complete agreement on the noting of categories for estimating degree of "social responsibility".

9. There was 90% agreement with regard to the "reason for referral" categories.

The final instrument used was therefore the end product of repeated examination of item content, and the information presented from the schedule is regarded as being reliable, in as much as it was produced independently of interviewer and time of interview.

Appendix 2

HEIM'S AH4 INTELLIGENCE TEST

This test was developed by Heim (1970): it attempts to provide an indication of general ability by assessing a person's verbal and numerical abilities on the one hand and his ability to manipulate spatial relationships on the other.

The test is divided into two parts and, according to Heim, it aims to "incorporate as many different biases and principles as is consistent with a reasonably short test". Part I consists of 65 questions which are biased towards verbal and numerical abilities. [These items include "verbal opposites, numerical series, verbal analogies, simple numerical computations and synonyms".] Part II is made up of 65 questions all of which have a diagrammatic bias [and involve "analogies, sames, subtractions, series and superimpositions"]. All answers are in the form of multiple choice alternatives with five possible solutions being provided for each problem.

Test performance is measured by totalling Parts I and II, although separate norms exist for both halves of the test. Deductive reasoning underlies most of the test items and in Part I the testee is also expected to be able to understand the meanings of certain fairly simple words. The first part of the test is more dependent than the second upon educational factors. Heim reports correlations between the two parts of the test which range from 0·60 (110 university students) to 0·81 (1414 industrial subjects).

1. Reliability

Test-retest — 0·92.

Heim obtained this result using a population of 100 industrial subjects who were retested after one month.

2. Validity

(a) *Criterion Related*

The table presents the relationship which has been found to exist between the AH4 and other intelligence tests:

Table*

	AH4			Groups
	Part 1	Part 2	Total	
NIIP group test 33	0·65	0·45	0·59	114 Scots university students
Progressive Matrices	0·66	0·68	0·69	273 naval entrants
G.V.K.			0·76	302 aircrew entrants

*Reproduced from "Manual for the AH4" — NFER 1970.

Heim also reports significant correlations between performance on the AH4 and examination results in populations of school children and university students.

(b) *Construct*

A simple centroid factor analysis of the relationships between the various principles used in item construction, revealed a strong general factor with which each principle was highly correlated — between 0·80 and 0·86 (Heim, 1970). In Part I, the correlation of each principle with total score for the part ranged from 0·83 to 0·89 and in Part II correlations ranged from 0·86 to 0·92.

The test was accepted as being both reliable and of sufficient validity for the purpose for which it was intended in the present study, i.e. as a general indicator of intellectual ability and functioning.

3. Test Procedure

The AH4 was originally chosen because it was suitable for presentation to groups. However, group testing was abandoned after several rather unsuccessful attempts had been made to test the first Grendon intake men in this fashion. Testing thereafter was normally completed individually. Each man was asked to read and complete the examples provided on page 1 of the question booklet. It was explained that he had to complete the trial questions on this page and help was given if any difficulty was expressed with these 12 items. Once he had completed the examples for Part I he was asked to begin working through the 65 items until told to stop. He was instructed to go on to the next question if he was really stuck with a particular problem. Ten minutes were allowed for the completion of Part I.

A similar procedure was carried out for Part II of the test, examples being provided before the test proper was started.

Appendix 3

CRIMINAL PROFILE

It will be appreciated that official records do not represent the actual amount of offending behaviour in which a man may have engaged. In an attempt to circumvent this problem a series of 5-point rating scales were devised, and these were developed in the pilot work carried out on the social history interview. The scales covered the following areas of behaviour: theft, fraud, sex, violence, motoring, drink and drugs. A man's position on each scale was determined both by the number of convictions incurred in that particular area, and by the offending to which he admitted in interview but for which he had not been convicted. Details about the reliability and validity of the scales and also a revised version of the scales are given in Gunn and Robertson (1976). The scales used in the research are reproduced below.

One further scale was developed in order to assess the degree of each man's previous financial dependence on crime. This scale was originally constructed as part of an attempt to measure motivation for treatment (see Appendices 5 and 7). It had been pointed out in a number of letters received from experienced prison medical officers, that the extent to which a man had depended upon crime for a living was probably related to his motivation for giving up crime. A 5-point scale was therefore developed in order to measure the extent to which a man had been financially dependent on crime.

Theft (includes TADA)

0   No convictions or reported behaviour.
1   No convictions but self-confessed occasional theft or one or two juvenile convictions for petty theft.
2   One theft conviction or self-confessed frequent stealing.
3   Several theft convictions but only small amounts of money involved.
4   Substantial **gains** by stealing (£1000 or more).

Fraud

0   No convictions or reported behaviour.
1   No convictions but self-confessed occasional fraud.
2   One fraud conviction or self-confessed frequent fraud behaviour.
3   Several fraud convictions but only small amounts of money involved.
4   Substantial gains by fraud behaviour (£1000 or more).

Sex

0   No convictions for illegal sexual behaviour.
1   One conviction for indecent exposure.

2   Several exhibitionism convictions or one indictable (other than in 4).
3   Several indictable convictions (other than in 4).
4   Rape/S.I. with children.

Violence

0   Never been convicted of violence. Never gets into fights.
1   Some evidence of violence, but only to a minimal degree, i.e. occasional fights or damage to property. No convictions for violence.
2   One or two convictions for violence, or repeated acts of violence to a person or property without convictions being brought, neither the conviction offences nor the repeated acts to have caused serious personal damage to life or health.
3   Three or more convictions for violence, none of which amounts to severe violence (4).
4   One or more severely violent episode in which someone's life or health has been seriously endangered.

Motoring

0   No motoring convictions.
1   One-three offences for speeding or traffic sign offences or self-confessed no licence or insurance.
     One-three offences for no insurance or driving licence or L plates or careless driving.
2   Four + offences for speeding or traffic sign offences or no insurance or driving licence or L plates or careless driving.
3   Driving whilst disqualified or one conviction for dangerous driving.
4   More than one conviction for dangerous driving or causing death or serious injury by dangerous driving.

Drink

0   No convictions or self-confessed drunkenness.
1   No convictions but occasional drunkenness.
2   One drinking offence or self-confessed frequent drunkenness.
3   Two or three drinking offences.
4   Four + drinking offences.

Drugs

0   No conviction or self-confessed breaches of drug laws.
1   No convictions but self-confessed illegal drug activities on more than one occasion.
2   One drug conviction or frequent self-confessed illegal drug activities.
3   Two or three drug convictions with oral or subcutaneous drugs.
4   Four + drug convictions or any use of intravenous drugs.

Assessment of Financial Gain Involved in Criminal Behaviour

0   His criminal behaviour has never involved financial gain.
1   Has made some financial gains from his criminal activities but these have been very small and/or incidental, and man has not been dependent upon these gains.
2   Has at times made money from crime but for the most part financial gain has come from legitimate activities.
3   Has largely been financially dependent upon crime. Activities have been regular and may have been planned but they are not "large scale" in the sense of "4".
4   Is a professional criminal who has been involved in large scale, well-planned crime (usually with evidence of adult gang activity).

Appendix 4

PERSONALITY ASSESSMENT USING THE MINNESOTA MULTIPHASIC PERSONALITY INVENTORY

The MMPI was chosen as a measure of personality in the present research largely because, as Hathaway (1959) pointed out ". . . if an investigator uses the MMPI, or another widely employed test . . . then more information is easily added to the substantial fund already accumulated and the tool, to use in replication and further work is readily available". By the same token, using a test which already has a large amount of data relating to it, puts the investigator into a better position for evaluating the specific results obtained. However, although, as Ellis (1970) points out, there is no other personality inventory on which so much theoretical and practical work has been done, the MMPI does have the disadvantage from the point of view of the present study that normative data has never been collected on a sample of British people. American norms have to be relied upon for the purposes of comparison. The importance of this deficiency varies with the type of scale used and, in the present research, only those scales which are regarded as being minimally dependent upon cultural factors have been selected.

The wide range of areas of behaviour covered by the MMPI and the existence of many symptom self-rating items made the test particularly suitable as an instrument for measuring attitudinal change. This quality, i.e. the ability to reflect change, made the test more attractive than its possible alternatives, e.g. the 16 PF (Cattell and Scheier, 1961) and the EPI (Eysenck, 1963). The latter of these, whilst having the advantage of having been standardised on a British population, is designed to measure stable personality traits which are not particularly influenced by present circumstances or feelings. As Passingham (1967) points out, the neuroticism measured by the EPI is emotional stability, whilst the neuroticism measured by the MMPI is the amount of anxiety being felt and expressed by the individual. In fact, the MMPI contains items and scales which reflect both present state and underlying emotional stability. We considered that psychiatric intervention could be expected to effect the former rather than the latter.

An additional factor in choosing the MMPI was that men coming to Grendon were already required to complete both the 16 PF and the EPI as part of the battery of tests which are given as a routine by the prison authorities on admission and departure. Moreover, there was a risk that the information obtained from the group testing involved in these tests was liable to deliberate false reporting because of the impersonal nature of the testing procedure. Completion of the MMPI, however, was a personal procedure; the men were given the forms only after they had talked at length to one of the inverviewers, and the results can be regarded as a personal communication between the respondent and the person who presented him with the test.

Thus the MMPI was selected as a suitable test for assessing areas of behaviour and interaction which experience at Grendon could reasonably be expected to influence.

The Hofmann-La-Roche company provided computer facilities for analysing the MMPI answer sheets. The main purpose of these facilities is a clinical one, and each respondent's printout includes a list of clinical statements which are designed to produce a description of possible areas of pathology for further investigation by the clinician. The method adopted to develop the program is described by its originator (Fowler, 1969).

Somewhere in the region of 220 scales have now been derived from the original MMPI pool, and the Hofmann-La-Roche printouts, as well as listing clinical statements for each respondent, gave his score on the ten clinical scales and on 63 derived scales and indices. (An example of the full printout is reproduced in Robertson, 1974, App. II p. 413). The empirical reduction of this wealth of material was carried out in three parts. First, the clinical statements were examined; secondly, the ten clinical scales were each examined to see whether in terms of validity, reliability, normative data, etc. they would prove suitable for use in the research as measures of either personality dimensions or of pathological traits; and finally the 63 derived scales and indices were looked at for the same purpose.

1. Clinical Statements

It was decided to analyse these statements in terms of frequency of occurrence within the population and thus provide a general picture of the most frequent pathology presented by that population. These statements were designed to indicate areas of pathology or distress and were not intended to provide a personality profile in the usual meaning of the term.

2. Clinical Scales

The ten clinical scales were examined for their validity as measures of either a personality dimension or a pathological trait. Only details of the scales used in our analysis are included in this appendix. Details of the excluded scales are to be found in Robertson (1974).

(a) *Hypochondriasis (Hs) (33 Items)*

This scale was designed to measure the characteristics associated with the neurotic disorder labelled hypochondriasis; the latter term was defined as "abnormal concern over bodily health" (Welsh and Dahlstrom, 1956).

It has been shown to be stable over short periods of time (mean for 10 such reliability studies is 0·66) and has been found to be internally consistent when this is measured by the split/half method.

Evidence relating to validity is minimal and sometimes conflicting. A factor analysis by Comrey (1957a) revealed a principal factor of "health concern". It was decided to use the scale as an indicator of the variable of concern for health but not as a diagnostic instrument for assessing the presence of the hypochondriacal state.

(b) *Depression (D) (60 Items)*

Depression was defined by Hathaway and McKinley (1956) as "a state of mind . . . characterised by poor morale, lack of hope in the future and dissatisfaction with the patient's own status generally". The construction of the test was elaborate and extremely thorough; the reported short term reliability correlations range from 0·66 to 0·85 with a mean of 0·72.

Factor analyses of the scale have been carried out by Comrey (1957b) and O'Connor *et al.* (1957). Both analyses demonstrate a major component which is made up of items related to the definition of depression supplied by the authors of the scale. Independent validity studies by Leverenz (1943) and Brown and Goodstein (1962) are consistent in their opinion that the scale is a valid measure of the depressed state.

(c) *Social Introversion (Si) (70 Items)*

This scale is the only member of the 10 clinical scales which was not developed by Hathaway and McKinley. No explicit statement about the nature of "social introversion" was made by Drake (1946) when he published the scale. However, it may be deduced from the criterion groups used in his cross validation studies, that he has defined the social extravert as someone who takes part in a number of group activities and is generally gregarious.

Drake's construction of the scale and the validity studies carried out are impressive. No information is provided as regards short-term stability. However, as most items in the scale are to be found within the scale of Hathaway and McKinley, this is not an important deficiency.

It is accepted that high scores on the scale reflect unwillingness to take part in group activities and a withdrawal from social activities generally. The scale has been used in its own right in the present description of personality characteristics.

3. Derived Scales

As some 63 derived scales and indices were produced in the Roche printout, and there was a considerable amount of redundancy present even upon visual inspection, a principal components analysis was carried out in order to reduce the pool of possible variables. The programe used was BMDO3M (Biomedical Computer Programme:

University of California Press). This analysis was performed using the results obtained from the Grendon sample (N = 106). The following results were obtained:

Principal Component 1 (this factor accounted for 41% of the total variance)

Scale	Loading
Manifest anxiety scale	0·95
College maladjustment	0·94
Depression (Wiggins)	0·93
Welsh first factor (neuroticism)	0·92
Causality	0·92
Alcoholism	0·90
Dependency	0·90
Factor 1 (neuroticism)	0·90

(Only scales with factor loadings of at least 0·90 have been listed.)

The majority of the 63 scales had a fairly high loading on the first component, the nature of which may be deduced from examining those scales which load most highly on the factor. All are fairly self-explanatory except "College maladjustment". This scale was devised by Kleinmuntz (1961) to identify potential breakdown cases in a student population. The principal characteristics of the breakdown group were found to be "pessimism, anxiety and worry with a tendency to somatize".

The nature of the first component is interpreted as being "Neuroticism" and of the scales which load most highly on the factor, the Manifest Anxiety Scale (0·95) and Barron's Ego Strength scale (−0·85) have been chosen for presentation. The reason for these scales being chosen was the high standard of validity, reliability and normative data available.

The Manifest Anxiety Scale

(a) Construction

This scale was originally developed by Taylor (1953) as an instrument for the selection of subjects for experiments in the relationship between drive and anxiety. Two hundred items of the MMPI were submitted to five clinicians who were asked to "designate the items indicative of manifest anxiety". The 65 items chosen after this procedure were then reduced to 50 after stability and internal consistency studies had been carried out by Ahana (1952). A test-retest coefficient of 0·82 (5-month interval) was reported by Taylor.

(b) Validity

Confusion about the nature of the scale has arisen because of the original purpose for which the scale was devised, i.e. to measure "here and now" anxiety. Studies by Erikson and Davids (1955) and a study by Rosin and Townsend (1958) demonstrated support to the hypothesis that the MAS is a measure of anxiety potential rather than chronic state of anxiousness and should be regarded as such.

The conclusions of these workers are based upon the general finding that in non-stress conditions, subjects differing on the MAS scale produce similar performances on a learning task. Under stress conditions however, the same subjects perform differently on the learning task with relatively poorer performances being obtained from those who score highly on the MAS. It is argued that if MAS scores reflected a chronic condition, different performances should be obtained regardless of stress. In other words, the MAS measures not so much a state of anxiousness as the potential to react in a neurotic maladaptive fashion.

The scale has been found to be related to the Psychaesthenia scale ($r = 0.92$) (Erikson and Davids, 1955) and Rosin and Townsend (1958) demonstrated the inability of the scale to differentiate between 57 "anxiety reaction" patients and 25 "psychoneurotics" who were not suffering from an anxiety reaction. The observed means for the two groups were 21·9 and 23·2 respectively.

It seems clear from all this that the MAS is a measure of underlying stability or neuroticism, rather than a measurement of "here and now" anxiety. It has been used as a measure of the neurotic dimension in the present study.

The Ego Strength Scale

This scale was chosen because of its specific applicability to the present work. It was presented by Barron (1953) as an instrument designed "to predict the response of psychoneurotic patients to psychotherapy". Barron's term "ego strength" is synonymous with "good personality". The 68 items of the scale cover a broad range of behaviour including attitude to religion, ability to share emotional experiences, attitude towards minority groups, sexual morality and personal feelings of adequacy and vitality.

There is a large neurotic component in the scale as is evidenced by its loading on component 1. However, the much broader range of items in the scale have been found by Barron to contribute to the prediction of which cases respond well to a fairly brief period of psychotherapy. The ego-strong individual reports little ill-health, is emotionally "open", is not dogmatic in his religious beliefs, expresses "permissive" views as regards sexual behaviour, is in good contact with reality, feels adequate and self confident and is physically courageous.

Items were selected on the basis of their relationship with rated improvement during six months psychotherapy in an out-patient clinic. Thirty-three cases, representing a variety of neurotic disorders, comprised the sample.

Test-retest reliability was reported as 0·72 (N = 30) and an internal consistency coefficient of 0·76 was obtained by Barron. A number of validation studies have been carried out, e.g. Taft (1951) and Gottesman (1959). Gottesman was concerned to establish the construct validity of the scale.

It is accepted that low score on the scale reflects a constricted, neurotic outlook on life, and it is for the measurement of this dimension that it is used in the present study.

The second principal component to be produced by the analysis accounted for 12% of the total variance.

The eight scales with the highest loadings on the factor are listed below.

Scale	Loading
Extraversion	-0.73
Second factor (Welsh)	-0.61
Factor three (introversion)	0.64
Authority conflict	-0.58
Manifest hostility	-0.55
Impulsivity	-0.50
Social responsibility	-0.49
Social maladjustment	0.48

The second factor is interpreted as being extraversion with there being a strong anti-social component in the scales listed. The "Extraversion" and "Manifest Hostility" scales were chosen to represent both elements in the component.

The Extraversion Scale

This scale was produced by Giedt and Downing (1961) to be a measure of extraversion which would be independent of the ego-strength (neurotic) dimension. Their work was based upon a factorial analysis of the MMPI which had been carried out by Kassenbaum et al. (1959). This latter research had produced two principal factors within the MMPI — neuroticism and extraversion. Only the "R" scale of Welsh was found to be independent of the neuroticism dimension and as the interpretation of this scale was uncertain, Giedt and Downing set out to develop a "pure" extraversion scale.

Two independent analyses were carried out to establish item content for the scale. In the first place, a group of 120 male psychiatric protocols were scored and the top and bottom 20 were compared. A similar procedure was employed with a population of students. The criterion groups used were chosen on the basis of their performance on the Hypomania and Sociability scale (Gough, 1952) as it had been reported by Kassenbaum that these two scales had equal loadings on the extraversion dimension but had opposite loadings on neuroticism. It was reasoned by Giedt and Downing (1961) that people scoring highly on both Hy and "Sociability" scales would be extraverts of about average neuroticism; similarly, introverts would score lowly on both scales. Forty-one items were chosen as discriminating between high and low scores for both student and psychiatric populations at the 5 per cent level.
One study has been conducted by Giedt and Downing (1961) to establish criterion-related validity for the test. Scale scores were correlated with staff ratings on a five point "extraversion" scale for 50 patients. A significant correlation of 0.35 was reported.

Someone scoring highly on the scale would be "the stereotype of an extravert . . . someone who is socially aggressive, full of energy and likes to be with people". In the present study, the scale has been used as a measure of social extraversion.

The Manifest Hostility Scale

This scale is one of thirteen scales developed by Wiggins (1969) in his attempt to take "a first step in the direction of classifying the content of the MMPI item pool". Starting with the original content classification of Hathaway and McKinley (1956), both psychometric and "intuitive" procedures were employed in the development of a set of scales designed to be internally consistent, mutually independent, and representative of the major substantive clusters that appear to exist in the total MMPI item pool.

The first stage in the development of the scales involved listing the original McKinley/Hathaway classifications. Each item in these was scored in the direction of deviance (i.e. infrequency) and the internal consistency and factor structure of these scales were calculated using the protocols of 500 students (250 male and 250 female). The results of these preliminary analyses proved to be encouraging and, according to Wiggins, "it seemed fruitful to attempt a more substantively consistent grouping of items within categories as a basis for subsequent development of actual content scales". Items were regrouped with the emphasis being placed upon "rational" consideration. Procedures were intuitive and "no claim is made for their replicability". After assessment, the eighteen scales produced were reduced to fifteen and a further two scales were dropped from analysis because of low internal consistency. The thirteen scales left were internally consistent and relatively independent of one another. The manifest hostility scale was one of these.

Some validity data has been produced by Wiggins, although as he himself points out, any criterion-related validity check will serve only to "enhance rather than define" the meaning of the content scales. This work is reported in Butcher (1969). A factor analysis of the structure of the thirteen scales revealed high loadings for all scales on a general "neurotic" or maladjustment factor.

The Manifest Hostility scale is described by Wiggins in the following terms, "High MHS admits to . . . a tendency to be grouchy, competitive, argumentative, uncooperative and retaliatory in his interpersonal relationships". The scale is accepted as being internally consistent and as being a measure of the social hostility which a man expresses.

Summary

The results from the MMPI are presented in two ways in this study. In the first place, the most frequent clinical statements printed by the Roche programme are outlined. Secondly, nine individual scales are used to describe the personality characteristics of the population. These nine scales are made up of (a) Four Neurotic scales: (1) Depression; (2) Hypochondriasis; (3) Ego Strength; (4) Manifest Anxiety. (b) Three "extraversion" scales: (1) Extraversion; (2) Social Introversion; and (3) Manifest Hostility.

Appendix 5

ATTITUDE TO PSYCHIATRY QUESTIONNAIRE (AP)

Because of the specific nature of the attitude which we wished to measure, namely, desire for psychiatric treatment within a prison setting, and the difficulties which this imposed with regard to obtaining a large enough number of items for discrimination purposes, it was decided to use a Likert (1932) type model in the construction of the scale. Five alternative answers were provided for each item, ranging from strongly positive through "uncertain" to strongly negative.

The development of the final scale took place in three stages: (1) Pre-pilot; (2) Pilot enquiry and collection of normative data, and (3) Statistical analysis.

1. Pre-pilot

Eight items — culled from suggestions made by the prison doctors we had canvassed, and from our own ideas — were put into a Likert-type scale and all the men in one of the wings in Grendon (N = 43) were asked to complete this and make any comments which they felt were appropriate to the improvement of the scale.

The existence of two major errors was discovered in this pre-pilot enquiry. Firstly, it was found that we had included items of a historical nature which were thus unable to reflect change; and secondly, we concluded from comments which we received from the men, that several of our items were ambiguous and open to misinterpretation. The appropriate changes were made to the scale and also, one item was added which had been chosen from suggestions made by the men on the wing.

2. Pilot Enquiry and Collection of Normative Data

A new seven-item scale was constructed, on which respondents were asked to indicate the extent of their agreement or disagreement with the following items: (1) psychiatry is useful for people who have problems; (2) my criminal behaviour has nothing to do with psychological illness; (3) for me, personally, psychiatry is useful; (4) in general psychiatric treatment has to be short if it is to be useful; (5) most crime is related to psychological illness; and (6) in the light of my own experience I consider that for the most part criminals are perfectly normal; (7) I should not mind having psychiatric treatment when I leave prison, if I need it. On each item, the five possible responses were: strong agreement, agreement, undecided, disagreement, and strong disagreement.

The response to each item was scored on a five-point scale; strong agreement with "pro-psychiatry" statements being given four points and strong disagreement none: the maximum possible score for the questionnaire was thus 28.

The new scale was circulated to seventy men in Grendon, forty men receiving psychiatric treatment at Wormwood Scrubs, and fifty Wormwood Scrubs prisoners who were not receiving psychiatric treatment. It was hoped that a population would thus be obtained which would be representative of the final total population which we intended to investigate: i.e. from our original distribution we hoped to collect at least 100 cases, one-third of which would come from Grendon, one-third from the Wormwood Scrubs psychiatric population and one-third from the general (non-treated) population. However, because many man either failed to return forms or returned blank forms, our final group of 100 was made up of 38 men from Grendon, 35 treated men from Wormwood Scrubs and 27 men from the "non-psychiatric" Wormwood Scrubs population.

3. Statistical Analysis

Table *a* presents the means obtained by the sub-groups on the scale.

Table *a*

	N	Mean	s.d.
Grendon	38	20·70	4·413
Wormwood Scrubs psychiatric	35	19·09	3·000
Wormwood Scrubs non-psychiatric	27	15·67	4·952
Total	100	18·57	4·53

4. Reliability

(a) *Test-Retest*

This was obtained by asking the Grendon population to complete the scale again after a two-week interval. A Pearson Product Moment correlation of 0·95 was obtained (N = 20).

(b) *Internal Consistency*

Three statistical devices were used to assess internal consistency. In the first place the scale items were subjected to Edwards "t" test (Edwards, 1957). This method of item analysis assumes that by taking the top and bottom 25 per cent of the population distribution, criterion groups are provided against which individual items may be evaluated for their discriminatory value. Edwards regards any "t" value equal to or greater than 1·75 as indicating that the average response of the high and low groups to a statement differs significantly. Table *b* presents the "t" scores obtained by each item in the final revision of the "Attitude to Psychiatry" scale.

Table *b*

Item number	"t"
1	4·247
2	8·051
3	5·073
4	5·714
5	8·347
6	3·892
7	7·938

The second assessment of internal consistency was made by calculating item-total correlations for each item on the scale. These are presented in Table c.

Table *c*   Item-Total Correlations

Item number	"r"
1	0·73
2	0·79
3	0·41
4	0·40
5	0·67
6	0·45
7	0·60

All values of "r" are statistically significant at the 1% level.

A final evaluation of the scale's internal consistency was performed by carrying out a simple centroid factor analysis. The results of this are presented in Table *d* below.

Table *d*   Factor Analysis of Items in the Attitude to Psychiatry Scale

Item number	Factor I
1	0·72
2	0·49
3	0·98
4	0·35
5	0·47
6	0·46
7	0·56

All items load highly on the scale and the two items with the highest loading are item (3) "For you personally do you think psychiatry is useful?" (0·98) and item (1) "For people who have problems I think psychiatry is useful." (0·72).

On the basis of these results, the attitude to psychiatry scale is presented as being internally consistent and as having short-term stability.

5. Validity

Content validity is concerned with the systematic investigation of test content to determine whether it covers a representative sample of the behaviour domain to be measured. It should be built into a test from the outset through the choice of appropriate items and this was attempted by constructing the test only after surveying as wide and experienced a population as possible for their opinions.

For the purposes of establishing criterion-related validity for a test, performance on that test must be checked against a criterion, i.e. an independent measure of that which the test is designed to predict. Applying this principle to our normative population one would predict that, if the test was a valid reflection of desire for treatment, the psychiatric sub-groups investigated should have responded in a significantly different and predictable direction from the non-psychiatric population. This was tested by comparing the means of the groups which were given in Table a above. When the mean score of the Grendon sample was compared with that of the non-psychiatric Wormwood Scrubs men, the difference was highly significant: $t = 3.891$, $p < 0.001$; similarly, comparison of the psychiatric Wormwood Scrubs men with the non-psychiatric showed a significant difference, $t = 3.419$, $p < 0.01$. But between the mean scores of the two psychiatric samples in Grendon and Wormwood Scrubs there was no significant difference ($t = 1.607$, $p < 0.1$). This demonstration of predictive power indicates that the scale can, and at a gross level does, discriminate between groups receiving psychiatric treatment and those who are not. However, the extent to which it meaningfully discriminates within groups and between individuals is not known.

The extent to which the scale measures "motivation for treatment" represents its construct validity. Construct validity is perhaps the most useful and certainly most difficult to demonstrate and requires a lengthy accumulation of relevant data from a large number of sources. Of particular relevance in this case is the work which was carried out in establishing the internal consistency of the scale. Whilst it is realised that the relative homogeneity of the scale demonstrated by use of the criterion-related Edwards "t" and item total correlations is of limited value, the simple centroid factor analysis which was carried out does shed light on the nature of the underlying construct or trait. An examination of item loadings on Factor I reveals very high loadings on this factor for items (1) and (3), i.e. "For you, personally, do you think psychiatry is useful?" and "For people who have problems, do you think psychiatry is useful?". This would indicate that the trait or construct measured by the scale is, in fact, desire for psychiatric treatment.

Items of the Attitude to Psychiatry (AP) Scale

Please read the following statements and questions and place a tick against the answer which you think is the right one *for you*. You are asked to avoid ticking the "undecided" category if possible.

Please remember that your answers and opinions are *entirely confidential* and are not made known to the prison authorities.

1. For people who have problems I think psychiatry is: —

Very useful   _____

Useful   _____

Undecided   _____

Of little use   _____

A waste of time _____

2. My criminal behaviour has nothing to do with psychological illness.

Strongly agree   _____

Agree   _____

Undecided   _____

Disagree   _____

Strongly disagree_____

3. For you, personally, do you think that psychiatry is: —

Very useful   _____

Useful   _____

Undecided   _____

Of little use   _____

A waste of time _____

4. In general, psychiatric treatment has to be short if it is to be useful.

Strongly agree   _____

Agree   _____

Undecided   _____

Disagree   _____

Strongly disagree_____

5. Most crime is related to psychological illness.

Strongly agree   _____

Agree   _____

Undecided   _____

Disagree   _____

Strongly disagree_____

6. In the light of my own experience I consider that, for the most part, criminals are perfectly normal.

Strongly agree   _____

Agree   _____

Undecided   _____

Disagree   _____

Strongly disagree_____

7. I should not mind having psychiatric treatment when I leave prison, if I need it.

Strongly agree   _____

Agree   _____

Undecided   _____

Disagree   _____

Strongly disagree_____

Appendix 6

INTERVIEWER'S ASSESSMENT OF DESIRE FOR TREATMENT

We initially constructed a very long and detailed interview which attempted to trace the history of how a man came to be having psychiatric treatment. After about fourteen men had been interviewed in this way, both interviewers concluded that the extent of a man's desire for treatment could be assessed without undertaking so laborious a procedure. A much shorter interview was therefore constructed, using the experience which had been gained on this first exercise.

Our objectives were two-fold: (a) to establish whether or not the man wanted psychiatric treatment and (b) if he wanted it, then to attempt to determine why he wanted it. The main problem with regard to whether the assessment is a valid measure of motivation, lies in whether the men are telling the truth. Since it had been made plain to them that nothing from the interviews would be divulged to the prison authorities, there seemed to be no particular incentive for the men to mislead us. But the objection that we can never know if the individual is telling the truth is perfectly legitimate. However, it is an objection which holds more for the individual than for any group. It is not suggested that every individual told us the truth about the reasons for his seeking psychiatric help, but we believe that for the majority of men, the answers which we received were honest and reflected what they themselves believed to be their reasons for seeking treatment.

Like the social and criminal history interview, the motivation interview was tried out on a pilot basis on a mixed population. This consisted of men from Grendon (some newly arrived, some who had been there for a while), men from the treatment population in Wormwood Scrubs, and men in Wormwood Scrubs who were not receiving psychiatric treatment. Reliability of the rating scale used (inter-rater and test-retest combined) was found to be $0 \cdot 86$ (N = 20) when two weeks were allowed between the interview occasions.

The format of the interview and the rating scale used is set out below.

Interview for Assessment of Desire for Treatment

Interviewer should assess

(a) whether man wanted (or wishes to have) treatment.

(b) If answer to (a) is in the affirmative, assess the extent to which other factors, e.g. peripheral benefits, fear of the authorities, are important in the desire for treatment.

If of no importance rate (4). If of some importance (e.g. 75:25) rate (3). If 50:50 or if the man expresses a very ambivalent attitude towards psychiatric treatment rate as (2).

If answer to (a) is negative, assess degree of negative attitude by asking if he would consider the idea, if the opportunity for treatment were given to him. If definitely "not" rate (0). If he would consider and possibly accept treatment although still maintaining that he was in no way "ill", rate (1).

(0) No desire for treatment.

(1) No desire for treatment but would accept if offered for whatever reasons.

(2) Expresses ambivalent attitude towards personal suitability for treatment.

(3) Wishes (or is having) treatment partly for other side benefits.

(4) Strong desire for treatment. Expresses little or no interest in peripheral benefits.

Appendix 7

THE ATTITUDE TO CRIME SCALE (AC)

The methods used for the construction of this scale were identical to those used in the construction of the attitude to psychiatry scale, and work on both was carried out simultaneously. As before, development was in three stages.

1. Pre-pilot

Seven items, chosen from a larger pool of potential items supplied to us by the prison medical officers, etc., and from items which we ourselves felt to be useful on *a priori* grounds, were formed into a Likert-type scale. This was presented to the men on one of the wings at Grendon and the replies of these men were examined for possible flaws in the construction of the scale. The appropriate changes were then made.

2. Pilot Enquiry and Collection of Normative Data

A new questionnaire was circulated to the pilot population (N = 160) described in Appendix 5, and normative data was collected from the same 100 men (38 from Grendon, 35 treated and 27 untreated men from Wormwood Scrubs).

The questionnaire contained five items, and respondents were asked to indicate the extent of their agreement with each. The items were: (1) If I had the choice of moving to another town, or getting mixed up in the sort of thing that I am now in prison for, I would move readily; (2) I like mixing with criminals; (3) I feel guilty when I think of my offences; (4) I would like to make a lot of money from crime; and (5) Under the circumstances, I consider my offences to have been wholly unreasonable. To each item there were five possible responses: strongly agree, agree, undecided, disagree, and strongly disagree. Responses were scored on a 5-point scale: strong agreement in the "anti-crime" direction scoring 4 points and strong disagreement scoring none. Thus the maximum possible score on the questionnaire was 20.

3. Statistical Analysis

Table e presents the means of the three subgroups on the scale.

Table e

Prison	N	Mean	s.d.
Grendon	38	15·08	3·37
Wormwood Scrubs psychiatric	35	14·88	3·75
Wormwood Scrubs non-psychiatric	27	12·63	3·56
Total	100	15·21	6·09

4. Reliability

(a) *Test-Retest*

The correlation obtained after a two week interval was 0·72 (N = 20).

(b) *Internal Consistency*

The procedures which were applied to the attitude to psychiatry scale were used to assess the homogeneity of the criminality scale.

Table f presents the "t" scores obtained by the items of the final scale.

Table f

Item number	"t"
1	5·797
2	7·977
3	5·840
4	4·821
5	5·732

The item-total correlations for this scale are presented in Table *g*.

Table *g*   Item-Total Correlations

Item number	"r"
1	0·61
2	0·62
3	0·75
4	0·30
5	0·50

All values of "r" are significant at the 1% level.

The simple centroid factor analysis carried out on the five items of the scale is presented in Table *h*.

Table *h*

Item number	Factor 1
1	0·41
2	0·46
3	0·63
4	0·58
5	0·53

All items load highly on the scale. The two items with the highest loading are item (3) — "I feel guilty when I think of my offences" — and item (4) — "I should like to make a lot of money from crime".

5. Validity

The difficulty about ensuring content validity for the scale is the almost limitless number of possible items of peripheral relevance for inclusion: attitude to crime is a far more diffuse concept than attitude to psychiatry, and there are consequently greater problems about establishing validity at any level. Moreover, whilst the opinions of doctors and psychiatrists had been of specific relevance in the construction of the attitude to psychiatry scale, no comparable expertise was available for us to draw on, when we set about listing the possible items (some of them supplied by prison doctors) that were relevant to attitudes to crime.

There are also difficulties about establishing the predictive validity of the scale. Whereas with the attitude to psychiatry scale there were distinct populations which could be used for its validation, there is less reason to suppose that populations chosen on the basis of having or not having psychiatric treatment, should differ with regard to their desire to change their criminal behaviour. However, it is not unreasonable to suppose that desire for psychiatric help and desire to abandon crime are related, and so the means for the "psychiatric" and "non-psychiatric" sub-groups were compared: they were given in Table *e* above. When the mean score of the Grendon sample was compared with that of the non-psychiatric Wormwood Scrubs men, the Grendon score was found to be significantly higher (i.e. more "anti-crime") (t = 2·783, p< 0·01). Similarly, when the Wormwood Scrubs psychiatric men were compared with the non-psychiatric, their mean score was significantly higher (t = 2·258, p <0·05). But between the two psychiatric samples themselves there was no significant difference (t = 0·028). Thus there is evidence that "psychiatric" prisoners differ from "non-psychiatric" in their performance on the attitude to crime scale, in a direction which one would have expected. However, as one would also have expected, these differences are less than those found when the two groups were compared for performance on the attitude to psychiatry scale.

To establish true predictive validity for the attitude to crime scale is a difficult problem. Had it been possible (which it was not) to follow up the normative sample after they left prison, an indication of their subsequent criminal behaviour would have been obtained, but the usefulness of such a procedure is not self-evident, since it can be argued that attitude and behaviour are distinct, the latter being susceptible to many forces which do not affect the former. In that case the criterion variable (offending behaviour) would be a result of many factors, only one of which is the individual's attitude to that behaviour. At one point in the study it was hoped that a measure of concurrent validity could be extracted by correlating the attitude to crime scores, with assessments of the men made by the prison therapists. Unfortunately, the latter were found to have such low inter-rater reliability that this procedure could not be used.

Construct validity must thus rely upon the work which was carried out in the establishment of the test's internal consistency. The factor analysis which was carried out demonstrated that all items had high loadings on the first factor, and the two items with the highest loadings were (a) I feel guilty when I think of my offences, and (b) I would like to make a lot of money from crime. This finding is encouraging but it is not suggested that it is in any way conclusive evidence as to what the scale is measuring. The overall state of our knowledge with regard to the validity of the attitude to crime scale leaves something to be desired. However, it is presented as being a stable and internally consistent instrument which, as far as we have been able to demonstrate, is a measure of attitude to crime.

Items of the Attitude to Criminality (AC) Scale

Please read the following statements and questions and place a tick against the answer which you think is the right one *for you*. You are asked to avoid ticking the 'undecided' category, if possible.
Please remember that your answers and opinions are *entirely confidential* and are not made known to the prison authorities.

1. If I had the choice of moving to another town, or getting mixed up in the sort of thing that I am now in prison for, I would move readily

Strongly agree   _____

Agree   _____

Undecided   _____

Disagree   _____

Strongly disagree_____

2. I like mixing with criminals

Strongly agree   _____

Agree   _____

Undecided   _____

Disagree   _____

Strongly disagree_____

3. I feel guilty when I think of my offences

Strongly agree   _____

Agree   _____

Undecided   _____

Disagree   _____

Strongly disagree_____

4. I would like to make a lot of money from crime

Strongly agree   _____

Agree   _____

Undecided   _____

Disagree   _____

Strongly disagree_____

5. Under the circumstances I consider my offences to have been wholly unreasonable

Strongly agree   _____

Agree   _____

Undecided   _____

Disagree   _____

Strongly disagree_____

Appendix 8

MEASUREMENT OF ATTITUDES BY A SEMANTIC DIFFERENTIAL

A semantic differential was constructed in order to measure the attitude of the men towards certain key figures. The objective was to develop an instrument that would be reliable and yet allow change to be assessed.

The semantic differential technique (Osgood *et al.*, 1957) was chosen for a number of reasons. In the first place, it is much simpler to construct than the more traditional Likert- or Thurstone-type of attitude scales and offers the opportunity of examining attitude towards a variety of individuals, each of whom would have required an individual scale had the more traditional methods been employed. Secondly, the willingness of Dr. Patrick Slater and his assistant, Dr. Jane Chetwynd, to allow us to use their programmes for grid analysis (Slater, unpublished; Slater, 1969) meant that standard and objective assessments could be made of the results obtained. A brief summary of the programme used is provided in Robertson (1974) p. 411.

1. Construction

Perhaps the commonest procedure used to construct a semantic differential is for the experimenter to choose constructs or adjectives from a table of factor loadings provided by the originators of the technique. These constructs, once chosen, are then used as the basis of the test. Dr. Slater, in a personal verbal communication, had made it clear that a more useful and often more valid way of obtaining constructs, was to carry out some pilot studies to ascertain which constructs were used most frequently by the population being studied, about the elements (figures) being assessed. The method chosen to obtain a number of suitable constructs was Kelly's Role Title List (Kelly, 1955) and in a pilot procedure, the men were presented with three figures and asked to say in what way they thought that two of them were alike and yet different from the third. About a dozen men were interviewed in this way before it was decided to abandon the procedure because of the paucity of responses being received. However, it was still felt that the most appropriate constructs would be obtained from the prison population. Two short questionnaires were therefore constructed and distributed within Grendon. Sixty men were contacted in this way, 30 of whom received questionnaire "A" and 30 of whom received questionnaire "B".

Questionnaire "A" was designed to tap the pool of constructs used to describe people with whom the man would usually have had close personal ties: father, mother, best friend, wife, etc. Questionnaire "B", on the other hand, contained the same instructions as form "A" but contained a list of people normally regarded as being authority or establishment figures. The format of the questionnaires is presented below.

2. Form A

These pages contain a list of people, most of whom you have known well. We should like you to think about each individual mentioned below and then describe what they were like in the space provided.

It would help us a great deal if you would make a list of their characteristics rather than writing in sentences which only contain one characteristic.

e.g. SISTER — good, kind (etc.)

rather than

SISTER — My sister is a very good person, etc.

You may use as many (or as few) descriptive words as you wish.

If, for any reason, you do not know the people concerned very well then please leave the appropriate space blank.

Please remember not to consult any of your friends when completing this questionnaire.

There then followed a list of people including the following figures: father; mother; brother(s); sister(s); wife/girl friend; good friend; someone you know who doesn't like you.

3. Form B

Form B was very similar to Form A with regard to instructions for completion. However, the list of characters to be described consisted of people in authority: social workers; prison officers; prison doctors; politicians; prison governors; magistrates; probation officers; policemen.

Of the 60 forms distributed, 43 were returned completed.

It was decided at this stage that it would be relatively fruitless to continue with the idea of developing a differential for "personal" elements. This decision was made because it became clear that many men had not known all the figures which were necessary to complete a semantic differential. In addition, a large number of men were no longer in contact with their families and it would therefore not have been useful to look for any change of attitude. One element of a personal nature was, however, put into the authority figure differential: this was "Myself".

The constructs finally chosen to form the differential were those which appeared most frequently within the population of adjectives supplied by the men in the pilot study. Only those adjectives supplied in response to form "B" were used; 181 constructs were supplied, the average response per man being 8·2.

A semantic differential with eight elements was constructed. They were: (1) social workers, (2) prison officers, (3) magistrates, (4) governors, (5) psychiatrists, (6) myself, (7) prison doctors, (8) police. Ten constructs were used, each to be rated on a seven-point scale. The constructs were: (1) helpful/not helpful, (2) insincere/sincere, (3) hardworking/lazy, (4) dishonest/honest, (5) considerate/inconsiderate, (6) narrow minded/broad minded, (7) friendly/unfriendly, (8) inhumane/humane, (9) good/bad, (10) rude/polite. Both elements and constructs were presented in the order in which they appear above. An attempt was made to reduce response bias by alternating the positive and negative ends of the scales.

4. Reliability

A short-term stability study was carried out in Grendon. Thirty men were asked to complete semantic differentials on two occasions, there being a two-week interval between testings. Eighteen men returned completed forms on both occasions. The reliability coefficients obtained are presented in Table i.

Table i Reliability coefficients for Semantic Differential Elements

Element	"r"
Social workers	0·84
Prison officers	0·82
Magistrates	0·81
Governors	0·75
Psychiatrists	0·58
Myself	0·56
Prison doctors	0·83
Police	0·65

Although the correlations for "psychiatrist" and "myself" were rather low, all elements were accepted as being stable.

The individual grids of the men in the Grendon sample which were completed at initial assessment were analysed using the "Ingrid" program (Slater, 1976).

The essence of the analysis is to ". . . specify the relationships of the constructs to one another, of the elements to one another and the relationship between the elements and the contructs". In addition to the individual "Ingrids" which were carried out, a concensus "Ingrid" was produced. This computes all of the above relationships but for the total group. The scores of the sample are treated as one and the "average" relationships are calculated.

Part of the analysis provided by the Ingrid program is a principal components analysis of the construct/element interaction. The results of this for the concensus grid are provided in Table *j*.

Table *j*   Principal component analysis from Concensus Grid of Grendon
Intake sample N = 96

Component	Root	%
1	7·98	79·76
2	1·17	11·72
3	0·48	4·77
4	0·19	1·96
5	0·08	0·86
6	0·06	0·62
7	0·03	0·30
8	0·00	0·01

As Table *j* indicates, one major component was found to account for almost 80% of the total variance within the grid. The loadings of the individual constructs on component 1 are presented in Table *k*.

Table *k*

Construct	Loading on Component 1
1. Helpful	0·97
2. Sincere	0·98
3. Hardworking	0·74
4. Honest	0·50
5. Considerate	0·99
6. Broad-minded	0·83
7. Friendly	0·96
8. Humane	0·95
9. Good	0·94
10. Polite	0·95

All constructs were found to load highly on the first component, although the "honesty" construct loaded considerably less highly than all others.

On the basis of these findings it was decided that the honesty dimension should be dropped from further analysis and that the total score obtained by an element on the nine remaining seven-point scales should be regarded as the "popularity" score for that element. In other words, component 1 was regarded as being evaluative, with all constructs, save honesty, contributing almost exclusively to it.

The results of the semantic differential analysis are therefore presented in this study as a series of scores on a unidimensional scale. This scale is regarded as representing an evaluative factor and any difference between elements on the scale is taken to represent a difference in "popularity" or evaluation. By the same token, changes in score between testing occasions are regarded as being changes in popularity. High score reflects high (good) opinion and low score represents low (poor) opinion.

Appendix 9

RE-INTERVIEW SCHEDULE

The men were re-interviewed after they had been receiving treatment for three months; the interval chosen was fairly arbitrary, but was based on the assumption that three months would allow a man sufficient time to settle down. Further interviews were held nine months after treatment began, and finally, before the men were released (or, in the case of long sentence men, fifteen months after the start of treatment).

At each re-interview, the men were asked about the treatment they had been having and also whether they had been involved in any fights. The items covered are shown below, as is their combined test/retest and inter-rater reliability. For this, a cross-over design was used, and two weeks elapsed between the interview occasions.

Reliability of Re-interview Schedule N = 24

Item	Categories	"r"
1. Do you feel that the treatment you have been receiving is helping you at all?	1. A waste of time 2. Doesn't feel it is helping 3. Finding it useful 4. Very helpful	0·83
2. Do you feel that you have learned anything about yourself?	1. Nothing at all or a little 2. Quite a lot or a great deal	No discrepancies
3. Have you been involved in any fights since coming to Grendon/beginning treatment?	Yes/No	1 Discrepancy
4. How many?		As above
5. Who is your doctor?	Name	No discrepancies
6. How many times have you been to see him for private talks?	Number	0·70

Appendix 10

MOOS SOCIAL CLIMATE SCALE FOR CORRECTIONAL INSTITUTIONS

Studies concerning the validity and reliability of the Moos Social Climate scale (Moos, 1968 and 1971) have been rather limited, and before deciding whether to use the scale in our own research, it seemed necessary to examine these aspects further. Although throughout our study the 140-item Form B of the Moos questionnaire was issued to respondents, all the analyses were made on the basis of the later version C of the test, which is a shorter and neater revision of form B: it comprises nine scales, each composed of ten items.

1. Short-Term Stability

Inmates and staff of the Grendon borstal wings were asked to complete the questionnaires on two occasions, and 25 inmates and 7 staff members did so. There was a two-week interval between testings. The results for the nine scales are shown in Table *l*.

Table *l*   Test-retest Correlation for Borstal Inmates and Staff
N = 32   Interval — two weeks

Scale	"r"
Involvement	0·69
Support	0·76
Expressiveness	0·86
Autonomy	0·79
Practicality	0·65
Insight	0·91
Order	0·80
Clarity	0·68
Control	0·88

As is clear from the table, all nine sub-scales in the questionnaire were found to be reasonably stable over time. Test-retest correlations ranged from 0·65 (practicability) to 0·91 (insight) and all scales were regarded by us as being sufficiently stable. Matched "t" test comparisons were carried out between occasions 1 and 2 in order to find out whether performance on the scales moved in a statistically significant (i.e. consistent) direction over time. Boys and staff were analysed separately and significant results are presented in Table *m*.

Table *m*   Differences between Testing Occasions

Sample	Scale	1st occasion		2nd occasion		t	p
		Mean	s.d.	Mean	s.d.		<
Boys (25)	Practicality	6·32	1·9	5·56	2·2	2·16	0·05
Staff (7)	Clarity	5·43	1·5	6·43	1·3	4·58	0·01
Staff (7)	Control	0·43	0·5	1·29	1·0	3·29	0·05

As far as the boys on the wings were concerned the extent to which their wings were rated as being "practically" oriented fell significantly over time. This scale attempts to measure ". . . to what extent the resident's environment orientates him towards preparing himself for release". Staff rated the wing environment differently on second testing in terms of the "Clarity" and "Control" sub-scales. The "Clarity" sub-scale is designed to reflect "the extent to which the resident knows what to expect in the day-to-day routine of his programme and how explicit its rules are". The "Control" scale deals with "the extent to which the staff use measures to keep the residents under necessary controls". For both these scales there was a significant increase in staff perceptions of wing environment.

It is not really possible to provide any adequate reason as to why these particular changes should have occurred between testing occasions. A large amount of discussion must have taken place on the wings after the first testing occasion and this discussion may have influenced the opinions expressed at second testing.

2. Internal Consistency and Scale Homogeneity

Eighty-five protocols were used to establish the internal consistency of the nine sub-scales in the test: they were the responses of the men on the three adult Grendon wings, at the first testing occasion. Item total correlations were calculated and an item was considered to be unsuitable if the correlation between the item and the scale total failed to reach significance at the 1% level. Such items are listed in Table *n*.

Table *n*   Inconsistent Items

Scale	Item	r
Practical Orientation	1. This wing emphasises job training	0·12
	2. Staff care more about prisoners' feelings than about practical problems	0·09
	3. Prisoners are expected to work towards their goals	0·23
Clarity	1. When prisoners first come, someone shows them round to explain how the wing operates	0·13
Control	1. Prisoners call staff by their first names	0·02

Of the five items listed in the table only one (item 2 in "Practical Orientation") gives any real cause for concern in terms of internal consistency. The very low correlations produced by the other four items are attributable to the fact that almost all men responded in the same direction to these items, presumably because of the homogenous nature of the Grendon regime. The only item which did not fall into this category is probably ambiguous from the point of view of both content and purpose. The item refers to staff caring about practical problems less than they care about "feelings". One would presume that a good officer will care about both aspects of a man's treatment and that the conflict and relative confusion engendered by asking a man to make such a distinction is reflected in the low item total correlation produced. It would probably be better if this item were to be removed from the scale.

3. Correlations between Scales and Other Variables

On the first occasion of testing, men were asked to state on their questionnaires details of age, length of time in Grendon and number of months left to serve. Similarly, staff were asked to state their age, length of time in Grendon and length of time in the prison service. These variables were correlated with the Moos scales. As far as the men were concerned there was only one correlation of significance: age was found to be positively related to the clarity scale ($r = 0.37$ $p < 0.01$ N = 69). Older men seemed to be more sure of their role on the wing and it is interesting that it was age rather than length of time in Grendon which related to the certainty of role definition. Moos had found that age was negatively related to the clarity scale ($r = -0.25$).

Only one significant correlation was produced by the staff analysis. The length of time which an officer had spent in Grendon was negatively related to his score on the order scale ($r = -0.46$ $p < 0.01$ N = 32). In other words, the more time he had spent in Grendon, the more inclined he was to rate the regime as being non-authoritarian.

Table o presents the correlations between the nine sub-scales.

Of the 36 correlations in the table, 20 (56%) are significant at the 0.10% level and 12 (33%) at greater than the 5% level. Of all nine scales, only "Control" and, to a lesser extent, "Clarity", are independent. On the basis of this result it was felt that it would be worthwhile to attempt to reduce the number of scales, and therefore, items, in the test.

A principal components analysis was carried out and it was found that 50% of the variance of the test could be accounted for by the first factor (Table p).

Most scales were found to load highly on the first component, which suggests that a considerable reduction could be made in the number of scales used in the test. For example, it seems fairly obvious that only one of the first six scales listed above would be necessary to represent the type of evaluation being made by all six scales. In our opinion, those scales labelled by Moos as Involvement, Support, Expressiveness, Autonomy, Practicality, and Insight, all reflect the general factor or concept of "goodness" so that their individual contributions to knowledge of wing atmosphere is minimal.

Three scales did not load highly on the first factor. Two of these — "Order" and "Control" — form the basis of component II, along with Involvement, and Autonomy which has a significant negative loading on the factor. We would suggest that this second component be regarded as reflecting the amount of freedom of action which is allowed in the environment. Clarity, Order and Insight scales all load highly on the

Table o Scale Intercorrelations

	Inv.	Sup.	Exp.	Auto.	Prac.	Inst.	Ord.	Clar.	Control
Involvement	1·000								
Support	0·724	1·000							
Expressiveness	0·580	0·645	1·000						
Autonomy	0·437	0·635	0·567	1·000					
Practicality	0·363	0·618	0·553	0·513	1·000				
Insight	0·555	0·674	0·635	0·467	0·617	1·000			
Order	0·559	0·491	0·290	0·845	0·307	0·278	1·000		
Clarity	0·327	0·386	0·292	0·349	0·338	0·231	0·432	1·000	
Control	0·051	0·225	0·256	−0·440	−0·177	−0·161	−0·059	−0·234	1·000

Table p Principal Components Analysis   N = 85

Scale	Factor I	II	III	IV	V	VI
Involvement	0·36	0·37	0·02	0·42	0·28	0·01
Support	0·42	0·09	−0·08	0·10	−0·04	−0·03
Expressiveness	0·38	−0·07	−0·27	0·08	0·38	−0·23
Autonomy	0·36	−0·33	0·04	0·16	−0·34	−0·66
Practicality	0·35	−0·07	−0·23	−0·59	−0·43	0·12
Insight	0·37	0·04	−0·40	−0·11	0·15	0·46
Order	0·28	0·39	0·50	0·19	−0·47	0·26
Clarity	0·25	−0·02	0·63	−0·53	0·47	−0·11
Control	−0·16	0·76	−0·24	−0·29	−0·03	−0·46
Cumulative proportion of the variance	50	62	74	81	87	91

third component, the latter having a negative weighting. The first two scales in particular reflect the degree of organisation which exists in the environment under examination.

In view of the results produced by the correlation and factor analyses, it seemed legitimate to reduce the number of scales used to three, these being Support, Control and Clarity; this was done for our study. We are not, however, suggesting that other workers should necessarily do likewise. If the Moos scale is to be fundamentally changed then several samples and factor rotations will be required.

4. Validity

During the period of this study the borstal section of Grendon was divided into two wings, which for experimental purposes were run on different lines. One wing was community- and group-oriented, and functioned as a therapeutic community. The other wing was run on strict, traditional borstal lines, with treatment consisting of individual psychotherapy.

It was possible for us to examine the criterion validity of the Moos scales by comparing the performance of the two groups of borstal inmates. In particular we hypothesised that group differences should be apparent for the "Control" sub-scale. Table q gives the mean scores for each wing on the three scales selected for use.

Table q Responses of Inmates in Two Different Types of Borstal Wing

Scale	Traditional (17)		Therapeutic Community (27)		t	p <
	Mean	s.d.	Mean	s.d.		
Support	5·00	2·32	6·81	2·31	2·47	0·05
Clarity	3·88	2·35	5·85	1·55	3·27	0·01
Control	7·06	1·35	2·11	1·34	11·61	0·001

The two treatment groups differed on all three scales although the most highly significant difference was in terms of the authoritarian (control) dimension. The staff on the two wings also differed in terms of "Control" but not in regard to the other scales (Table r).

Table r   Responses of Staff in the Two Borstal Wings

Scale	Traditional (6)		Therapeutic Community (9)		t	p <
	Mean	s.d.	Mean	s.d.		
Support	8·50	1·50	8·78	1·31	0·35	NS
Clarity	5·67	1·24	5·89	1·59	0·27	NS
Control	5·50	1·10	0·33	0·47	8·45	0·001

5. Summary

Because of the high correlations between many of the nine scales, we decided to employ only three — Control, Clarity and Support — each of which we regarded as being relatively independent, and each of which had been shown to have short-term stability. As regards the validity of these scales, we were impressed both by content validity (as reflected by inter-item correlations) and by the criterion related validity produced from the borstal wing comparison.

Appendix 11

POST RELEASE FOLLOW-UP ENQUIRY FORM

Section 1

1. Are you working at present? — please circle

                                    Full Time   Part Time   Not Working

2. How long have you had your present job?

3. Is your employer (or are you, if you are self-
employed) paying National Insurance Stamps?

                                            Yes   No

4. How many jobs have you had since leaving
prison?

_____

5. What has been your longest time in any one job?

_____

6. For the period since you left prison how many
weeks have you been out of work?

_____

7. If you have been out to work, has this been
through

                                            a) Sickness
                                            b) No Jobs
                                            c) Not Tried

(Please give details)

Section II

1. Who are you living with at the moment?
(please underline)

                                            a) Wife
                                            b) Girl friend
                                            c) Friends (male or female)
                                            d) Alone (in a flat or bedsit)
                                            e) Alone (in a probation
                                                hostel)
                                            f) Alone (in a hostel/lodging
                                                house or sleeping rough)
                                            g) Other (please give details)

2. (a) Are you happy with your present living
       arrangements?

                                              Yes   No

   If not why not?

3. This section applies only to those men who were living with their wives or regular
   girl friends before their last sentence.

   a) Are you still living with your wife?   Yes   No

   b) If 'No' to 3 (a) could you please say what has
      happened?

   If 'Yes' to 3 (a) are you getting on well together?

Section III

1. Have you had anything to do with psychiatrists or doctors since leaving prison?
   (Cross out those possible answers which do not apply)

   a) I have been admitted as an inpatient to a
      hospital   *Name of*
                                              Date   *Hospital*

   b) I have been seeing a psychiatrist fairly regularly   *Name*   *Hospital*

   c) I have been to see a doctor for
      (please tick)   (i) Nerves
                                             (ii) Depression
                                             (iii) Headaches

   d) I have had no dealings with any doctors for
      'psychological' things since leaving prison

2. a) Have you tried to kill yourself since leaving   Yes   No

   b) If yes, by what means and why?

c) Has your drinking been—

Very heavy—since leaving
prison
Heavy
Moderate
Very little
Not at all

(Once again, please circle the answer which is correct for you)

d) Have you started taking drugs since leaving
   prison?
   (or returned to taking drugs)   Yes   No

If 'Yes' then which ones and in what sort of
amount?

Section IV

1. Have you been in any trouble with the law since
   leaving?

(Please cross out the answers which do not apply)

a) I have been charged and convicted

Offence   *Date*   *Sentence*

1.

2.

3.

b) I have been charged but am still on remand
                        Offence   *Date*

c) I have not been charged with any offence but
   have been committing offences again**

                                        Type of offence

**Please remember that your replies are in the strictest confidence.

d) I have not been charged with any offences and
    have not committed any

(Once again please circle)

(a) Since leaving prison have you been in contact
    with a probation or aftercare officer?

                                    Regularly

                                    Occasionally

                                    Not at all

(b) If 'not at all' do you think it would have
    helped you to have had some such
    contact?

(c) If 'regularly' or 'occasionally' have you found
    your contact helpful?

Since leaving prison have you been gambling —

                                    Very heavily

                                    To excess

                                    Moderately

                                    Not at all (i.e. hardly anything)

Appendix 12

SOCIAL PERFORMANCE SCALES

These three scales have been selected from a series of twenty which were originally
constructed for this research. The reliability and validity of them have been
commented on elsewhere (Gunn and Robertson, 1976).

Family Relationships

0 = No interpersonal problems in the family. Good contact between most of the living close relatives by visits or letters. Only occasional short-lived rows.
1 = Mild interpersonal problems in the family. Rows and strained relationships confined to only one area of the family (say with an aunt or cousin) but close relationships largely harmonious.
2 = Moderate interpersonal problems in the family. Difficulties and occasional significant rows with three or four close members of the family (e.g. mother or brother).
3 = Severe interpersonal problems in the family. On friendly terms with no-one, or only one member of the family. Most of his family relationships are a series of protracted arguments and rows.
(Test-retest reliability (N = 20) r = 0·69).

Personal Relationships

0 = No interpersonal difficulties. Actively enjoys other people. Plenty of friends, some of which are close and seen frequently. Occasional disharmony between subject and others.
1 = Mild interpersonal difficulties. Evidence of distinct disharmony between subject and others to a signficiant degree. However, proper close friendships maintained with some people in spite of this.
2 = Moderate interpersonal difficulties. Disharmony with others more in evidence than friendships. Finds it difficult to relate to more than one or two people in a close way and most friendships are superficial and inactive.
3 = Severe interpersonal difficulties. No friendships. Avoidance of other people. Subject regards these problems as a significant disability.
(Test-retest reliability (N = 20) r = 0·62).

Alcohol Problem

0 = No drinking problem. No evidence of uncontrolled drinking. Abstains or only drinks socially (some sub-cultures, e.g. salesmen demand more social drinking than others, this should be allowed for).
1 = Mild drinking problem. Evidence of some kind of psychological need for drink (e.g. to calm the nerves). Patients in this category will not be regarded as in need of medical treatment but they could be considered vulnerable. Patients who have had a pathological problem but who have mastered it should be rated here.
2 = Moderate drinking problem. Pathological drinking to a moderate degree. Only occasional dependency or withdrawal symptoms. No real craving or loss of control.
3 = Severe drinking problem. Two or more repeated dependency or withdrawal symptoms. Drinking is a dominant feature of the subject's life. Very likely to have evidence of periods of craving or loss of control.
(Test-retest reliability (N = 20) r = 0·88).

Appendix 13

CENSUS MEDICAL HISTORY QUESTIONNAIRE

MEDICAL HISTORY

Please circle *YES* or *NO* to the answers below as appropriate. Remember all the answers you give are confidential and are not revealed in any way to the prison authorities or the police.

Have you (or do you now) suffered from sugar diabetes?	YES	NO
Have you ever had a serious head injury involving *both* loss of consciousness and admission to hospital?	YES	NO
Do you suffer from epileptic fits or take medicines for epilepsy?	YES	NO
Have you ever received out-patient psychiatric treatment in the National Health Service?	YES	NO
Have you ever been an in-patient at a mental hospital?	YES	NO
Have you ever been to Grendon Prison?	YES	NO
Have you had any other kind of psychiatric treatment during any imprisonment?	YES	NO
Would you like (or would you have liked) some psychiatric treatment during your present sentence?	YES	NO
Would you like (or would you have liked) to go to Grendon psychiatric prison during your present sentence?	YES	NO
Are you a heavy drinker (of alcohol)?	YES	NO
Do you have a drink problem?	YES	NO

Are you a heavy gambler?   YES   NO

Do you have a gambling problem?   YES   NO

Have you ever taken drugs other than those
prescribed by the doctor?   YES   NO

If yes — please tick which ones
                    Hashish or cannabis (pot)
                    LSD (acid)
                    Amphetamines (blues, etc.) or Methedrine
                    Pethidine
                    Cocaine
                    Others (please state which): —

Have you ever tried to kill yourself?   YES   NO

Comments (if any)

Appendix 14

THE SELF RATING SYMPTOM SCALE
(35 item scale)

This is the shortest version of a 90-item scale currently under development (see Derogatis *et al.* (1973), Derogatis *et al.* (to be published)). Unfortunately we chose the brief scale before we realised that most of the reliability data available applies to the longer 58-item or 90-item versions (Lipman *et al.* 1965; Uhlenhuth *et al.* 1966). The check-lists have been factor-analysed into five primary factors — somatization, obsessive compulsive, interpersonal sensitivity, depression, and anxiety. Test-retest correlations (period unspecified) for the five sub-scales ranged from $r = 0.75$ to $r = 0.84$ (Lipman, personal communication).

We have not subsequently used the five sub-scales. Unfortunately we have no data on the test-retest reliability of the 35-item version used, although it seems highly unlikely that it would be below $r = 0.75$.

The questionnaire is reproduced below.

SELF-RATING SYMPTOM SCALE

INSTRUCTIONS: Listed below are 35 symptoms of problems that people sometimes have. Please read each one carefully and decide how much the symptoms bothered you *during the past week, including today.*

Decide how much the symptom affected you: NOT AT ALL? A LITTLE? QUITE A BIT? EXTREMELY? and place a tick in the appropriate column to the right.

HOW MUCH WERE YOU BOTHERED BY THE FOLLOWING SYMPTOMS: (Do not leave out any items)

SYMPTOMS	NOT AT ALL	A LITTLE	QUITE A BIT	EXTREMELY
	1	2	3	4
1. Sweating				
2. Trouble getting your breath				
3. Suddenly scared for no reason				
4. Difficulty in speaking when you are excited				
5. Feeling low in energy or slowed down				
6. Pains in the heart or chest				
7. Trouble remembering things				
8. Hot or cold spells				
9. Blaming yourself for things				
10. A lump in your throat				
11. Feeling fearful				

SYMPTOMS	NOT AT ALL	A LITTLE	QUITE A BIT	EXTREMELY
	1	2	3	4
12. Numbness or tingling in parts of your body				
13. Feeling critical of others				
14. Having to avoid certain things, places or activities because they frighten you				
15. Having to do things very slowly in order to be sure you are doing them right				
16. Heavy feeling in your arms or legs				
17. Faintness or dizziness				
18. Crying easily				
19. Nervousness or shakiness inside				
20. Your feelings being easily hurt				
21. Constipation				
22. Loss of sexual interest or pleasure				
23. Feeling easily annoyed or irritated				
24. Poor appetite				
25. Difficulty making decisions				
26. Difficulty in falling asleep or staying asleep				
27. Feeling hopeless about the future				
28. Feeling blue				

SYMPTOMS	NOT AT ALL	A LITTLE	QUITE A BIT	EXTREMELY
	1	2	3	4
29. Feeling lonely				
30. Temper outbursts you could not control				
31. Headaches				
32. Heart pounding or racing				
33. Trouble concentrating				
34. Your mind going blank				
35. Thoughts of ending your life				

References

Ahana, E. (1952) *A Study on the Reliability and Internal Consistency of a Manifest Anxiety Scale.* M.A. Thesis (unpublished).

American Psychiatric Association (1968) *Diagnostic and Statistical Manual of Mental Disorders,* 2nd edn. Washington, D.C.

Baly, W. (1852) In *Report of the Directors of Convict Prisons for 1851.* HMSO.

Barron, F. (1953) "An Ego-Strength Scale which predicts Response to Psychotherapy". *Journal of Consulting Psychology,* 17, 327-33.

Bennett, L. A. (1974) "Application of Self Esteem Measures in a Correction Setting". *Journal of Research in Crime and Delinquency,* 11, 9-15.

Billewicz, W. Z., Chapman, R. S., Crooks, J., Day, M. E., Gossage, J., Wayne, N. E. and Young, J. A. (1969) "Statistical Techniques Applied to the Diagnosis of Hypothyroidism". *Quarterly Journal of Medicine, New Series,* 38, 255-66.

Bluglass, R. (1966) *A Psychiatric Study of Scottish Prisoners.* M.D. Thesis (unpublished).

Bolton, N., Smith, F. V., Heskin, K. J. and Bannister, P. A. (1976) "Psychological Correlation of Long Term Imprisonment IV: A Longitudinal Analysis". *British Journal of Criminology,* 16, 38-47.

Bowden, P. (1975a) "Liberty and Psychiatry". *British Medical Journal,* 4, 94-6.

Bowden, P. (1975b) "Reliability of Prisoners' Attitudes to their Drinking Behaviour". *Psychological Medicine,* 5, 307-13.

Branthwaite, R. W. (1903) In *Report of Commissioners of Prisons and Directors of Convict Prisons (1901-2).* HMSO.

Brody, S. R. (1976) *The Effectiveness of Sentencing.* London, HMSO.

Brown, R. A. and Goodstein, L. D. (1962) "Adjective Checklist Correlates of Extreme Scores on the MMPI Depression Scale". *Journal of Clinical Psychology,* 18, 477-81.

Butcher, J. M. (1969) *MMPI Research Developments and Clinical Applications.* McGraw-Hill.

Campbell, J. (1856) In *Report of the Directors of Convict Prisons for 1855.* HMSO.

Campbell, J. (1884) *Thirty Years' Experience of a Medical Officer in the English Convict Service.* Nelson, London.

Cattell, R. B. and Scheier, I. A. (1961) *The Meaning and Measurement of Neuroticism and Anxiety.* Ronald, New York.

Clarke, R. V. G. and Cornish, D. B. (1972) *The Controlled Trial in Institutional Research: Paradigm or Pitfall for Penal Evaluators?* Home Office Research Studies No. 15. HMSO.

Clarke, R. V. and Sinclair, I. (1974) "Toward More Effective Treatment Evaluation". In *First Criminological Colloquium on Methods of Evaluation and Planning in the Field of Crime*. Council of Europe.

Clemmer, D. (1940) *The Prison Community*. Holt, New York (1958).

Commissioners of Prisons (1921) *Report for 1919-20*. HMSO.

Commissioners of Prisons (1924) *Report for 1922-3* (p. 50). HMSO.

Commissioners of Prisons (1930) *Report for 1929*. HMSO.

Commissioners of Prisons (1939) *Report for 1938*. HMSO.

Commissioners of Prisons (1945) *Report for 1942-4*. HMSO.

Commissioners of Prisons (1947) *Report for 1946*. HMSO.

Commissioners of Prisons (1948) *Report for 1947*. HMSO.

Commissioners of Prisons (1949) *Report for 1948*. HMSO.

Commissioners of Prisons (1950) *Report for 1949*. HMSO.

Commissioners of Prisons (1951) *Report for 1950*. HMSO.

Commissioners of Prisons (1957) *Report for 1956*. HMSO.

Commissioners of Prisons (1958) *Report for 1957*. HMSO.

Commissioners of Prisons (1961) *Report for 1960*. HMSO.

Commissioners of Prisons (1963) *Report for 1962*. HMSO.

Commissioners of Prisons and Directors of Convict Prisons (1902) *Report for 1900-01*. HMSO.

Commissioners of Prisons and Directors of Convict Prisons (1905) *Report for 1903-4*. HMSO.

Commissioners of Prisons and Directors of Convict Prisons (1910) *Report for 1908-9*. HMSO.

Comrey, A. L. (1957a) "A Factor Analysis of the Items on the MMPI Hypochondriasis Scale". *Education and Psychological Measurement*, 17, 568-77.

Comrey, A. L. (1957b) "A Factor Analysis of the Items on the MMPI Depression Scale". *Education and Psychological Measurement*, 17, 568-77.

Cornish, D. B. and Clarke, R. V. (1975) *Residential Treatment and Its Effects on Delinquency*. HMSO.

Deese, J., Lazarus, R. S. and Keenan, J. (1953) "Anxiety, Anxiety Reduction and Stress in Learning". *Journal of Experimental Psychology*, 46, 55-60.

Derogatis, L. R., Lipman, R. S. and Covi, L. (1973) "SCL-90: An Outpatient Psychiatric Rating Scale (Preliminary Report)". *Psychopharmacological Bulletin*, 9, 13-28.

Derogatis, L. R., Lipman, R. S., Rickels, K., Uhlenhuth, E. H. and Covi, L. "The Symptom Distress Check List (SCL): A Measure of Primary Symptom Dimensions". In *Psychological Measurements* (P. Pichot, ed.). To be published.

Directors of Convict Prisons (1874) *Report for 1873*. HMSO.

Directors of Convict Prisons (1875) *Report for 1874*. HMSO.

Directors of Convict Prisons (1879) *Report for 1878*. HMSO.

Drake, L. E. (1946) "A Social I—E Scale for the MMPI". *Journal of Applied Psychology*, 30, 51-4.

Du Cane, E. (1874) In *Report of the Directors of Convict Prisons for 1873*. HMSO.

East, W. N. (1932) In *Report of the Commissions for Prisons for 1931*. HMSO.

East, W. N. (1949) *Society and the Criminal*. HMSO.

East, W. N. and Hubert, W. H. de B. (1939) *The Psychological Treatment of Crime*. HMSO.

Edwards, A. L. (1957) *Techniques of Attitude Scale Construction.* Appleton-Century-Crofts, New York.

Elkin, W. A. (1957) *The English Penal System.* Penguin, Harmondsworth.

Ellis, A. (1947) "Questionnaire versus Interview Methods in the Study of Human Love Relationships". *American Sociological Review,* **12,** 541-53.

Ellis, A. (1970) "A Review of the MMPI". In *Personality Tests and Reviews* (O. K. Buros, ed.). Gryphon Press, New York.

Erikson, C. W. and Davids, A. (1955) "The Meaning and Clinical Validity of the Taylor Anxiety Scale and the Hysteria-Psychasthenia Scales from the MMPI". *Journal of Abnormal and Social Psychology,* **50,** 135-7.

Eysenck, H. J. (1963) *The Eysenck Personality Inventory.* Educational and Industrial Testing Service. San Diego.

Eysenck, H. J. (1964) *Crime and Personality.* Routledge & Kegan Paul, London.

Finn, J. D. (1968) *Multivariance: Univariate Analyses of Variance, Co-Variance and Regression (A Fortran IV Program, Version 4).* Suny/B Mimeograph. Computing Center, State University of New York at Buffalo.

Fowler, R. D. (1969) *MMPI Research Developments and Clinical Applications,* Chapter 6 (J. M. Butcher, ed.). McGraw-Hill.

Fox, L. (1952) *The English Prison and Borstal Systems.* Routledge & Kegan Paul, London.

General Penitentiary Millbank (1822) *Rules and Regulations.* Hansard, London.

General Register Office (1968) *A Glossary of Mental Disorders.* HMSO.

Gibbens, T. C. N. (1966) "The Development of Forensic Psychiatry". In *Concepts of Crime and Its Treatment* (Hugh Klare, ed.). Pergamon Press, Oxford.

Giedt, F. N. and Downing, L. (1961) "An Extraversion Scale of the MMPI". *Journal of Clinical Psychology,* **17,** 156-9.

Glasse, (1968) 53 CR App. R. 121

Glatt, M. (1974) Letter in *British Medical Journal,* ii, 56.

Goffman, E. (1961) *Asylums.* Penguin, Harmondsworth.

Goldberg, D. (1972) *The Detection of Psychiatric Illness by Questionnaire.* Oxford University Press, London.

Goldberg, D. P., Cooper, B., Eastwood, M. R., Kedward, H. B. and Shepherd, M. "A Standardised Psychiatric Interview Suitable for Use in Community Surveys". *British Journal of Preventive and Social Medicine,* **24,** 18.

Gordon, M. (1922) *Penal Discipline.* Routledge, London.

Gottesman, I. I. (1959) "More Construct Validation of the Ego-Strength Scale". *Journal of Consulting Psychology,* **23,** 342-6.

Gough, H. G. (1952) "Predicting Social Participation". *Journal of Social Psychology,* **35,** 227-33.

Gray, W. J. (1973a) "The English Prison Medical Service". In *the Medical Care of Prisoners and Detainees.* Ciba, Elsevier, Amsterdam.

Gray, W. J. (1973b) "The Therapeutic Community and Evaluation of Results". *International Journal of Criminology and Penology,* **1,** 327-34.

Gunn, J. (1971) "Forensic Psychiatry and Psychopathic Patients". *British Journal of Hospital Medicine,* **66,** 1133-5.

Gunn, J. (1973) "The Evaluation of Violence". *Proceedings of the Royal Society of Medicine,* **66,** 1133-5.

Gunn, J. (1974) "Disasters, Asylums and Plans: Forensic Psychiatry Today". *British Medical Journal*, 3, 611-3.

Gunn, J. (1977) *Epileptics in Prison.* Academic Press, London.

Gunn, J. and Robertson, G. (1976a) "Psychopathic Disorder, a Conceptual Problem". *Psychological Medicine.*

Gunn, J. and Robertson, G. (1976b) "Drawing a Criminal Profile". *British Journal of Criminology*, 16, 156-60.

Hamblin-Smith, M. (1922) *The Psychology of the Criminal.* Methuen, London.

Hamblin-Smith, M. (1923) In *Report of Commissioners of Prisons for 1921-2* (þ. 39). HMSO.

Hamblin-Smith, M. (1925) In *Report of Commissioners of Prisons for 1923-4* (p. 39). HMSO.

Hamblin-Smith, M. (1926) In *Report of Commissioners of Prisons for 1924-5.* HMSO.

Hamblin-Smith, M. (1934) *Prisons and a Changing Civilisation.* John Lane, London.

Hansard (1974) Volume 877, 18 July, Columns 225-6.

Hathaway, S. R. (1956) Chapter 10 in *Basic Readings on the MMPI in Psychology and Medicine* (G. S. Welsh and W. G. Dahlstrom, eds). University of Minnesota Press, Minneapolis.

Hathaway, S. R. and McKinley, J. C. (1956) Chapter 7 in *Basic Readings on the MMPI in Psychology and Medicine* (G. S. Welsh and W. G. Dahlstrom, eds). University of Minnesota Press, Minneapolis.

Heim, (1970) *Manual for the AH4 Group Test of General Intelligence.* NFER Publishing Co., Windsor.

Heron, A. (1956) "The Effects of Real-Life Motivation on Questionnaire Response". *Journal of Applied Psychology*, 40, 65-8.

Heskin, K. J., Bolton, N., Smith, F. V. and Bannister, P. A. (1974) "Psychological Correlates of Long Term Imprisonment. III: Attitudinal Variables". *British Journal of Criminology*, 14, 150-7.

Hobhouse, S. and Brockway, F. (1922) *English Prisons Today.* Longmans, London.

Hochstim, J. (1962) "A Comparison of Three Information Gathering Strategies in a Population Study of Sociomedical Variables". *American Statistical Association, Social Statistics Proceedings*, 154-9.

Home Office (1895) *Report from the Departmental Committee on Prisons (The Gladstone Committee)*, C.7702. HMSO.

Home Office (1932) *Report of the Departmental Committee on Persistent Offenders*, Cnmd 4090. HMSO.

Home Office (1959) *Penal Practice in a Changing Society*, Cnmd 645. HMSO.

Home Office (1964) *Organisation of the Prison Medical Service.* HMSO.

Home Office (1969) *People in Prison.* HMSO.

Home Office (1971) *Report of the Working Party on Habitual Drunken Offenders.* HMSO.

Home Office (1972) *Report on Work of the Prison Department 1971.* HMSO.

Home Office (1973) *Report on Work of the Prison Department 1972.* HMSO.

Home Office, DHSS (1974) *Interim Report of the Committee on Mentally Abnormal Offenders*, Cnmd 5698. HMSO.

Home Office, DHSS (1975) *Report of the Committee on Mentally Abnormal Offenders*, Cnmd 6244. HMSO.

Hood, R. and Sparks, R. (1970) *Key Issues in Criminology*. World University Library, London.

Howard, J. (1777) *The State of the Prisons in England and Wales*. Warrington.

Kassenbaum, G. G., Gough, A. S. and Slater, P. E. (1969) "The Factorial Dimensions of the MMPI". *Journal of Consulting Psychology*, **23**, 226-36.

Kelly, G. A. (1955) *The Psychology of Personal Constructs*. Norton, New York.

Kleinmutz, B. (1961) "The College Maladjustment Scale Norms and Predictive Validity". *Education and Psychological Measurement*, **21**, 1029-33.

Leverenz, C. W. (1943) "MMPI: An Evaluation of Its Usefulness in the Psychiatric Service of a Station Hospital". *War Medicine*, **4**, 618-24.

Lewis, A. (1953) "Health as a Social Concept". *British Journal of Sociology*, **4**, 109-24.

Likert, R. (1932) "A Technique for the Measurement of Attitudes". *Archives of Psychology*, No. 140.

Lipman, R. S., Park, L. C. and Rickels, K. (1965) "Sensitivity of Symptom and Non-Symptom Focused Criteria of Outpatient Drug Efficacy". *American Journal of Psychiatry*, **122**, 24-7.

Mannheim, H. (1965) *Comparative Criminology*. Routledge & Kegan Paul, London.

Mark, R. and Scott, P. D. (1972) *The Disease of Crime*. Royal Society of Medicine, London.

Martinson, R. (1972) "What Works?". *The Public Interest*, **35**, 22-54.

Meehl, P. E. and Hathaway, S. R. (1946) "The K Factor as a Suppressor Variable in the MMPI". *Journal of Applied Psychology*, **30**, 525-64.

Merton, R. K. (1938) "Social Structure and Anomie". *American Sociology Review*, **3**, 672-82.

Ministry of Health (1961) *Report of the Working Party on Special Hospitals*. HMSO.

Moos, R. (1968) "Assessment of Social Climates in Correctional Institutions". *Journal of Research in Crime and Delinquency*, **5**, 174.

Moos, R. (1971) *Revision of Ward Atmosphere Scales*. Technical Report

Newton, M. (1971) *Reconviction after Treatment at Grendon*. Chief Psychologist's Reports: Home Office Series B No. 1 (unpublished).

Northfield Experiment (1949) A series of papers by Main, T. F., Bridger, H., Dion, W. R., Dewar, M. C. and Foulkes, S. H. in the *Bulletin of the Meninger Clinic*, **10**, 66-89.

O'Connor, J. B., Stefic, E. C. and Gresock, P. J. (1957) "Some Patterns of Depression". *Journal of Clinical Psychology*, **13**, 122-5.

Osgood, G. E., Suci, G. J. and Tannenbaum, P. H. (1957) *The Measurement of Meaning*. University Press, Illinois.

Parliamentary Papers (1872) *Report from the Select Committee on Habitual Drunkards. House of Commons Paper No. 242*. HMSO.

Parliamentary Papers (1893) *Report from the Departmental Committee on the Treatment of Inebriates, C. 7008*. HMSO.

Passingham, R. E. (1967) *Crime and Personality: A Review of Professor Eysenck's Theory*. M.Sc. Thesis (unpublished).

Penrose, L. (1939) "Mental Disease and Crime: Outline of a Comparative Study of European Statistics". *British Journal of Medical Psychology*, **18**, 1-13.

Prewer, R. R. (1974) "Prison Medicine" In *Progress in Penal Reform* (L. Blom-Cooper, ed.). Clarendon Press, Oxford.

Redlich, F. C. and Freedman, D. X. (1966) *The Theory and Practice of Psychiatry*. Basic Books, New York.

Robertson, G. (1974) *An Examination of the Psychiatric Services in Two British Prisons*. Ph.D. Thesis (unpublished).

Roethlinberger, E. J. and Dickson, W. F. (1939) *Management and the Worker*. Harvard University Press, Cambridge, Mass.

Rollin, H. R. (1968) *The Mentally Abnormal Offender and the Law*. Pergamon Press, Oxford.

Rosin, H. and Townsend, A. H. (1958) "The Taylor Manifest Anxiety Scale in Differential Diagnosis". *Journal of Clinical Psychology*, 14, 81-3.

Royal Commission (1908) *The Care and Control of the Feeble Minded*, Cnmd 4202. HMSO.

Royal Commission (1932) *Report on Licensing (England and Wales) 1929-31*. HMSO.

Royal Commission (1958). *The Law Relating to Mental Illness and Mental Deficiency*, Cnmd 169. HMSO.

Sinclair, I. (1971) *Hostels for Probationers*. HMSO.

Slater, P. (1976) *Explorations of Intrapersonal Space*. Wiley, London.

Solzhenitsyn, A. (1968) *One Day in the Life of Ivan Denisovich*. Penguin, Harmondsworth.

Stanton, H. E. (1971) "The Taylor Scale: a Measurement of Chronic Anxiety or of Emotional Reactivity". *Australian Journal of Psychology*, 23, 69-72.

Taft, R. A. (1951) "The Validity of the Carron Ego Strength Scale and the Welsh Anxiety Index". *Journal of Consulting Psychology*, 14, 81-3.

Taylor, J. A. (1953) "A Personality Scale of Manifest Anxiety". *Journal of Abnormal and Social Psychology*, 48, 285-90.

Thomas, D. A. (1970) *Principles of Sentencing*. Heinemann, London.

Uhlenhuth, E. H., Rickels, K., Fisher, S., Park, L. C., Lipman, R. S. and Mock, J. (1966) "Drug, Doctors' Verbal Attitude and Clinic Setting in the Symptomatic Response of Pharmacotherapy". *Psychopharmologia*, 9, 392-418.

Walker, N. (1968) *Crime and Insanity in England*, Vol. 1. Edinburgh University Press.

Walker, N. (1970) *Crime and Punishment in Britain*. Edinburgh University Press.

Walker, N. and McCabe, S. (1973) *Crime and Insanity in England*, Vol. 2. Edinburgh University Press.

Walton, H. J. and Presly, A. S. (1973) "Use of a Category System in the Diagnosis of Abnormal Personality". *British Journal of Psychiatry*, 122, 259-68.

Webb, S. and Webb, B. (1922) *English Prisons and Local Government*. Longmans, London.

Welsh, G. S. and Dahlstrom, W. G. (1956) *Basic Readings on the MMPI in Psychology and Medicine*. University of Minnesota Press, Minneapolis.

Wheeler, S. (1961) "Socialisation in Correctional Communities". *American Sociological Review*, 26, 697-712.

Wiggins, J. S. (1969) Chapter 7 in *MMPI Research Developments and Clinical Applications* (J. M. Butcher, ed.). McGraw-Hill.

Wing, J. K., Birley, J. L. T., Cooper, J. E., Graham, P. and Isaacs, A. D. (1967) "Reliability of a Procedure for Measuring and Classifying Present Psychiatric State". *British Journal of Psychiatry*, 113, 499-515.

Wootton, B. (1959) *Social Science and Social Pathology*. Allen & Unwin, London.

Government
Reports and Legislation

Figures after titles refer to page numbers

1774, An Act for Preserving the Health of Prisoners in Gaol and Preventing Gaol Distemper, 1

1808, County Asylum Act, 4

1872, Departmental Committee on Inebriety, 12

1889, Home Office Circular, 7

1893, Departmental Committee on Inebriety, 12

1895, Gladstone Committee Report, 8-10

1898, Inebriates Act, 12

1904-8, Royal Commission on the Care and Control of the Feeble Minded, 11

1908, Departmental Committee on Inebriety, 11

1908, Royal Commission on Mental Deficiency, 13

1909, Royal Commission on the Poor Laws, 11

1913, Mental Deficiency Act, 13, 14, 15, 18

1927, Mental Deficiency Act, 13

1931-2, Departmental Committee on Persistent Offenders, 19

1932, Royal Commission on Licensing, 13

1939, East-Hubert Report, 19-22

1946, National Health Service Act, 23

1948, Criminal Justice Act, 24

1958, Royal Commission on the Law Relating to Mental Illness and Mental Deficiency, 26-27

1959, Mental Health Act, 26-31

1961, Working Party on Special Hospitals, 29

1964, Working Party on the Organisation of the Prison Medical Service, 31

1967, Criminal Justice Act, 13

1972, Criminal Justice Act, 13

1975, Butler Committee Report on Mentally Abnormal Offenders, 29, 259

Index

Adjustment to prison, *see* Prisonisation

Affective psychosis, 220

After care, *see* Community care

Age,
  of Grendon sample, 53-4, 172
  of South East Region sample, 217, 235, 238, 239
  of Wormwood Scrubs sample, 129

Alcohol problems, *see also* Inebriate offenders, 12, 13, 144, 175, 180, 185, 186, 187, 194, 198, 202-3, 213, 220, 222, 224, 234-6, 238, 239, 241-6, 256, 301

Alcoholism, *see* Alcohol problems

Amygdelectomy, *see* Brain surgery

"Any Questions", 99, 195, 200

Asylums, 4, 6, 7, 9, 256

Attempted suicide, 175, 180, 198, 213, 217, 220, 222, 234, 244

Attitudes, *see also* Moos Social Climate Questionnaire
  of staff, 89-91
  to authority, 47, 67-8, 113-6, 119, 120, 138-9, 154, 160-1, 176, 183, 185, 188, 190-2, 200, 286-90
  to crime, 46-7, 66-7, 120-1, 139-40, 150-1, 167, 175, 185, 188, 190, 212, 217, 234, 236, 239, 245, 281-6
  to doctors, *see* Attitudes to authority
  to psychiatry, 46, 65-6, 120-1, 139-40, 150-1, 175, 177, 183, 188, 190-3, 212, 217, 220, 221, 225, 226, 234, 236, 239, 245, 274-9
  to self, *see* Self esteem
  to social workers, *see* Attitudes to authority
  to treatment, *see* Desire for treatment

Aversion therapy, 25

Aylesbury State Reformatory, 12

Behaviour therapy, 257

Birmingham prison, 16, 17

Borstal system, 10

Brain surgery, 257

British Medical Association, 27

Broadmoor, *see also* Special Hospitals, 6, 7, 230

Butler Report, 29, 259

CRO data, 182, 188-9

Case histories, 194-205

Case identification, *see also* Census, 41-3, 44, 218-24, 226, 238, 255

Census,
  discriminant function analysis, 221-3
  drinking behaviour, 241-6
  factor analysis, 247
  false negatives, 222-3, 224
  false positives, 222-3, 223-4
  gambling, 247
  Home Office Research Unit, 41, 209, 214-7, 227, 231, 247-9
  illegal drug taking, 236-40
  medical history, 211-2, 218, 227, 302-3
  questionnaire, 42, 211-4, 217-24, 227, 302-3
  questionnaire refusers, 219
  responders v. non-responders, 214-7
  sample bias, 214-7
  sentence length factors, 233-6, 241, 242
  validation by interview, 218-24

Clemmer, D., 117, 138

Community care, 258, 259-60

Compulsory treatment, 210

Control study, 169-79, 181, 251-3

Crime prevention, 253-4, 258, 259-60

Criminal activities after release, *see also* Reconviction, 181, 188-9
Criminal histories,
  method, 44-5, 261, 291-3
  of Grendon sample, 56-8, 68-71, 73, 156, 157, 172, 173, 176-7, 185, 188, 189, 190-1, 192-3
  of South East Region sample, 213, 215, 216, 217
  of Wormwood Scrubs sample, 129-30, 133-6, 156, 157, 185, 188-9, 190-1
Criminal Profile, 45, 265-7
  drink rating, 266
  drugs rating, 173-4, 185, 266
  financial gain, 173-4, 185, 267
  fraud rating, 183, 191, 265
  motoring rating, 266
  sex rating, 265-6
  theft rating, 173, 183, 185, 189, 191, 265
  violence rating, 266
Criminality, 247-9, 255-7
Criminogenesis, 167-8

Dartmoor prison, 6
Demand for services, 209, 226-7, 256
Depression Scale, 63-4, 106, 108, 138
Desire for treatment, 46, 65-6, 67, 139-40, 175, 188, 190-1, 192-3, 199, 211-2, 213, 216, 217, 218, 220, 221, 222, 223, 224, 225, 226, 230, 234, 236, 238, 239, 243, 246, 251, 280-1
Deterrence, 166, 168
Distemper, gaol, 1
Doctor-patient relationship, 5
Drinking habits, *see* Alcohol problems
Drug dependence, *see* Drug taking
Drug taking, *see also* Criminal histories, 144, 156, 173, 180, 187, 195, 196, 201, 213, 217, 220, 234, 236-40, 243, 244, 248-9, 256
Drunkenness, *see* Alcohol problems
Du Cane, Edmund, 3, 4, 10

ECT, *see* Physical treatments
East-Hubert Report, 19-22

Education,
  of Grendon sample, 54, 172
  of Wormwood Scrubs sample, 136
Ego strength, *see* MMPI
Employment,
  during follow-up, 180, 186
  of Grendon sample, 55, 171
  of South East Region sample, 215, 216
  of Wormwood Scrubs sample, 136-7
Environmental influences, 167
Epilepsy, 213, 217, 256
Ether abreaction, 25
Expectations about treatment, 226-7
Extroversion, *see* MMPI

Family histories,
  of Grendon sample, 53, 172
  of South East Region sample, 215
  of Wormwood Scrubs sample, 136
Family relationships, *see also* Family histories, 184-5, 301
Feeble minded persons and prisoners, *see also* Mental defectives, 6, 7, 8, 11, 13, 18
Fetishism, 230
Follow-up studies, 169-79, 180-193, 296-300
  reconvicted *v* non-reconvicted, 188-193
  re-offenders *v* non-offenders, 184-7
  responders *v* non-responders, 182-3

GHQ, *see* General Health Questionnaire
Gaol fever, 2
Gambling, 217, 234, 243, 244, 247, 256
General Health Questionnaire, 49-50, 111-3, 132, 147-8, 162-3, 174, 180, 182-3, 186-7, 212, 217, 220, 221, 227-8, 230, 231, 234, 239, 245
Gray, Dr. William, 52, 65-6, 76-9, 83, 259
Grendon,
  follow-ups, *see also* Follow-up studies, 166-79, 181, 194-205
  Grendon effect, 46, 166, 170, 177, 179, 194-205, 253, 254, 257, 259
  history of, 30, 31

regime, 76-101, 157, 159, 194, 252, 253, 257, 258
sample, 52-75, 78, 80, 102-123, 156-65, 170, 171-2, 179, 192-3
staff, 78-9, 88-92
unsuitable men, 71-4
Group psychotherapy, *see also* Grendon regime, 23, 145-6, 150-3, 257, 258
Groups, Statistics of, 254-5

Hamblin-Smith, Dr. M., 16-17, 32, 46
Heim Intelligence Test, 50, 54-5, 263-4
Holloway prison, 30
Home leave, 99-100
Hormone treatment, *see* Physical treatment
Hospital order, 28, 29
Howard, John, 1, 2, 4
Hulks, 3, 6
Hypochondriasis, *see* MMPI, *or* Psychiatric interview

Illiteracy, 215, 216, 219
Imbeciles, *see* Mental defectives
Inebriate offender, 9, 11, 12, 13
Insight, 103, 147, 159
Intelligence, *see also* Heim Intelligence Test,
of Grendon sample, 53-4, 156, 172, 177
of Wormwood Scubs sample, 136, 156
Introversion, *see* MMPI

Length of Sentence, *see* Criminal history
Living arrangements after release, 171, 180, 186
Long term prisoners, 233-6

MMPI, 45, 61-5, 73, 102, 103-9, 119, 137-8, 174, 184, 187, 188, 190, 267-73
clinical statements, 268
Ego Strength Scale, 63-4, 105, 106, 108, 138, 183, 271-2
Extroversion Scale, 63, 65, 106, 108, 137-8, 272
Extroversion scales, 63, 65, 105-6, 108-9, 138
F Validity Scale, 107-9, 174

Hypochondriasis Scale, 63-4, 106, 108, 138, 269
Manifest Anxiety Scale, 63-4, 105, 106, 108, 138, 270
Manifest Hostility Scale, 63, 65, 106, 108, 119, 137-8, 273
Neuroticism scales, 63-4, 105-7, 108-9, 137, 138, 269
Social Introversion Scale, 63, 65, 105, 106, 108, 137, 138, 269
Manifest anxiety, *see* MMPI
Manifest hostility, see MMPI
Manslaughter, *see also* Violent offenders, 224
Marital histories,
after release, 186-7, 199
of Grendon sample, 55, 171
of Wormwood Scrubs sample, 136
Matching, 170-6, 176-8, 180-1
Medical myth, 168
Medium term prisoners, 233-6
Mental defectives, *see also* Feeble minded persons and prisoners, 8, 9, 11, 13, 15, 16, 18
Millbank Penitentiary, 3, 6
Minnesota Multiphasic Personality Inventory, *see* MMPI
Moos Social Climate Questionnaire, 93-8, 291-6
Moral defectives, *see also* Psychopathic disorder, 13, 14, 26, 27, 28, 36
Moral imbeciles, *see* Moral defectives
Motivation, *see* Attitudes and Desire for treatment

Narcoanalysis, 25
Neurosis, *see also* MMPI, *or* Psychiatric characteristics, 220
Non-Sane, Non-Insane, 17-19
Northfield Experiment, 23, 258

Open door policy, 28

Parental separation, *see* Family histories
Parkhurst prison, 7, 8, 10, 259
Parole, 215, 216, 258
Parole board, 31
Parole index, 170-1, 176

Personal relationships, *see also* Family histories, 184-5, 301

Personality characteristics, *see* MMPI

Personality disorder, *see also* Psychopathic disorder, 36-8, 41, 220, 225

Physical treatments, 25, 28, 257

Postal enquiry, *see* Follow-up studies

Prevalence of psychiatric disorder, 223, 224-6, 227-9, 256

Previous psychiatric histories, 58, 133-4, 175, 187, 211, 212, 213, 215, 216, 217, 218, 220, 221, 222, 226, 229, 238, 239, 243, 244

Prison diet, 4, 5, 8, 10

Prison surgeon, 3-5

Prisonisation, 117-20, 228, 257

Probation, 24

Psychiatric characteristics,
  as a cause of crime, 168, 187, 247-9, 255-7
  of Grendon sample, 58-61, 109-13, 156, 162-4, 168, 174, 184, 188, 190
  of South East Region sample, 60, 148, 163-4
  of Wormwood Scrubs sample, 130-3, 147-50, 156, 162-4, 184, 188, 190

Psychiatric diagnoses,
  of Grendon sample, 61
  of South East Region sample, 209-10, 219-20
  of Wormwood Scrubs sample, 132

Psychiatric interview, *see also* Psychiatric characteristics, 48-9, 102, 174, 187, 218, 220

Psychiatric problems after release, 180, 186-7

Psychiatric social workers, 24

Psychologists, 24, 84, 90, 91

Psychopathic disorder, *see also* Personality disorder, 28, 36-8, 41

Psychopaths, *see also* Moral defectives, 14, 18, 23, 26, 27

Psychotherapists, visiting, 25, 31, 33, 157

Psychotherapy, *see also* Group psychotherapy, 14-17, 19, 20, 21, 22, 23, 24, 25, 30, 39-40, 46, 80, 83-5, 91-2, 127-8, 133, 143-6, 153, 154, 157, 158, 159, 227, 257

Psychotropic drugs, *see* Physical treatments

Random allocation, 178, 251-2

Rape, *see also* Sex offenders, 224, 230

Recidivism, *see also* Criminal histories, 247-9, 256

Reconviction, 166-79, 180-93, 253-4, 254, 259

Referral agencies, 71, 128-9

Reform, 167

Re-interview schedule, 50-1, 290

Reliability, *see also* individual scales, 48, 214

Revolving door, 28

Risley remand centre, 30

Royal Medico-Psychological Association, 27

"Rule 43", 157, 158

SRSS, *see* Self Rated Symptom Scale

Sadism, 202

Schizophrenia, 220

Secure hospital units, 29

Self esteem, 47, 67-8, 113-6, 118-9, 120, 138-9, 150-2, 153, 160-2, 176, 188, 286-90

Self Rated Symptom Scale, 212, 217, 220, 221, 222, 234, 239, 245, 303-6

Semantic differential, *see also* Attitudes, 47, 68, 103-20, 150-2, 160, 190, 286-90

Sexual deviation, *see also* Sex offenders, 220, 257

Sex offenders, *see also* Criminal histories, 84, 125-6, 156, 158, 190-1, 248-9, 256

Short term prisoners, 233-6

Silence, 4, 6

Social class,
  of Grendon sample, 55, 172, 176, 177
  of Wormwood Scrubs sample, 137

Social histories, 44-5, 188, 291-3, 300-1

Social performance, 50, 300-1

Solitary confinement, 4, 6, 166

Special Hospitals, *see also* Broadmoor, 29, 72

Statistical analyses, 44

Stigma, 226

Subnormal prisoners, *see* Feeble minded persons and prisoners, *and* Mental defectives

Suicidal ideas, *see also* Attempted suicide, 230

Therapeutic community, 23, 258
Transportation, 2, 3
Treadmill, 4, 10
Typhus, 2

Unemployment, *see* Employment

Vagrancy, 215, 216
Violence in prison, 78, 80-1, 87, 157-8
Violence ratings, 157

Violent offenders, 12, 157, 198, 202, 256

Wakefield prison, 24, 30
Warwick State Reformatory, 12
Weak minded convicts, *see* Feeble minded persons and prisoners
Welfare officers, 92
Wheeler, Stanton, 117-8
Wing meetings, 79, 85-6, 92, 94, 99, 157
Woking prison, 7
Wormwood Scrubs,
    follow up, 181
    new therapeutic community, 155, 257, 259
    psychiatric unit, 22, 23, 24, 25, 30, 124-8, 156-7, 159, 257
    sample, 128-42, 156-65, 180-1